CORPORATE
PERSONALITY DISORDER

Also by Eli Sopow

The Critical Issues Audit

The Age of Outrage: The Positive Power of Public Protest

CORPORATE PERSONALITY DISORDER

SURVIVING & SAVING
SICK ORGANIZATIONS

ELI SOPOW, PhD

iUniverse, Inc.
New York Lincoln Shanghai

Corporate Personality Disorder
Surviving & Saving Sick Organizations

iUniverse books may be ordered through booksellers or by contacting:

iUniverse
2021 Pine Lake Road, Suite 100
Lincoln, NE 68512
www.iuniverse.com
1-800-Authors (1-800-288-4677)

ISBN: 978-0-595-42560-0 (pbk)
ISBN: 978-0-595-86889-6 (ebk)

Printed in the United States of America

CONTENTS

PREFACE

This introduction is short, because you probably already know each other well. Too well, you may think. I'm talking about the galaxy of organizations we deal with on a regular basis, including our workplace, financial institutions, schools, hospitals, local shopping malls, community police departments, phone company, gas company, numerous government agencies—and the list goes on.

Although there are many outstanding corporations, institutions, and organizations around, places that treat others well and with respect, there are many bad ones that do not. In some cases, we do not like what we know about these places. Perhaps we get along with them because we have to, but if we had our druthers, they'd behave a lot better.

It's not uncommon to see and experience examples of organizations behaving badly. Just think about Hurricane Katrina and FEMA and the executives from Enron who went to jail. Think about government agencies that cut funds to local programs and health care agencies that strangle patients in red tape. (A litany of such sins is found in Marianne Jennings' excellent book *The Seven Signs of Ethical Collapse*.)

The wonder of it all is that many people think such behavior is not uncommon. It's just the way it is. Worst of all, there are those who believe *they* are the problem when dealing with organizations—and not the organization. It's *they* who need to shape up, get with the program, be a team player, and suck it up. And why shouldn't we think this way? Bookstore shelves are overflowing with self-help books whose key theme is that we need to fix *our* behavior in order to get along with our organization's personality. We can also pick one of the zillion management and leadership books espousing the latest flavor-of-the-month theory related to the daily ethics and actions of organizations, completely ignoring the fact that actions are a product of long-established culture and learning.

All this finally dawned on me after spending thirty-five years in the workplace. Some people can't hold a job, but in my case I can't hold a career. I have worked as an award-winning newspaper and television reporter, a senior advisor to a government cabinet, vice-president of an international consulting firm (where I received more awards), an advisor to a national police force, and an academic teaching university students about systems theory and change management. I have a doctorate in human and organizational systems, master's degrees in both human development and organizational leadership, and training as a peer counselor. But my *real* education has come from my daily interactions with both fellow employees and bosses. And that's what finally led to my epiphany.

Here's a secret, and it's why this book is different from most. It's not the individual that's the problem, at least in most cases; it's the *organizational personality* that behaves badly. By organizational personality, I mean all the things that combine to influence the actions of most organizational structures. Organizations behave the way they do for a number of very specific reasons, which also make it difficult for many of them to do otherwise. In fact, in many cases, the modern organization has very little awareness of why it behaves the way it does.

The behavior of all organizations—their organizational personality—is shaped by their history and the lessons it has learned, just like our *human* personality is shaped by hereditary and developmental influences. Trouble is, the modern organization has a very unhealthy history.

Imagine a person whose family tree is rife with physical and emotional abuse, psychotic behavior, anti-social tendencies, and an inability to show or recognize emotions. Imagine that that person is also in denial about his or her past. It would certainly be a challenge to share a life with that person. But the fact is, that's exactly what the *Organizational Family Tree* (as I call it) looks like.

Many organizations behave badly because they are strongly influenced (often unconsciously) by their history and by actions from the past. We often call this aspect of organizational life its "culture," but in many cases we haven't dug deep enough, to the roots of the Organizational Family Tree, to see what strains of sap are still negatively influencing current behavior.

This book is a survival guide to dealing with root rot within the Organizational Family Tree. The pages ahead will help us assess the personality of the organizations we deal with, understand what causes them to behave the way they do, and most importantly be happier in the relationship we currently have with organizational personalities.

Thank you for joining the journey.

ACKNOWLEDGMENTS

This book was possible because many people are brave enough to care. They show they care by respectfully saying "no" to those who don't like people contradicting them and questioning their dictates. They show they care by asking "why" and "why not" when pressured by people demanding sycophantic loyalty. And they show they care by showing genuine empathy, love, and sincere attempts to understand what's going on emotionally with others.

At the top of my list of caring people is my wife, Lindsay Wilde, who helped me think through this book, who offered (and offers) shelter from my many personal storms, and whose wisdom, experience, humor, and patience brought sensible content to what were otherwise random ravings. This book would not have been possible without Lindsay's support. I only wish we had met twenty-five years ago.

Writing a book is a process of storytelling, of sharing, and of revealing to strangers the author's insecurities and fears. The thoughts and insights that you may like in this book have come from many. They have been seeded in me by the galaxy of wonderful professors at the Fielding Graduate University in Santa Barbara, California, a safe place of collegiality, support, and continual questioning. In particular, my friend Dottie Agger-Gupta, associate dean of the School of Human and Organizational Development, stands out.

Of continuing influence are colleagues and friends at Royal Roads University in Victoria, BC, where, as an instructor, I gain more from learners than they gain from me. Particular thanks goes to Peni Hambrook, Karen Fiorini, and Richard Bruce, three seasoned-with-many-years-of-life graduate students whose research on organizational change and human emotions has kept my own creative juices flowing.

A large group of colleagues and friends at the Royal Canadian Mounted Police must also be acknowledged, specifically at the Pacific Region command. The RCMP is Canada's national police force and a unique organizational model, steeped in history, tradition, and some growing pains. Like a giant supertanker navigating a delicate chain of fragile islands, the police force is comprised of many brilliant, hard-working individuals whose planning and leadership skills are without par. There are many I can name, but the only one I will embarrass with my tribute and thanks is Staff Sergeant John Ward. John is a great friend, supporter, and mentor. He also has that unique ability to apply street-cop smarts to the far more dangerous world of senior management politics.

I also want to thank the many colleagues and bosses I've had over the past decades, in four different professions and well over twenty different jobs. I've been lucky enough to work as a construction worker, journalist, advisor to a government cabinet, senior manager of a major professional association, vice-president of an international firm, and academic. The beauty of being in the trenches of everyday work life and management, rather than just peering down from the safety of academia, is that you get to taste the reality and not just the theory. The many corporations, associations, institutions, and government agencies that have put up with my moods, boat rocking, and downright obstinacy have shown me firsthand the good, the bad, and definitely the ugly of leadership and management. Those experiences have provided a rich and deeply personal backdrop to this book.

A huge thanks goes to the staff and management of iUniverse, an organization with the foresight to appreciate that book publishing and marketing is not the exclusive domain of a few well-established corporations. This book is about personal empowerment and breaking from the narrow constraints of organizational life. It stands to reason, then, that I chose the self-publishing route, and iUniverse was a perfect fit. The philosophy of iUniverse is that writers should have access to the tools they need to share their thoughts and words with others, including assistance with editing, cover design, marketing, and numerous other technicalities related to book publishing. Because of the depth of expertise offered by Susan Driscoll, Diane Gedymin, Rachel Krupicka, and others at iUniverse, this project is more a "co-publishing" than a "self-publishing" venture. I especially want to single out David Bernardi at iUniverse. David is not only a master wordsmith and editor, but has that unique ability to draw deeply from the disciplines of philosophy, history, psychology, and rock and roll, just to cite a few content challenges in this book. Having finally completed this project, I believe more strongly than ever that iUniverse is the way of the future for book publishing, just like independent movie and music producers are carving out exciting new ground in those creative fields.

There are many real-life stories cited in this book. In some cases, I have changed the names of those profiled to protect their current jobs, and in other cases I have provided a composite case of what people are going through rather than reveal specific details that would blow their cover with their bosses. But in all cases, the stories are only too real, and those experiencing them were only too happy to share their journey.

Last, but foremost, I want to thank *you*, the reader, for venturing into this journey into the organizational psyche. While many have helped shaped my thoughts and ideas, the opinions I bring you are mine alone, and therefore I must accept the blame and barbs for things that seem awry.

Eli Sopow

1

MOST ORGANIZATIONS MAKE POOR FRIENDS

o o o o o o o o o o o o o o o o o o o o o o o o o o o o o o o o o o o o

For the great majority of mankind are satisfied with appearances, as though they were realities, and are often even more influenced by the things that seem than by those that are.

—Niccolo Machiavelli, 1527

Psssst! Are you *really* sure you know that person? I don't mean your best friend, your passion partner, or Auntie Sally. I mean that *other* person–the *corporate* personality—the one that represents all the traits and behaviors and idiosyncrasies of the organization you have to deal with every day.

Chances are you have a pretty good idea *what* this corporate personality is like, but not *why* it behaves as it does. I'm going to tell you why. But watch out. You may never be the same again. You may have trouble accepting the status quo, rightfully demand that your emotional needs be recognized, and even find it easier to say "no" to that corporate personality. In other words, you are on the cusp of becoming a "boat rocker," a "naysayer," and maybe even a "shit disturber."

If you're happy with the status quo, if you're happy keeping your head down and waiting to be told what to do, if you're okay with sucking it up and waiting it out, then quickly slam closed the cover of this book, throw it in a dumpster, switch off your brain, and pull up the covers. But if you're starting to think that maybe it's not *you* that's the problem; maybe it's the way an organization or corporation or institution is designed and operates—maybe *it's* the problem—then put on the coffee, take a big breath, let it out slowly, and let's get started on a wild journey into what *really* makes an organization tick (and why this clock metaphor is so darn perfect to describe a very *imperfect* system structure).

By the way, "you" can mean floor sweeper, computer code writer, director of sales, manager of new gizmos, butcher, baker, or candlestick maker. You can occupy the top, bottom, or middle rung of your organization. You can be just out of university (or technical college) and scrutinizing a potential employer to see if its corporate personality fits with your human personality. Perhaps you've had your job for a number of years now and have pretty well had it with the dysfunctional behavior of the place. Or you might be close to retirement and, instead of keeping your head down and slipping out quietly, you've decided to stand up on your hind legs and tell it like it is.

But one thing's for sure. We're not alone. Despite our differences, we have a lot in common with thousands of others who are touched daily by organizational life. This journey will show just how much we do have in common, how much our personalities overlap, and just how hugely different our *human* personality can be from the *organizational* personality we think we know.

I'm going to say a few things that may at first sound crazy. They might even sound, well, a little "out there"—like something dreamt up in some academic ivory tower by latte-sipping tenured professors with leather patches on the elbows of their dirty tweed jackets. For example, I'm going to say there's an "eco-alarm" ringing in our head, deep in our subconscious, that's telling us to do things that will protect the planet or, at the very least, our health and welfare. (No, this eco-alarm isn't a new tune on our iPod.) I'm saying this neurobiological alarm bell is what's behind social protests, peace marches, and our escalating concern over climate change, as well as our deep desire to give some organizations a swift kick in the butt. And I'm going to prove it with sound science and documented facts.

I'm also going to expose the fact that many people are living in a totally false reality, sort of like those human pods hanging around in the movie *The Matrix*, who are constantly programmed by their machine masters to think they're actually cutting the lawn or making love with their dream partner. A major part of this false reality is believing that we need tight control and containment of events around us and believing that we fear change—especially change in our organization.

I'm going to prove that thinking this way is no accident—that we've been purposefully conditioned to accept this logic—and yet we're probably not even aware of who or what is conditioning us and why. So steel yourself. You're going to discover why this has happened and who made it happen—but also why a lot of wise people today think it's wrong. You're going to discover that for the majority of the time that people have lived on this planet, things were very different—organizational systems were far more natural, wholesome, and healthy, not just for regular folks but for Earth itself.

And you're going to find out (as if you didn't know already) that some organizational personalities are big, fat liars. Some of the biggest lies are woven into the lexicon of corporate-speak and business-talk. For example, consider the following lies:

- "All things being equal, then [x] will happen."
- "We need to have a level playing field."
- "In a perfect world …"
- "Anybody can do it if they work hard enough."

Well, things are *never* equal, it's *impossible* to have a perfectly flat playing field, our world will *never* be "perfect," and, sorry to say, sometimes no matter what we do or how hard we work, we simply *won't* be able to "do it." All of this, by the way, is perfectly okay. What's *not* okay is thinking that everything is tightly predictable, entirely possible, and perfectly programmable.

But first I'm going to tell a story about Charlene and Katrina—both powerful in their own right. The devastation of Hurricane Katrina was wild-eyed frightening to Charlene, who lived with her three young children in the heart of residential New Orleans, but it didn't destroy her resolve, not even as the dirty, smelly water rose and poured through her small single-level home, destroying everything she owned. Even the immediate aftermath of Katrina—the stench, the body count, the missing friends, and Charlene's lost job—didn't stifle her spirit, for she was one tough thirty-nine-year-old single mother who had learned to survive many human tragedies.

But that was August 29, 2005, and this was August 2006. On that day in August, the diseased waters, the bodies, the stench, and the devastation had long since ebbed back into the sea. But another stench grew even stronger, emanating not from natural weather systems but from manmade organizational systems. Hurricane Katrina filled Charlene with fear, but it didn't bring her to tears. It was a human organizational system that left Charlene beyond simple frustration, beyond anger and comprehension, and in tears as she shuffled through her house that had no water or heat a year later—while sitting next to it was a shiny new mobile home filled with all the modern amenities, delivered just for her and her family through the generosity and planning of the Federal Emergency Management Agency (FEMA).

The only problem was that the trailer was locked and Charlene had not been able to get the keys from FEMA for what seemed like months, and so there it sat—shiny and white and useless—while she and her children suffered through the hot New Orleans day, the bugs, and the muggy night, with no water, no sanitation, and a shell of what had once been a home.

Katrina showed just how gummed up the machine works of modern organizations (in this case, FEMA and related federal agencies) can become. Charlene, while in tears over the trailer that wasn't, at least had something to beat her fists of frustration upon. Almost twenty-five thousand other manufactured homes never even got to the distraught and destroyed victims. After spending $879 million on the homes, FEMA was forced to store them around America because its own bureaucracy and rules said such housing could not be allowed on a flood plain such as New Orleans. In the end, nearly eleven thousand perfectly new manufactured homes were left to deteriorate on old runways and in Arkansas farmers' fields.

The colossal blunders of FEMA's system structure in the aftermath of Katrina are now legendary, from spending $3 million on four thousand beds that were never used to spending $10 million to renovate and furnish rooms in Alabama that ultimately housed just six victims before being shut down. Yet the truly tragic story is that the complete meltdown of FEMA's system structure was in no way a bizarre aberration in Western civilization.

It couldn't have been any other way. FEMA was doomed to failure because its basic organizational genome, its foundational structure—similar to the organizational design of most institutions, corporations, and agencies in the Western world—was maladapted to its environment and especially to the needs and expectations of people within that environment.

What this also means is that all the committee hearings, investigations, finger pointing, and staff firings in the world won't do anything to prevent a similar performance disaster in the future unless FEMA's deeply imbedded organizational structural dysfunctions are addressed. But to address it would require looking at FEMA's meltdown with a mindset far different from the one in place when the government agency was created.

The case of FEMA is different because of the immediate, short-term severity of the crisis, the obscene amount of tax dollars it wasted, the devastation inflicted upon innocent lives, and the international news media focus. But the reality is that dysfunctional organizational behavior is inflicting pain and suffering on people every day. It's just that the collective magnitude of such behavior has become so enormous that many of us can no longer see it, and the impact has become so pervasive that many of us now consider it just part of life, just like abusive relationships that go on for years, until those being beaten down forget what a healthy existence is like.

CORPORATE PERSONALITY DISORDER

If some companies and organizations were people, it's unlikely we'd want to be friends with them. In fact, if some companies were people, we'd most likely be afraid of them. We'd see them as big bullies, violent and unpredictable, and we'd have good reason to feel this way. We'd be afraid of these bully personalities because they push us around. Some even threaten us with bodily or psychological injury. And, as you've heard or read or maybe even know firsthand, the behavior of some bullyboy organizations has even caused death.

If some companies were people—vicious, intimidating personalities or simply mindless, insensitive individuals that hurt us—something would be done. For starters, our brain would turn fear into anger and outrage. There would be the natural tendency to flee or freeze—just keep our head down and hide—but there would also be the natural tendency, inculcated deep within the most primitive region of our brain, to fight back, on our own or along with others who are also afraid and outraged.

If some companies were people, they'd be in deep trouble with those they threatened and hurt and intimidated. The fact is, almost all of us believe companies and organizations of all sorts—from government agencies to giant associations and formal religions—have the same personality traits humans have. And that's why many corporations and organizations today in the Western World, particularly those in North America, are having trouble with employees, customers, clients, parishioners, and voters. We simply don't like who they are.

The *Oxford Dictionary of Psychology* describes "personality disorder" as

> *n.* A category of mental disorders, with onset no later than early childhood, characterized by pervasive, inflexible, and enduring patterns of cognition, affect, interpersonal behavior, or impulse control that deviate markedly from culturally shared expectations and lead to significant distress or impairment in social, occupational, or other important areas of functioning.

We find a similar definition in the American Psychiatric Association's *Diagnostic and Statistical Manual of Mental Disorders*, 4th edition (2000):

A personality disorder is an enduring pattern of inner experience and behavior that deviates from the expectations of the individual's culture, is pervasive and inflexible, has an onset in adolescence or early childhood, is stable over time, and leads to distress or impairment.

The above definitions relate to people. But organizations also have a "personality," the human attributes we label them with, such as "greed," "caring," "trustworthiness," or "aggressiveness." When we look at the behavior of some organizations today, including certain corporations, government agencies, religious groups, and even volunteer organizations, we won't find it too hard to recognize the clinical descriptions of *corporate* personality disorder as well as the positive traits.

It's easy. For example, think of Starbucks. I've had folks describe this ubiquitous corner coffee dispenser as "friendly," "trendy," and "comforting" but also as "greedy," "corporate," and "pushy." It's the same with any company or institution. Most of us just naturally ascribe human personality traits to them, and in fact the corporations spend billions of collective dollars hiring slick advertising and marketing consultants to cultivate just the right "brand image," which is really their personality.

Now think of where you work or an organization that you have had to deal with. What kind of *personality* does the place have? Does *your* personality get along with this organizational personality? Many such relationships are at best "okay" and at worst severely dysfunctional. However, if you're having trouble with an organization, don't be too quick to blame yourself, because that's exactly what a bullyboy organizational personality is good at getting others to do.

This book is a journey inside the corporate psyche—what makes it behave the way it does and, especially, what makes it sometimes behave in strange and even mean ways. On this journey, you'll learn that corporate personality disorder is behind many *human* personality disorders and dysfunctional conditions, including depression, anxiety, and even suicide, and is the cause of public protests, workplace strikes, and consumer boycotts.

This is not something you'll find in a standard university MBA program, but the reality is that an organization's personality—its identity or brand—gets formed just like our human personality. As every counselor knows, a human personality is shaped by historical factors originating with our parents (and theirs before them) as well as the hugely influential formative years of our life, which shape our development as individuals. An organization too has historical factors that it was "born" with when first created, and it is strongly influenced—particularly in its early years—by developmental factors or lessons learned.

These historical and developmental factors end up shaping the organization's structure, including delegation of authority, responsibility, and accountability, as well as the emphasis it places on your emotion and knowledge needs. Organizational historical and developmental factors in particular create what is commonly called "corporate culture." This is the big-picture stuff, the long-ingrained values and beliefs and way of doing things, which we will explore in detail in chapter 2 when we probe the nature of culture versus climate. (If you want an even deeper, more academic pool of information on this, I strongly recommend the *Handbook of Organizational Culture and Climate*, 2000.)

The importance an organizational system structure places on specific human emotion and knowledge factors constitutes what is commonly called the "corporate climate," with varying levels of commitment to communications, cooperation, and connectivity to others. This is the "here and now" stuff—the way things feel in the workplace, which is often influenced by how authority, responsibility, and accountability are apportioned. The combination of corporate culture and climate is what creates the organizational *environment* and shapes organizational *personality*.

THE ORGANIZATIONAL FAMILY TREE

Just as the influence of our personal history and the lessons learned throughout life shape our *human* personality, an organization's history and lessons learned shape its *corporate* personality. An organization is born, grows, and develops behavioral patterns much as people develop behavioral patterns.

I call this overall concept of organizational life the *Organizational Family Tree*. This idea is the central theme of our journey. It's the metaphor that will help us understand why organizations behave the way they do. The idea is that the modern organization—rather than being a mechanical clockworks—is a holistic, living, breathing body of fluctuating power and energy, much like our human body, which builds and disperses energy based on the traits we were born with and our experiences throughout life.

Looking at an organizational structure this way is very different from trying to figure out what makes an organization tick by simply studying its "organization chart." An organization chart is the "skeletal structure," showing how an organization is put together. But what's missing when we gaze upon the quintessential organization chart is any sense of the company's "heart and soul." What the Organizational Family Tree provides is not the skeleton of the organizational body but its nervous and circulatory system, its deep roots and its current behaviors—the systems that bring it to life and give it meaning and vibrancy.

The Organizational Family Tree is the source of power and energy for all forms of organization, from multinational corporation to small nonprofit group. The nature of the Organizational Family Tree is what makes an organization successful or a failure. It's what determines whether the organization is trustworthy and can easily make friends and build relationships or it is cold and untrustworthy. You're going to hear a lot about the Organizational Family Tree as we explore the organizational psyche, and eventually I'll twist this handy metaphor into one that also includes energy and power sources and things like resistors and conductors.

Okay. Right now you might be thinking, "What the heck is he talking about, and how is this of any use to me in dealing with an insensitive boss and dumb cubicle?" Well, here's the deal. For the first time, you're going to see your organization—or one that affects you a lot—from a different perspective. You're going to understand why that organization has the personality it has. And once you know that, you might ask yourself a few questions, not the least being "Do I really want to continue my relationship with this place?"

But here's another thing. In relationships between two humans, this kind of self-assessment and pause for thought (a) makes for a healthier relationship, (b) exposes the need for counseling, or (c) results in divorce. It's the same in the relationship between our human personality and the organization's personality. Regardless of whether you pursue option (a), (b), or (c) above, or decide on all three, the odds are you'll be happier than now. And if you poke your head up and look around—around the entire country, the entire planet—you'll quickly see the urgent need for many of us to start looking hard at organizational behavior, to discover the root rot settling into the Organizational Family Tree, and to start doing something about it.

Over hundreds of thousands of years, the structure of humans—including our physique, our processes of reasoning, and our ability to adapt to the environment by carefully rebalancing and redirecting our human power and energy systems—has changed in order to allow us to survive as a species. It has taken many millennia for humanity to evolve in response to the world around us—and in the process, especially of late, to negatively suppress elements in our natural environment, destroying other species so we may survive and thrive or meet self-decreed definitions of "success." In lockstep with human evolution came an evolution in organizational system structures, "progressing" from hunting and gathering societies to the Industrial Revolution and beyond.

Along the way, human emotions and an affinity with nature were displaced in favor of mechanistic models of management and a suppression of human feelings in the workplace. But lately, something good is starting to happen, and not a second too early. Today, a natural correction is beginning to occur to organizational system structures, one that is also realigning sources of power and energy. But unlike the evolution of mankind, the change to organizational life in Western society is neither gradual nor subtle. The change to organizations is very often dramatic and immediate, such as when an entire senior management team is dismissed (or sent to jail), when angry shareholders rise up in revolt, or when corporations lose massive market share.

Going into Emotional and Organizational Meltdown

When people end up having emotional problems, when they suffer great anxiety, and when they start acting a little out of sorts, they might say to themselves and others, "I'm having a meltdown!" How many times, when facing the severe pressures of home life, children, or your work environment, have you yelled out in frustration, "I'm having a meltdown!" People around you usually get it. That's because all of us have been there. Maybe we still are, right now. Maybe *you* are, right now. I know *I* am.

The term "meltdown" is very fitting. Taken from the atomic energy industry, it describes uncontrollable nuclear fission in a power reactor due to a malfunctioning or decaying coolant system, which in turn causes a massive overheating of the reactor's core, resulting in release of radioactive material into the atmosphere.

This was the case with Three Mile Island on March 28, 1979, and with the Chernobyl nuclear disaster in the Ukraine on April 26, 1986. At Three Mile Island, a series of operational and human error calamities prevented vital cooling water from being directed to the reactor's core. The nuclear fuel overheated, the zirconium cladding (long metal tubes that hold nuclear fuel pellets) ruptured, and very small amounts of radioactive gases were released into the atmosphere, causing widespread panic but negligible impact on human and plant life.

Chernobyl was far worse. On April 25 and 26, 1986, the world's worst nuclear power accident occurred. While testing one of the four reactors, employees disregarded all manner of safety procedures. At 1:23 AM, a chain reaction led to an out-of-control meltdown, creating explosions and a fireball that blew off the reactor's heavy steel and concrete lid. The result was four thousand deaths, hundreds of billions of dollars in damage, and million of acres of soil contaminated. Sheep as far away as Scotland had to be quarantined or slaughtered, and today thousands of people, many of them young children, are still suffering from radiation poisoning.

With Three Mile Island, a report by a presidential commission into the accident concluded that both human systems and organizational systems were at fault. Organizational systems melted down long before the reactor accident. The Commission stated, "Many factors contributed to the action of the operators, such as deficiencies in their training, lack of clarity in their operating procedures, failure of organizations to learn the proper lessons from previous incidents, and deficiencies in design of the control room."

Human systems melted down because organizational systems had gone into meltdown. It was disclosed that the company was badly managed, that some employees had cheated on exams to become licensed operators, and that those with the company who had warned of potential disaster to come had been ignored.

Today many *organizational* systems are experiencing a "meltdown" due to a lack of effective organizational "cooling systems." Volatile, angry energy is erupting due to a clash of organizational personalities and human personalities. As the crazed character Howard Beale in the movie *Network* screamed out, "I'm mad as hell, and I'm not going to take it anymore!"

The personality clash between mechanistic organizations and real people is creating an eruption unprecedented in history. It's an eruption of power and energy seen with placard-packing protesters on the streets of New York and Los Angeles, on Internet Web sites and blogs, in anti-corporate shareholder resolutions, in class-action lawsuits, and, sadly, in the shattered lives of millions of people each year.

What's happening is a natural, emotion-driven reaction to sick organizational systems. Just like when an abused partner in a human relationship finally says, "No! That is enough!" people who feel abused in organizational relationships are fighting back. Like the relief valve in a nuclear reactor, which automatically opens to prevent pressure from reaching explosive levels, today's human reactions to unbearable pressures and meltdown within organizational structures will ultimately self-correct the nature of organizational life. And the system will never be the same again.

This journey into the corporate psyche is about how many people today are standing their ground and, in many cases, trying to save badly behaving organizational personalities that are in deep meltdown and exhibiting corporate personality disorder. If you happen to be one of those people, this journey is going to give you a little help. It will give you a set of proven tools to diagnose the current personality of an organization; it will help you gain a greater understanding of why an organization behaves the way it does and, most importantly, what you can do to help it—or, if necessary, to stop it.

And that's my point. We *can* do something to re-nourish the Organizational Family Tree, to bring some sanity and stability to our workplace even if it does nothing more than make our little cubicle a better place to be or make us feel better when we wake in the morning and go to bed at night.

This journey is about creating positive energy within organizations through communication, connectivity, and cooperation. It's about the balanced application of authority, accountability, and responsibility. It's about the role of human resistors and conductors within a living energy system called the Organizational Family Tree. And this journey is about creating hope. It's about how we can detect and treat organizational decay and, just as we would with some human personalities, direct dysfunctional behavior and conflict-ridden relationships into something positive, and lasting, and hopeful.

But before we go further, I want to share a few stories about people who've had to deal with sick systems and corporate personality disorder. These are people who have figured out how to either re-nourish the Organizational Family Tree or delicately prune its offensive branches. I know these people through my years of journalism, my service as a senior bureaucrat in government, my time as a vice-president of an international consulting and corporate coaching firm, and my academic research and teaching. I've worked with them closely in many cases to find solutions to challenges in their lives. I'm using pseudonyms to protect their privacy, but the quotes attributed to them are unaltered and their tales are indeed starkly real.

Robin the Family Doctor

Let me introduce you to Robin, age thirty-eight, a family physician in Vancouver. Robin is having a personal meltdown. His busy medical practice occupies him constantly. His children, ten-year-old Robert and eight-year-old Samantha, weave in and out of his professional life like the ebb and flow of a turbulent tide. Robin's wife, Sarah, put her elementary school teaching career on hold twelve years ago to bring at least one element of constancy and stability to a chaotic household.

But families are not separate silos of existence where success can depend on one strong pillar. Families are interlaced systems where success, depression, hope, and disappointment shape-shift depending on the synergy created by the connectivity, communication, and cooperation among all elements in the system. However, in Robin's family the strength of one member was not enough to fuel positive energy within the whole—not enough to lessen the burden pressuring the young doctor.

Robin tells me that he feels like a stretched elastic band—stretched so tight that the normal brown rubber is white and narrow, so taut that when plucked the sound is high-pitched and strained. Taking precious time from his clinic and patients, Robin says,

I feel terrible. I am overweight, out of shape, stressed, and about to lose my relationship with my wife. I know it's important for me to have a balance between my personal and professional life but I have great difficulty in achieving this. My work preoccupies my mind, even when I am off. I have no time for hobbies or interests. My friends never see or hear from me.

There is a serious crisis in health care. All my patients want more time with me but I can't give it to them because of all kinds of bureaucratic restraints. There's pressure, pressure, pressure. Pressure to do more and more but at the same time to keep costs down. Patients see this and it contributes to a lessening of respect for what I do as a doctor. Increasingly, I see doctors cutting more and more corners.

Robin says he feels fearful, angry, trapped, and "screwed by the system." He says "the system" has disempowered physicians and turned control of medicine over to "paper-pushing bureaucrats" more concerned about fiscal than physical fitness. "If I had to do it again, I'd never be a doctor. Is everyone as tired as I am?" he asks rhetorically but at the same time looking for even a sliver of hope in his life.

Robin is drained of positive energy due to misalignment in what I call the *Triangle of Trust*—the core of the Organizational Family Tree. In the triangle, effective communications, connectivity, and cooperation is bound by a harmonious balance of authority, responsibility, and accountability. (We'll get into this in more detail in chapter 3.)

Robin's historical sense of *authority* as a physician within the health care system appears badly eroded to him, with bureaucrats and other health care providers playing a much larger role in the delivery and administration of care.

At the same time his *accountability* within the system has mushroomed in past years, particularly to the accountants, MBAs, and chief financial officers who have a direct say in his treatment of patients. On top of that, his *responsibility* to patients is stretched to a seemingly impossible extent. Robin doesn't have the time to treat patients with the care he wants to extend, he feels burnt out, and his responsibilities as a parent and husband have long since taken a backseat to his professional responsibilities and accountabilities.

There's plenty of energy and power in Robin's life today—all of it negative. The energy and power is created by the fear and anger over his personal meltdown and over the meltdown of a health care system in which authority, responsibility, and accountability no longer align themselves in positive-energy producing harmony. Ironically, it is the health care system—a place dedicated to healing—that is suffering from corporate personality disorder.

Robin's fear and anger over the organizational structure of health care has spurred him to join an upcoming protest by medical doctors, who are planning a news conference to announce that they will close their clinics for a day to get the attention of politicians and bureaucrats. Only a month earlier, a friend and colleague of Robin's—the president of a hospital's medical staff—resigned his post after citing "unsafe, unsanitary, and unsuitable for patient care" conditions at the hospital.

KAREN AND JOSH, THE PEACEFUL PROTESTERS

Five thousand miles away from Robin, Karen Wilcox and Josh McGregor are part of a giant energy surge, again created by an imbalance in the authority, accountability, and responsibility vested in a public institution. They are deep among the three hundred thousand or so protesters spilling through the streets of New York City on a fine spring day. The demographics of the undulating crowd fail to fit what police profilers had predicted in their carefully scripted Public Order Management strategy.

First, the sea of humanity is far larger than covert intelligence had predicted—an extra fifty thousand people to be exact. Second, the level of anticipated violence fails to materialize. This is *not* another Battle of Seattle, after all. There are no Molotov cocktails, no bandana-masked Black Bloc activists with handmade catapults hurling bags of steel ball bearings at police, and no smashed picture windows at the GAP or Nike or Starbucks. Suddenly, the five thousand police tactical troop officers dressed in their Darth Vader look-alike costumes look strangely out of place.

Karen, thirty-five years old, lives full time with Josh, forty-two. Both are college instructors. They are neatly dressed, nicely groomed, have no previous criminal records, are registered Democrats, and together with tens of thousands of others marching with them on this sunny day share a passionate distaste for America's invasion of both Afghanistan and Iraq. A crow sitting in a maple tree above the lacework of New York streets notices the average age is late thirties. Liberally sprinkled throughout the march are families with young children, old-timers with bald and graying hair, teenagers, those in wheelchairs and some who have just left their highchairs.

Drums are being beaten, songs are being sung, giant anti-capitalism puppets tower above the crowd, and banners, signs, placards, and balloons fill the air. Absent from the scene—a disappointment to both the news media and to a few police officers pumped up for battle—is any tone, tactic, or action that could be construed as overt violence. On one obvious level, what's occurring is a massive antiwar march and rally, complete with protestations against corporate globalization, the Bush administration, and verbal attacks against American geopolitical hegemony.

But something far deeper and far more significant is also unfolding. This is where I'm going to ask you to step out of your comfort space of organizational thinking. What I'm about to share may sound a little "out there," something you might even dismiss as outlandish. But the thing is, there's a strong body of neuroscientific fact that makes what I'm about to share hold water.

The emotional reaction we often have to badly behaving companies, to bad laws and government policy, and to really nasty managers and bosses is the same deep-seated protective emotional response we have to a rattlesnake suddenly jumping out of our desk drawer. We'll get into the science of this in later chapters, but for now, just hold on to this one fact: To our brain, specifically our emotional brain, danger is danger. And we react the same way to a snake that's literally coiled inside our desk as we do to a metaphorical venomous snake in a business suit.

This is why it's not coincidence or serendipity that has drawn at least three hundred thousand people to the streets of New York City. What's happening is both organizationally and consciously orchestrated, as well as biologically predetermined at an atavistic, unconscious level. What's happening is that deep within the hardwired limbic system of the protesters' brains, far in the recesses of their first-formed, ancient emotion-based core of consciousness, an alarm bell is clattering away. This natural alarm bell is also ringing loudly within many of our brains.

What's happening is that our naturally programmed and often unconscious instinct to perpetuate as a species—an instinct with roots stretching back millions of years—is activating an emergency survival plan, one that tightly links communications, connectivity, and cooperation. A nuclear reactor has multiple failsafe devices built into it to stop a meltdown. It's the same with the complex three-pound organic reactor stuffed between our ears—but in this case, the failsafe device is our primordial, hardwired instinct to survive through action and reaction.

Just as our human genome's immune system produces protective antibodies in the face of an attack by a dangerous virus or infection, our brain's primordial survival instinct creates a natural resistance to *organizational* threats. Large-scale public protest actions and individual backlashes against organizations in meltdown are as natural and necessary as the release of antibodies in our biological system, as automatic as the "scamming" in a nuclear reactor, in which control rods automatically drop down to halt nuclear fission.

What's happening today is that the meltdown in the structure of Western organizations is creating gigantic power and energy surges through both human resistors and conductors. These resistors and conductors manifest in the form of protests, boycotts, labor strikes, backlashes, and both peaceful and violent attacks against "the system." This atavistic, human need for survival is also making millions of us worry about the danger of climate change and global warming.

In Karen and Josh's case, what brought their protest actions to the streets of New York City was not the war in Iraq—which they opposed—but a meltdown in the college education system, where decisions by senior administrators were being made unilaterally behind closed doors, where budgets for liberal arts programs were being slashed, and where the organizational personality of their specific college was increasingly at odds with their own individual personalities and core values.

Although college instructors were being saddled with far greater classroom *responsibilities* in terms of meeting the rising expectations of students and the community, and although college instructors were being held far more *accountable* for the quality of education ultimately bestowed upon students, their *authority* to influence administrative decisions that directly affected their role had been dramatically curtailed.

The *positive* energy that could have come from a harmonious balance of authority, accountability, and responsibility ("Here's what we need to accomplish. How do you think we can make it happen?") had been short-circuited by a power imbalance with all the authority hoarded by senior managers ("Do it this way because I said so. You report to me.") Well, you can imagine the result. Frustrations boiled over, resulting in an emotion-based power surge, but this was really a very natural correction of an *organizational* meltdown that threatened the *human* personalities in its midst.

Karen and Josh were five thousand miles away from Robin the medical doctor, but their fear, outrage, and emotional and cognitive need for action was based on strong similarities and common ground—the debilitating impact of a dysfunctional and toxic organizational system.

CORPORATE PERSONALITY DISORDER LURKS IN THE SHADOWS

So, you've looked around your organization, thought about its personality for a minute, and concluded, "Things aren't too bad here." But there's also a really good chance you're saying, "Yeah, this company's personality sucks," or "Come to think of it, I have to deal with an organization with a personality like Dracula's." One thing is for sure: you didn't have to think about your answer very long. And if you've concluded that you're dealing with an organization with only one oar in the water, you're not alone.

Organizations that have plenty of top-down authority but little accountability or responsibility to us, that have poor communications and connectivity, and that don't care much about cooperation are in meltdown, and the impact of their "personalities" clearly shows it.

For example, drawing on a wide range of employee surveys, the American Institute of Stress reported in 2006 that 40 percent of workers saw their job as very or extremely stressful; 26 percent were often or very often burned out or stressed by their work; 34 percent had trouble sleeping because of stress; 62 percent complained of neck or back pain because of workplace stress; and an estimated one million workers are absent from work every day in America due to stress. Is this sounding familiar?

When workplace stress builds to a breaking point, the effects can be tragic. The U.S. Bureau of Labor Statistics tells us that up to a thousand workers a year are murdered on the job, making job-related murder one of the fastest growing categories of homicide.

The workplace can be an emotional toxic dump where violence and stress and burnout are so common that they now cost industry over $4 billion a year. For example, a national survey of Canadians by the research firm Ipsos Reid informed readers in 2004,

> The two top contributors to absenteeism and/or health costs in the workplace are depression/anxiety/other mental health disorders (66 percent) and stress (60 percent). The other ranked causes include relationships with supervisor/manager (44 percent), childcare issues (35 percent), co-worker conflict in the workplace (28 percent), parenting issues (21 percent), addictions or substance use/abuse (20 percent), and eldercare issues (19 percent).

In the report, human resource management experts agreed that "the most serious organizational issue," causing the greatest level of absenteeism and thereby impacting health benefits claims costs, is "stress," followed by "poor relationships with supervisors/managers." But there was also good news. The same experts pointed out how 64 percent of organizations were busy fixing the deadly threat to their financial bottom lines by instituting "leadership and management training programs."

In principle, there's nothing wrong with such programs. Many corporations understand the benefit and need of continuous learning, of mentorship programs, and of designing leadership and management programs that offer early exposure to a wide variety of experiences to young employees. But such well-meaning programs don't work when they try to deal with the short-term *climate* while ignoring the powerful influence of organizational *culture*. It's like going to the city of Calgary for the sub-zero winter, taking only short-sleeves and sandals, focused only on the fact that the city has the occasional Chinook—a weird aberration of meteorology that for a day pumps summer-like warm winds into town.

The reality is that any remedy involves more than a little happy talk, a tweaking of the machinery, and a burnishing of the cogs in the wheel with the hope that everything will hum along predictably, profitably, and on time. The sad fact is that flavor-of-the-month workshops often do nothing to alleviate or even recognize corporate personality disorder, because they focus on what to do about the current climate when it's the long-term culture that's the problem.

But it's not just what's going on *inside* the Organizational Family Tree. Dysfunctional organizational structures are also destroying the lives of those *outside* their walls. System structures with official policies, procedures, red tape, bureaucratic rubber-stamping, communication spin-doctoring, and box-like organization charts create system actions by which consumers and investors are robbed of life savings, safety and security is compromised, and cost-benefit analyses favor the death of families and children over the making of production-line changes.

Just think about the words Enron, WorldCom, Nortel, Arthur Andersen, *Exxon Valdez*, Bhopal, Three Mile Island, the Ford Motor Company's Pinto car (with its exploding gas tank), the disastrous space shuttle *Challenger*, the Dalkon Shield and toxic shock syndrome, and dozens of other examples, and you will see how corporate personality disorder takes its toll. You don't have to look very far for examples. Just ask yourself, "Am I happy in my job? Am I happy with how I'm treated by my organization—and by the organizations I'm forced to deal with, such as government agencies, my doctor's office, my lawyer, and my child's education system?"

It's not just big companies that suffer from corporate personality disorder. It's also government departments, not-for-profit groups, and even the structures in our society that are designed to help us in our misery and pain. In hospice settings, it is often noticed that loss of trust in others can accompany severe illness and disease. The same is true with sick organizational systems. When we're exposed to this organizational condition, one of the first symptoms is a loss of faith and trust in the institutions that have built the expectation that they will be there when we need them the most.

National surveys (www.pollingreport.com) showed that in 2006, North Americans had lost faith in many of their major institutions, with 83 percent agreeing that big companies have too much power and 71 percent agreeing that the news media have too much power. A national Harris Poll in 2007 (www.pollingrepoprt.com) also showed that only 16 percent of us had a great deal of confidence in major companies, 15 percent in organized labor, 12 percent in the news media, and only 10 percent in Congress.

As part of my research for a master's degree dissertation in 2000, I looked at how dysfunctional organizational systems might be affecting the self-image and hopefulness of medical doctors. This is where I discovered Robin. The study found that the impact of a health care system that was underfunded, badly administered, and inefficient created a measurable, clinical condition in those directly affected, including both patients and doctors. While it wasn't surprising that patients were suffering, my study showed that corporate personality disorder was also taking its toll on physicians, with many reporting cases of personal burnout, depression, and even thoughts of suicide.

The devastation that organizational environments can have on you is well documented in the late Peter Frost's 2003 book, *Toxic Emotions at Work*. In his detailed study of unhealthy workplaces, Professor Frost states, "Not just managers but organizations themselves create conditions for toxicity through policies and practices that fail to include the human factor in their execution."

Frost's book identifies many key sources of organizational toxicity, including company policies, the behavior and attitudes of managers, the psychological makeup of employees, and the general nature of today's organized life. While the sources identified by Frost are very real, they are often the symptoms of an institutional disease—not the cause. The *cause* of organizational toxicity is not the immediate dysfunctional actions of managers or employees that we must deal with.

No, the *cause* lies deeply embedded in the historical and developmental factors (the culture of an organization) that combine to shape the overall structure and personality of organizations, including the organizational personalities who treat us badly. In the next chapter, we're going to peel back some of the structural layers of the organizational onion and see why it makes you cry.

2

A HEALTHY, NATURAL REMEDY FOR SICK SYSTEMS

According to laws in most Western nations, a corporation is technically a person. It can own things, such as property and buildings, has legal rights, must have a unique name and registration number, is compelled to pay taxes, can be sued or sue others, and is responsible for certain actions (see Joel Bakan's 2004 book *The Corporation* for more on this). There are very specific legal descriptions of what a corporation is. Lawyers spend zillions of billable hours protecting or dissecting the legal intricacies of corporations, but I'm not a lawyer, and I'm lucky if my socks match. I'm what my two sons call a "feelings doctor."

As a social scientist with a doctorate in human and organizational systems and training as a peer counselor, I've spent the past thirty-five years in the trenches of everyday organizational life trying to figure out why corporate personalities behave the way they do. What I've discovered is this: there's really little difference between a *human* personality and an *organizational* personality. What causes people to melt down also causes organizations to melt down. This also means that what can help us mortals straighten out our attitudes and behavior is also what can help the illustrious corporate body behave a lot better.

Our individual background, family history, and developmental influences usually contribute to our personality, including how we behave and see the world. It's the same thing with organizations. There's a parallel between the development of human and organizational personalities, especially regarding how historical factors and early lessons learned (culture) shape today's behavior. But just as we don't have to be held hostage by the past—we can through self-reflection and effort change not only our behavior but also our attitudes about life—so too can organizations change for the better.

A continuing series of studies are showing that the way some organizations behave—particularly, the attention they pay to emotional needs—is leading to severe human anxiety, depression, burnout, and a wide range of physical and psychological maladies. These places are, in fact, showing clinical symptoms of a personality disorder. Why is this happening? And what's the treatment? To answer this, we must look at both the historical definition of what an organization is and particularly how—and why—organizations are structured the way they are.

What's an "organization"? Simply put, it's the *relationship* between people who apply various *processes* according to agreed-upon goals and behavior. (The word comes from the Greek word *organon*, meaning tool.) An "organization" can be formally defined by legally binding agreements with clearly articulated codes of conduct. Corporations, government agencies, sports teams, religious groups, and well-defined social movements are all examples of formal organizations. An organization can also be a less formally defined collection of individuals, such as a street gang, a neighborhood homeless shelter, or even your weekend joggers' group.

Your family is an organization, and so is an "organized crime" syndicate, which has a specific definition under the Criminal Code of Canada as "a group comprised of three or more persons which has, as one of its primary activities or purposes, the commission of a serious offence(s), which likely results in financial gain."

Organizations, just like us, have varying levels of power and energy based on who they are and how well they get along with others—their personalities and their relationships. Organizations exhibit unique behavior and are influenced by both historical and developmental factors, including the environment they are born into, strong "parents" (in the form of other organizations or powerful leaders), and ongoing events in their lives.

The healthy organization is an organic rather than a mechanistic system. It is living and breathing, ebbing and flowing with energy and power, *not* a deterministic mechanical device without soul or human substance.

If you hear the words "corporation" or "company" and automatically think of stupid bureaucracy, multilayered organization charts, and forty-minute hold times to get service, you're not alone or wrong. But let's forget the old machine metaphor for a while and think about organizations as *organic* beings.

Over the past several years, many management experts ranging from Ralph Stacey to Jeffrey Goldstein have increasingly viewed the structure of the modern organization as a natural system rather than a prescriptive, mechanistic model. A way of thinking called *complexity science* argues that organizations operate as networked, adaptive, nonlinear systems, much like biological organisms.

Now, this description is a real mouthful and I'll go into more detail later, but for now let me put it this way: A "complex adaptive system" (a.k.a., complexity science) is an organizational system whose parts come together not in some top-down box-like model but rather in a spider web-like structure.

It is not a straight-arrow system, despite the belief in many organizations today that there's just one path to tomorrow. Instead, it's "nonlinear," meaning growth and progress can meander around and what happened before won't necessarily happen again. And that means even a small action can create big results.

This notion, that organizations are not just clockworks but rather living, evolving places, has been getting a lot of attention in recent years—mostly because the old Industrial Age mechanical metaphor keeps breaking down. Some writers and researchers, using a similar metaphor, claim that organizations have distinct "DNA" or a "corporate genome" with a differentiated corporate personality and measurable attributes related to how organizations coexist with employees, customers, and others. This genetic metaphor is also the basis of what Richard Dawkins (1989) calls *memes*, defined as "an element of a culture that may be considered to be passed on by non-genetic means, especially imitation."

A common theme among complexity science's ideas of leadership and management is that organizations emulate principles of emergence, or evolution, found in natural biologic systems. This means that instead of you being stuck into a cubicle like a peg into a hole, where everything is expected to tick along predictably, something quite different takes place—there are ebbs and flows and, oh my gosh, even surprises! Such notions typically use language with terms like "interconnectivity," "nonlinearity," and "self-organization."

But don't let the multisyllabic mouthful of complexity-speak scare you away. As we'll discuss later, there's nothing at all complicated about complexity science. For example, "interconnectivity, nonlinearity, and self-organization" simply means working together and sharing information, understanding that very few things are totally predictable, and being creatively adaptable to changes that will indeed come.

Lessons from complexity science have much to offer the modern organization. However, the most practical lessons are not drawn from plant and insect life (despite my tree metaphor) but from patterns in human biology, such as those found in the metaphor of an organizational genome and Dawkins' concept of memes.

BRANCHES AND ROOTS ON THE ORGANIZATIONAL FAMILY TREE

The multilayered *Organizational Family Tree* helps us trace the growth and flow of power and energy within an organization (i.e., what makes it what it is) and spot potential decay, which can lead to corporate personality disorder. Once we get this insight into not only *what* we're dealing with but *why*, we can either think of ways to help the organization or decide that our very unique *human* personality would be much happier living with a different *organizational* personality.

In case you're wondering, the Organizational Family Tree has indeed left my mad scientist's laboratory of weird theories and is actually being applied to real life. To date, this model has been successfully used with a large national organization, is used daily as an issue identification tool by an international police force, has been applied to health care agencies, and was used in 2005 as the foundation for a major change-management initiative affecting over eight thousand personnel.

Organizations are like people in that their personalities (the sum of culture and climate) are susceptible to aberrant behavior—some are antisocial bullies while others are warm hearted, caring, and sensitive. Like a *human* personality, the *organizational* personality is prone to "illness" and often, again like humans, clues to why the organization is suffering can be found in its history.

What we'll find hanging from the Organizational Family Tree is a focus on the role of both historical and developmental factors in organizational behavior. What we'll *especially* find as we shuffle the leaves and branches around and dig into the roots is a strong focus on how organizational personalities intertwine with the *emotional* aspect of human personalities. In doing this, I'll be borrowing a lot of ideas taught in family and individual counseling. After all, a family is a family, whether it's an organizational one or a human one. Why not? In my experience, the same techniques used to help an individual overcome his behavior and outlook also work very well in helping an organizational personality deal with *its* behavior.

HISTORICAL FACTORS: THE ROOTS OF ORGANIZATIONAL BEHAVIOR

Ever think about your cousin Kenny and realize that his weirdo behavior is just like his uncle Benny's (who, by the way, is a lot like his grandfather George, who isn't playing with a full deck)? You've heard the expression "The apple doesn't fall far from the tree." In this case, the entire organizational apple cart sits directly under the sprawling Organizational Family Tree.

The Organizational Family Tree suggests that, as with humans, organizations have historical factors they were "born" with and developmental factors they have acquired from life experiences. Think of these factors as the vital nutrients of organizational growth. Historical factors include the early history and characteristics of the organization, including the culture and behavior of the sector or the category the organization was born into. This means a logging company will have different historical traits than a women's shelter or a financial institution.

Historical factors also include the regulatory environment that an organization was born into, including all the laws, regulations, and government codes, and rules that apply to it. So what happens during a corporate merger or the creation of a unique new department? Well, the same thing that happens in human families after the birth of a new child or after two divorced people get remarried and blend their existing families, including kids from previous marriages.

What often happens is that the strongest and deepest family structure is the one that dominates in a blended marriage. And when new children are born into a family, the existing environment, which is a mix of past culture and current climate, tends to influence them. It's the same with the organizational family. A new business line or branch born into, or adopted by, an existing organization inherits the current historical influences, including the mission, vision, and values of the existing organization, and is affected by the existing environment.

This is why many organizations run into trouble when they create new, specialized departments or branches that try to be "different" from the deeply imbedded factors influencing the Organizational Family Tree. It's also why mergers and acquisitions in the corporate world often run into "clashes of culture" when the adopted corporation finds that its Organizational Family Tree is significantly at odds with its new parent's background, history, and lessons learned.

Another set of historical factors that an organization possesses is the overall style and structure of its leadership and management, usually well entrenched in the sector the organization is part of. For example, military or paramilitary organizations (like police forces) have command-and-control structures and reporting relationships that are very well established, including systems of reward and punishment. On the other hand, credit unions have a strong culture of depositor participation in corporate decision making as well as a great deal of investor empowerment. Imagine a hard-assed, by-the-book retired military general taking over the running of a decentralized credit union. ("Listen up! You *will* vote according to these orders! That is all.")

There are many forms of leadership within the Organizational Family Tree, including transactional ("Do what I say and I will reward you"), transformational ("We're giving you the tools and mentoring you need to succeed"), situational crisis events calling for dynamic and very directed approaches ("Clamp that artery now!"), what Max Dupree calls servant leadership, wherein the leader sees service to others as his or her calling, and the "great person theory" of leadership, wherein leaders have larger-than-life, dynamic, and inspirational personalities (Winston Churchill and John Kennedy come to mind).

Finally, part of an organization's historical factors includes its meeting of long-prevailing public expectations. For example, financial institutions have a high degree of fiduciary responsibility (meaning you wouldn't expect the local branch manager to run off to the Grand Caymans) and health care organizations have a high trust factor ("Okay Doc, you can stick that needle in my eye").

As I mentioned earlier, historical factors also include what Dawkins refers to as memes—the concepts, ideas, beliefs, and behaviors than humans pass on to others through interaction and mimicry. Greed, envy, self-interest, and other factors provide fuel for memetic replication, which can be useful or destructive. When looking at how memes have moved through organizational evolutionary life, we discover that a major memetic historical strain is the continuing and sometimes unconscious influence of management and organizational structures dating back to the Industrial Revolution. Two particularly powerful continuing influences are Frederick Taylor's scientific management model of 1911 and Max Weber's model of bureaucracy of 1946.

Thus, the reason many managers always say, "This is the way we've always done it" is because, in fact, that *is* the way the organization has always done it—it's been repeating a memetic mantra for over a hundred years. And as we do with a lot of things, after a while we stop asking, "Why exactly are we doing this?" and just keep on trucking along, never minding that the truck is heading over a cliff.

Our personality and our daily behavior are heavily influenced by strong historical and developmental factors. This means some of our behaviors are harder to change than others (e.g., it's a lot harder to change how we cope with stress than our table manners). It's the same with organizations. The best intentions of leaders and managers, including efforts at creativity, "out of the box thinking," and emergence from the status quo, is severely restricted in an organization heavily laden with Industrial Age baggage—namely, mechanistic command-and-control structures.

When we try to change today's organizational climate, we're likely messing with conditions created by a culture deeply rooted in the Organizational Family Tree. There's no point in trimming a few discolored leaves or decaying branches when the cause is a long history of bad sap that just keeps on flowing (and I'm sure you know more than one decision-making sap).

DEVELOPMENTAL FACTORS WITHIN THE ORGANIZATIONAL FAMILY TREE

Let's now look at the *developmental factors* within the Organizational Family Tree. Just like us humans, organizations grow and define themselves according to developmental factors—the events that impact them throughout their life, sometimes purposefully created through internal decision making and leadership, sometimes through externally imposed regulations and laws, and sometimes through unexpected events, such as a major crisis.

The combination of historical and developmental factors creates what is commonly referred to as corporate culture. As Robert Kaplan and David Norton (2004) explain, culture is

> The symbolism, myths, stories, and rituals embedded in the organizational consciousness (or subconsciousness). Culture attempts to capture the systems of shared meanings, assumptions, and values in an organization.

In addition, Hiroaki Nagura and Hirofumi Honda (2001) point out that "corporate culture is supported by traditions that have been developed since the company's foundation, and have grown in succession."

Developmental influences in an organization's growth also include the pressures of public opinion, which in turn shape public policy. Major examples include environmental protection, gender issues, the treatment of minorities, and the protection of children. However, in many such cases of developmental growth, the advances had to first overcome major pressures exerted by an organization's historical factors, which stressed conformity, control, and predictability. And sometimes, as with the continuing need to address climate change, for civil rights, gay rights, and women's rights movements, some of those old stick-in-the-mud historical factors that served as the foundation of an organization are still obvious in the organization's current behavior—as witnessed in class-action lawsuits aimed at stopping discrimination in the workplace.

A good example of the replicator outcome of memes within an organization's developmental factors is the commonplace standard operating procedures (SOPs). SOPs are a codified way of dealing with a host of potential issues and crises based on lessons learned and the experience of others. While SOPs can be useful to deal with crises and to help define both responsibility and accountability, they can also be more of a problem than they're worth. This happens when the standards and procedures become so prescriptive and demanding that all they really do is anger users, who then ignore the SOPs. And when employees begin to ignore SOPs, the organization is SOL (sweet out of luck).

Why is there a propensity by many in so-called leadership roles to micromanage us, second-guess us, and look over our shoulder? Simple. That's the way a mechanistic mindset works. Those who believe that it's super important to second-guess us and micro-wordsmith every comma and syllable we write in a memo are looking for one thing—absolute control and containment of the world around them. Their sense of self—their small box of confidence and personal identify—is threatened by even the smallest uncertainty, by even the remotest chance of unpredictability. And so they try to tie everything down tight, triple-bolt the doors, secure the shutters, squeeze their eyes shut, and take shallow breaths.

Another example of a developmental factor is the ubiquitous organization chart—basically unchanged in design since the first one was created in 1846 to suit the needs of American railroads. (We're going to ride this rail a little longer, later on.) Developmental factors are also particularly profound in science, technology, medicine, and the judicial system, where past actions and outcomes create precedents that shape how future actions are developed and received. In fact, every formula, scientific method, list of instructions, and *Farmers' Almanac*—every document that we use to plan tomorrow's behavior based on yesterday's actions—is an example of a developmental factor.

We obviously can't do away with developmental factors. We can't wave a magic wand and evaporate our growth histories, including the impact others have had, the schools we have attended, and the lessons we have learned in life. But what we can do is acknowledge the presence and impact of developmental factors on our daily behavior and on the climatic factors of our existence.

It's the same with *organizational* personalities. We *can* take the temperature of an organizational climate and ask, "Why are we doing this anyway? To what end? Is there a better way of doing this? Why not?" (For example, why is it against the law to keep a donkey in a bathtub in Georgia? And why is it against the law to ride a bike in a swimming pool in California?) We can take stock of our organizational developmental factors and ask ourselves if they're contributing something positive or negative to the climate. And then we can dig even deeper into the Organizational Family Tree and, while our fingers are enjoying the cool soil, think about the following.

Much of today's organizational structure and behavior is influenced more by *historical* than *developmental* factors. Organizations certainly learn from experience, but that experience is perceived and managed through the lens of the organization's historical factors. Sometimes an experience is so profound that it offsets the influence of history ("I know we've always used a horse and plough, but this tractor thing seems to be working out okay.") But usually it doesn't.

While an organization certainly has an opportunity to learn from sudden and planned actions, and while it can incorporate such learning into new activities, the guiding forces behind most organizational development are often still rooted in the basic mechanical systems model introduced during the Industrial Revolution. And that means it's harder to shift an organizational paradigm than it is to shift my faded red 1952 Jeep truck from first to second gear. It's way harder because the continuing lesson of history is that the old system will keep us safe, stable, and secure. It won't, of course, but it's very scary to challenge that carved-in-stone logic. Better just to cruise along in neutral.

Even the most innovative training programs in the world will have trouble helping an organization if its personality is rooted in deep—and often unconscious—historical influences. Employees automatically put up barriers to learning when a training program presents information that conflicts with their well-enshrined way of seeing the world and doing things. I've seen this in gender and culture "sensitivity training" workshops, where the same sexist and racist louts who first walked into the room are the same sexist, racist louts who left six weeks later with their cute certificate of accomplishment.

The world is constantly changing, and the pace and type of change swirling around a corporation, a religion, a citizen's group, a government department, or some other form of organization can't help but affect, either now or later, how that place behaves. In some cases, the organization will hunker down in a defensive fetal position, wishing the change will simply go away. In other cases, the organization will aggressively resist change, fighting with all its might to preserve the status quo. And in other cases, the organization will embrace change as a natural, evolutionary stage of growth. The different responses by different organizations to the same conditions are, just as they are with everyday people, based on differing cultural influences (historical and developmental factors).

SYSTEM STRUCTURES AND THE ORGANIZATIONAL FAMILY TREE

If you have kids, as I do, I don't have to tell you about the importance of rules, boundaries, rewards, and consequences. Without them things can get pretty crazy, and even with such wonderful tools of family organization, you may still find yourself at the edge of chaos. The systems of organization families use have been around since the first cave family blinked at the sun and worried that their toddler was in danger of being abducted by something with huge teeth. It's the same with the Organizational Family Tree, and the dangers can be just as scary.

An organization's *system structure* is the technical management stuff that's supposed to help an organization understand and respond to its *systems environment*. The environment, in corporate terms, means all the economic, political, ecological, social, technological, and communications factors, expectations, and goings on that directly impact the organization's health. ("The Dow Jones is up today, crazy legislators have added a new tax, no one likes our moose burgers, and global warming means the lake is frozen forever.")

Will McWhinney (1998) describes a system as "a thing and the relations between and among its parts and the whole, a collection of parts that interact with each other to function as a whole." Fitjof Capra in his book *The Web of Life* (1982) describes a system this way:

> Systems are integrated wholes whose properties cannot be reduced to those of smaller units. Instead of concentrating on basic building blocks or basic substances, the systems approach emphasizes basic principles of organization. Every organism—from the smallest bacterium through the wide range of plants and animals to humans—is an integrated whole and thus a living system.

Capra looks at organizational systems from a complexity science perspective. He sees organizations as organic, interconnected entities rather than static machine works of predictable causes and effects. Management theorist Peter Senge (1990) offers a related description of a system:

> Anything that takes its integrity and form from the ongoing interaction of its parts. Companies, nations, families, biological niches, bodies, television sets, personalities, and atoms are all systems. Systems are defined by the fact that their elements have a common purpose and behave in common ways, precisely because they are interrelated toward that purpose.

In the average workplace, the organizational system structure includes

- Delegation and control of authority, including reporting lines
- Organization charts tied together with both solid and dotted lines
- Formal rules and policies
- Standard operating procedures
- Internal and external communication systems, including how new information is incorporated into actions
- Measures that dispense both rewards and penalties

In addition, a system structure often includes the common mission, vision, and values statements (those fading things stuck on a back wall that few read and even fewer implement) that supposedly represent the organization's philosophical direction. It also includes plenty of formal business and marketing plans that promise "strategic and tactical direction" but which are more like a shaman's best guess after analyzing a goat's entrails. Both human emotion and knowledge needs are key ingredients within an organizational structure. In fact, how this balance is achieved—if at all—speaks to the organization's *personality* and is the first indicator of a healthy or sick Organizational Family Tree.

EMOTION AND KNOWLEDGE WITHIN AN ORGANIZATIONAL FAMILY TREE

We humans have both an emotional makeup and an inherent need to know things—especially things that keep us safe and alive and that serve to either protect or polish our egos. But we're *especially* packed with emotion. The emotion part of our three-pound brain was the first area formed, in order to keep us attuned to danger, and it's still the first part that's triggered when we're stimulated by the various sights, sounds, tastes, and sensations around and in us.

Therefore, we're going to look at the importance of both emotions and knowledge within organizational structures, after which I'll offer a very *simple* checklist of emotion and knowledge factors. These are the ones that often surface in my work with people who are trying to make their human personalities gel with organizational personalities. I suspect that you may also have a few things to add to the list.

The powerful role emotions play in organizational life is of growing interest to researchers, counselors, and those trying to achieve better relationships between organizational personalities and human personalities. Paul Wieand, founder of the Centre for Advanced Emotional Intelligence, has a lot to say about the importance of emotions, relationships, and authenticity in leadership. In an interview with Pamela Kruger of *Fast Company* magazine (1999), he says this about senior executives to whom he provides counsel:

> They lose touch with their emotions, and they become insensitive to how they affect others and intolerant of others' weaknesses. If you idealize your role—which is what happens to most of the people I see—you fool yourself about what people really think of you.

Wieand advises people to communicate with emotion as well as logic. He draws upon findings in neuroscience that show the brain's limbic system, which governs feelings and emotions, plays a stronger role than the neocortex, where rational thought and logic reside. Drawing upon his past work in a psychiatric ward, Wieand says, "If creating an atmosphere of trust and authenticity can get acute schizophrenics to work together, think of what presumably less-fragile people can do."

Psychologist Daniel Goleman has written extensively on how emotional intelligence is rooted to emotions and the influence of the brain's limbic system, home to the almond-shaped amygdala. Goleman draws from the groundbreaking work of neuroscientist Joseph LeDoux, who focused specifically on the amygdala's role in the emotion of fear. In his work, Goleman has created an "emotional competence framework," which includes twenty-five personal competencies under five domains, including self-awareness, self-regulation, motivation, empathy, and social skills.

ORGANIZATIONAL ENERGY INDEX

never 1...2...3...4...5 always

EMOTION FACTORS

People treat each other with respect
There is supportive supervision of work
Individuals feel personally valued
Cooperation with others is a priority
Everyone is treated fairly
Candid feedback is encouraged
Help and support is easily available
There is a balance of work and personal life
Mistakes are quickly admitted and corrected
People are recognized for a job well done

KNOWLEDGE FACTORS

Responsibilities are clearly communicated
Workplace promises are met with action
Important information is openly shared
There is a clear link between tasks and goals
Assumptions are regularly reviewed
There is clear accountability for actions
Lessons learned are rolled into new actions
The organization connects well to other groups
A variety of opinions are often/widely sought
Knowledge and skills are often upgraded

The Organizational Family Tree suggests that all organizational behavior includes specific, baseline requirements related to both our emotion and knowledge needs. In other words, we want to be treated well and we want to know what's going on and have the knowledge to get on with it. One way to measure the state of these key factors is my *Organizational Energy Index*. What the Index does is measure the strength of ten emotion and ten knowledge factors that are key to organizational effectiveness. Why ten each, you ask? And why, you wonder, *these* ten each?

Recent management research is as rich as the Alberta tar sands, with references to the importance of recognizing human emotion in the workplace ranging from the popular concept of emotional intelligence to research connecting workplace efficacy to the state of our emotions. As Anat Rafaeli and Monica Worline (1996) state, "Emotional bonds are what produces organizations, rather than legal, financial, or geographical bonds."

The ten emotion factors in the Organizational Energy Index are those that collectively contribute to reducing our fears while contributing to a sense of common community, belonging, and emotional connectivity. They were distilled from the significant research on emotion and trust in organizations as well as my review of numerous national and regional employee surveys conducted in both Canada and the United States over the past ten years.

What the questions related to emotion factors recognize is the huge value we place on our sense of self—the very personal and important perception we have of who we are. Now, this self-image thing is huge. Research shows we'll do almost anything to protect our self-image, our positive notion of *who we are*.

And now we're getting down to the nitty-gritty of why changes to how an organization behaves can create problems. As Blake Ashforth and Fred Mael (1998) state, "In particular, resistance is often prompted by a perceived threat to identity, to a valued conception of self," and as Terrell Northrup (1989) states, "Events which threaten to invalidate the core sense of identity will illicit defensive responses aimed at avoiding psychic and/or physical annihilation."

It is possible for an organization to create a threatening and fearful work environment even if the threat to our self-image is an *unconscious* one. Our sense of insecurity, unease, or even fear because of what's going on can be flying below our radar like a stealth bomber, but our brain's internal self-defense system knows exactly what's going on, and it's opening the bay doors, ready to push out a few megaton surprises in the form of anything from a nasty e-mail to a red-faced toe-to-toe shouting match.

One rough measure of how uneasy or even threatened you're feeling right is how well you think your organization is responding to the ten *emotion* factors in the Organizational Energy Index. A major reason why emotion factors score low in some organizations is that their importance has historically been downgraded. It's an outcome of organizational culture, the continuing influence of historical factors that demand allegiance to mechanistic command-and-control structures of management and leadership.

The ten *knowledge* factors within the Organizational Energy Index include knowledge, skills, and abilities but much more. What the knowledge factors capture are attributes commonly associated with transformational leadership, trust, empathy, effective communication, and core managerial competencies. In addition, the ten knowledge factors are those organizational actions and ongoing behaviors that enhance empowerment, sense of self, and self-actualization.

If you score an organization high on this scale, you think you're getting the training you need, there are folks around to help you if necessary, "mistakes" are seen as learning opportunities and quickly rolled back into new action, and you have a good idea where the organization is going (and you actually get a chance to have a say in that direction).

Most organizations don't score too well on this scale (although most score better here than on the emotion factor scale). But some do, particularly places that have a reputation for corporate social responsibility, see their employees as partners with something to creatively contribute, and have a culture (historical and developmental factors) that values empowerment and adaptability.

When humming along with high scores, all ten knowledge factors contribute to a greater sense of stability, adaptability, and especially *trust* in an organization. Now, *trust* is very big stuff, whether the organization is the local Boy Scouts group or Dow Chemical. Trust is the glue that binds personal relationships and organizational life—whether the organization is a multinational corporation or my son's weekend soccer team.

The years of research on trust by a wide range of scholars shows that for trust to occur at least the following basic factors must be present—competence, predictability, reliability, honesty, and shared values. Do you trust your lover, spouse, or the person in the next office? If you do, those factors will be present. Just *how much* you trust that person will depend on how much importance you place on each of the criteria ("Now, I've never done this before, and I've just met you, but I want you to stand really still while I throw these hatchets around your head. Trust me. It'll be okay. I think.")

A key principle of the Organizational Family Tree is that *both* emotion and knowledge factors need to score high for an organization to be trusted, healthy, well performing, and innovative. In addition, the need for a balance of emotion and knowledge factors doesn't waiver based on circumstances or the nature of the organization. I've discovered this need for balance (and, if anything, a greater need for emotional availability) in surveys involving organizations as diverse as a national police force, a regional medical association, a national bank, an international food services chain, and an international environmental organization.

WHAT KIND OF ORGANIZATIONAL PERSONALITY ARE YOU HANGING WITH?

An indication of what kind of organizational personality you're dealing with can be found by applying the results of the emotion/knowledge scale to what I term the *Organization Personality Type* (OPT). There are four basic personalities within the OPT: visionary-adaptive, collaborative-supportive, cautious-controlling, and suspicious-defensive.

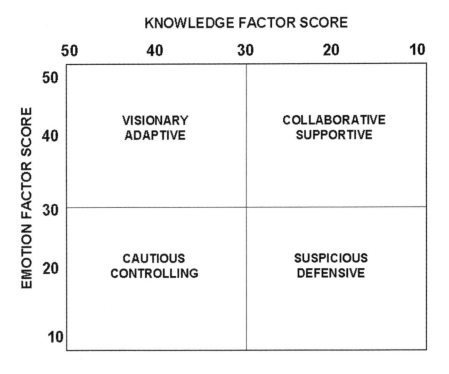

Here is a rundown of the various organizational personality types. But please don't see these descriptions as cut in stone. Organizational personalities, like human personalities, are often difficult to pigeonhole and often have characteristics found to varying degree in all four quadrants. Nevertheless, just as with the index, the Personality Type assessment will hopefully give you at least a general insight into the organization you are dealing with.

Type 1: Visionary-Adaptive Organizational Personality

In the visionary-adaptive organization we won't see displays of corporate personality disorder. High emotion and knowledge scores suggest an environment where change is encouraged and assumptions are constantly being challenged. Communications are open, inclusive, ongoing, and sought out, leading to double-loop learning (what's learned through two-way communications and feedback is reincorporated into what is done next). There's a high level of creativity and productivity, decision-making autonomy is highly decentralized, and the organizational layers of reporting are kept to a minimum.

The visionary-adaptive organization experiences low levels of workplace stress, absenteeism, and employee turnover. Teamwork and mentoring are common, and management strives to balance personal and workplace needs. Relationships are built on mutual trust, shared understanding, and collaboration. Leadership follows a transformational and servant-leadership style, which emphasizes getting the best out of people rather than issuing dictates and demanding performance based on intimidation.

Drawing from the Triangle of Trust model, we see in the visionary-adaptive organization a reasoned sharing of authority in which employees are not afraid of making decisions on their own and "thinking in a bigger box" when they have to. They know their responsibilities, and there's regular accountability for actions associated with all levels of authority. Communications are open, honest, and reciprocal, meaning individuals not only get the information they need when they need it but also have plenty of opportunity to provide input and feedback. There's broad connectivity to other organizations, community groups, and individuals that are impacted by the actions of the organization, and there's excellent cooperation among groups and individuals within and outside the organization.

Type 2: Collaborative-Supportive Organizational Personality

It's in the collaborative-supportive organization where we start to see examples of corporate personality disorder. A moderate to high emotion factor score combined with a low to moderate knowledge score is indicative of an organization in which two-way communication is inconsistent and only moderate levels of trust exist in leaders, managers, and the organizational personality.

There's often an emotional disconnect in such organizations, where, despite best intentions, the focus of senior managers and leaders is on meeting measurable targets rather than mentoring and nurturing. Change is generally accepted as a given but not necessarily well managed due to perceived threats to personal power, pride, and profit.

In the collaborative-supportive organization, the Triangle of Trust—comprised of responsibility, accountability, and authority—places a heavier demand on individual responsibility and accountability than on offering people authority. This can result in employees feeling powerless and frustrated. Although there are high expectations on employees, they're not given the tools and power necessary to do their job. In addition to communications being inconsistent in terms of quality and quantity, connectivity is also weak—the organization is not well networked to the community it serves and with those it impacts. Finally, cooperation among individuals and groups, both internally and externally, is not well nurtured and is often uneven and inconsistent.

Both crises and contentious organizational issues in the collaborative-supportive organization are viewed as things to be managed, contained, and controlled, and less emphasis is given to finding the internal reasons that such events occur. The person in such an organization might be feeling supported and respected—as long as they don't ask tough questions or offer criticism of goals and objectives—but they're also often unclear about the direction of the organization and how they fit in.

Type 3: Cautious-Controlling Organizational Personality

A low to moderate emotion score combined with a moderate to high knowledge score suggests an organizational environment where individual emotional needs are second to organizational objectives, which are usually driven by numerical performance targets and financial bottom lines. This can breed suspicion, a lack of peak productivity, higher than average turnover, and diminished morale. This type of organization is a fertile breeding ground for corporate personality disorder.

Change in the cautious-controlling organization is usually viewed with suspicion and defensiveness, and there is a strong emphasis on preserving the status quo; there is minimal creativity and innovation, because to do "something different" is to "buck the system"; communications are top down, with an emphasis on "selling the message" and spin-doctoring rather than engaging in a dialogue that could mean challenging old assumptions; and there is little opportunity for feedback and collaboration. Conflict is seen as a negative force that must and can be "managed" away.

Leadership in the cautious-controlling organization is usually of the command-and-control variety, also known as transactional leadership. Employees are expected to do what they're told, ask few questions, and be grateful for having a job. In applying the Triangle of Trust, we find that there's a great deal of accountability demanded but little independent responsibility and minimal authority to make things happen. Besides communications being top down with little perceived need for feedback, there are very weak ties—or connectivity—to groups and individuals impacted by the behavior of the organization. Finally, cooperation in this type of organizational personality occurs only when the organization sees a direct benefit to itself or when it's forced to cooperate.

Type 4: Suspicious-Defensive Organizational Personality

Low to moderate emotion factor and knowledge factor scores suggest an organization that is highly resistant to change and threatened by opposing viewpoints. This is a classic mechanical model of organization and transactional leadership. There's little innovation or creativity and strong protection of long-standing historical and developmental factors embedded in the status quo, regardless of whether what has worked before is useful. The suspicious-defensive organization is the worst case of corporate personality disorder.

Communications in the suspicious-defensive organization are directive based and often coercive, with no effort at relationship building or collaboration. Conflict or contrary views are seen as a threat that must be repelled, subdued, and punished. The workplace environment usually has high levels of stress and poor morale, with accompanying low levels of performance and commitment. Leadership is a classic military-style, transactional command-and-control model, where rank, reporting lines, and hierarchy rule the day.

In the suspicious-defensive organization, the Triangle of Trust is badly twisted. While there are high expectations of performance, accountability for actions is often unclear and frequently redirected through finger pointing. There's no independent responsibility allowing the exercise of creativity and innovation. And authority is entirely vested with the most senior management, which operates on a "need to know" basis. Besides communications being rare and mostly concerning dictates and orders, the organization maintains little positive connection with those it affects through its actions, and it views cooperation as capitulation.

IDENTIFYING AN ORGANIZATION'S PERSONALITY

Just as with people, an organization's personality is the result of an intertwined process rather than a nature-versus-nurture argument. All organizations and institutions in society—not just big corporations—have personality traits, and those traits ultimately reach maturity in an organization in much the same way that your traits reach maturity. Or, as individuals do, organizations can get stuck at a certain early developmental stage.

We are born with very specific traits and dispositions. Neuroscientist Joseph LeDoux in his book *Synaptic Self* (2002) says that genes account for about 50 percent of each personality trait (though not 50 percent of all traits), and fellow neuroscientist Steven Pinker from Harvard points out in his book *The Blank Slate* (2002) that there are five major ways our personalities can differ, and they are all heritable. As he says,

> Most of the 18,000 adjectives for personality traits in an unabridged dictionary can be tied to one of these five dimensions ... introverted or extroverted, neurotic or stable, incurious or open to experience, agreeable or antagonistic, and conscientious or undirected.... including such sins and flaws as being aimless, careless, conforming, impatient, narrow, rude, self-pitying, selfish, suspicious, uncooperative, and undependable.

Like our own personality development, organizational personality development includes early formative years, when there are both emotional and organizational system structure influences. An organization can be heavily influenced by its "parents"—which can be head offices, its major shareholders, and its top leadership. In addition, like our personalities, an organizational personality is often subject to peer pressure from other organizations with whom it has much in common, associates (business alliances, corporate clients, partner groups), or shares membership (business groups, trade associations, cartels, social movement networks, professional associations).

We developed our personalities throughout a learning process, which included the consequences of actions and of traumatic crisis events. Organizational personalities develop in exactly the same way, but with one notable exception. Organizational personalities are far less adaptable than human ones. That's one reason why, as Royal Dutch Shell found in a study that was later shared with me by a senior manager, the average lifespan of a large corporation is less than half that of an average, healthy human being.

Many of us tend to learn and adapt, but organizations are very slow learners. In his book *The Fifth Discipline* (1999), Peter Senge laments that many organizations have "learning disabilities" because their system structures are designed so that effective learning is actually inhibited. As Senge says,

> It is no accident that most organizations learn poorly. The way they are designed and managed, the way people's jobs are defined, and, most importantly, the way we have all been taught to think and interact (not only in organizations but more broadly) create fundamental learning disabilities.
>
> These disabilities operate despite the best efforts of bright, committed people. Often the harder they try to solve problems, the worse the results. What learning does occur takes place despite these learning disabilities—for they pervade all organizations to some degree.

Organizational personalities are also shaped, like our personalities, by the small and large crises that enter the life of an organization. In my years of offering counsel to organizations and individuals facing severe conflicts and crises, I've received ample confirmation that major crises are change agents, and often that change is for the better. Corporations and the people affected within them are never the same again (notwithstanding that *every* event in our life leaves us a different person to some degree).

A crisis that causes pain and impoverishment can leave us wiser, to be sure, leading to alterations in both our awareness and behavior, usually making us more vigilant and protective. But a crisis can also affect our attitudes about others and, most tellingly, about the person we thought we were. A crisis can leave us feeling less trustworthy of others and more risk-averse, but it can also make us feel subconsciously that we can't even meet our own and others' expectations of ourselves—that we failed to live up to our perfect self-image of being strong, smart, adaptable, and in control.

Imagine a child growing up who is born with aggressive and antisocial personality traits and whose developmental years leading to maturity are shaped by a variety of abusive relationships with his or her parents and family members. What kind of person would we be dealing with as an adult? How would such a person respond to sudden crises or significant changes in his life? How easy would it be for us to get along with her, to build trust and a long-term relationship? What if that person was our boss? What if that dysfunctional personality belonged to an organization?

The child described above has grown up into the personality manifested by many of the organizational structures of commerce and government that touch our lives daily. It's a personality born with, and now deeply troubled by, corporate personality disorder. If such an organization were a person, it would be diagnosed as "stuck" in an early developmental stage, unable and unwilling to mature and adapt. And predictably, as such organizations are found increasingly wanting in their behavior, we say we have a "crisis of confidence" in them.

In my work and research I find I'm not the only person who thinks that organizations display human characteristics. William Bridges (2000) developed a corporate personality assessment tool based on the human personality-linked *Myers-Briggs Type Indicator*, while Sandra Fekete and Lee Anna Keith (2003) use a much more elaborate and detailed personality-assessment tool that profiles such factors as "practicality, action, idealism, competence, leadership personality, and cultural diversity." Gary Neilson, Bruce Pasternack, Decio Mendes, and Eng-Ming Tan (2003), on the other hand, describe seven distinct corporate personalities shaped by "four bases of organizational DNA."

While other models of corporate personality assessment are all valid in their own way, what's often missing in such assessments is recognition of the powerful role that emotions play in everyday organizational life. Corporations, nonprofit groups, government agencies, and religions are not a neat array of boxes and reporting lines statically positioned on a flowchart. They are conglomerations of people—human beings with real needs, desires, hopes, and aspirations. It's this vital fact that underscores the emotion factor component in the Organizational Family Tree.

This is why, as you'll see in the next chapter, the task of changing organizational culture is incredibly difficult—far more than that envisioned by some practitioners who suggest that changes to an organization's strategy, structure, or human processes (its climate) will somehow magically and automatically result in a change to organizational culture.

While some successes may occur in the short term, a true understanding of what's behind organizational historical and developmental factors and an appreciation of the importance of both emotion and knowledge factors is required before any possible *lasting* improvements can be made to the structure and ongoing actions of an organization.

However, as we seek to understand the organization's personality, we must also hold the mirror up to our own personalities. The reason for this perhaps uncomfortable exercise is that our judgment of others' performance is often based on the level of our own expectations, which in turn are a reflection of our personal historical and developmental factors and our unique attention to both emotion and knowledge needs. But looking within, *honestly* looking within, is tricky business.

It's very difficult to see ourselves for who we are, because so much of our external behavior is not consciously available to us. We rarely see ourselves exactly as others see us, and how others see us is based on the unique lens through which they view the world, which has been formed through their own unique historical and developmental influences.

Depending on who we are—and especially who we *think* we are—the notion of seeing something different can be a very scary concept. It means exposing ourselves to truths that are hidden under multiple layers of protective lies, applied one small lie and one big lie at a time over the years, like successive layers of fine rice paper—white lies and gray lies and black lies that after many decades have become so rigid and protective, and especially so *comforting*, to us that we easily accept them as truth.

I believe, and this is especially true of my own experience, that too often we come to live a life of lies—not always glaring and obvious, but lies nevertheless. We lose sight of, and forget through purposeful determination, what lies are buried deep under our multilayered protective shellac. It was this notion of buried lies that inspired me to write the following while alone on a ferry churning through the waters of a rough West Coast winter night. It was taking me away from my son, who now lived with his mother following our divorce.

Lies

the lies we tell ourselves
are lighter than a secret whisper
invisible, inaudible, improbable
to us alone.

the lies we tell ourselves
shape the lives we share with others
and soon lies and living
and living lies, are one.

Inseparable
indistinguishable
invisible
to us alone.

Later in our journey into the corporate psyche, we're going to talk a lot more about this business of living a lie. I'm going to explain why we automatically think something is right about organizational behavior when we know in our gut, in our emotional brain, that it's all a bag of baloney. But for now, let's get into a little refined and not-so-refined culture and see what kind of climate exists in various environments, just so you know what to pack on this trip.

3

CULTURE, CLIMATE, AND ORGANIZATIONAL GROWTH

A few years ago a number of smaller financial institutions in Canada decided they would pool their resources and create a much larger national bank. The idea, which made great business sense and seemed very well planned, soon failed. There were all manner of technical reasons given for the failure, but a major reason was a clash of culture and climate.

The long-standing culture of the individual financial institutions was deeply rooted in local community control, with each customer being an official voting shareholder with plenty of say in how the institution supported such things as community projects. What I found as a consultant to the senior transition team was that many customers and even some managers saw the idea of a giant national bank being created from this grassroots organizational structure as anathema to everything they believed in.

Changing the *climate* of how everyday business was conducted was one thing; changing the *culture* was something else quite different to those who had both a financial and personal relationship with their local institution. Over the decades, I've continually seen how culture is vital to organizational climate and how the two combine to create what's called the "operational environment." I also continually see how the terms get mixed up. So I'm going to do a bit of a recap here, building on some of my explanations in chapter 1.

An organization's *culture* is its deeply rooted traditions, values, beliefs, and sense of self. An organization's *climate*, on the other hand, is the here and now. It includes rules and regulations, communication models, employee incentives, and other key factors that speak to both the emotion and knowledge needs of personnel. In my experience, I've found that the vast majority of an organization's climate is influenced by deeply imbedded organizational culture.

Daniel Denison, in his 1996 essay in *Academy of Management Review*, produced an excellent overview of culture and climate. He points out that despite the intellectual wars on the categories, culture and climate are often intertwined. In particular, early culture factors are very difficult to segregate from climate.

We humans all like to feel safe and we all like to have boundaries in our lives that contribute to that safety. A *positive* organizational culture often provides that sense of security and stability. When we feel fear, it's usually because we are facing the unknown and/or feel powerless. An organizational culture with roots deep in a well-defined past and whose actions incorporate lessons learned can give us a sense of empowerment, knowledge, and most importantly safety and security.

But there are also organizational cultures that are *not* so healthy, places where our interests—and those of employees, customers, and investors—are second to other corporate interests, including personal profit and ego aggrandizement. Such a culture usually leads to a toxic workplace and sick organizational systems. Rather than a sense of stability and security, the outcome is usually a climate of fear.

Dysfunctional cultures usually create organizational structures with power that is hoarded at the top of the organization chart, little sharing of authority, and asymmetrical top-down communications more intent on *telling* us what's happening than sharing or listening. In such cases, organizational climate—the here and now of how things are done—is almost entirely dictated by culture and extremely difficult to change in any meaningful way. Usually we get a lot of studies and surveys followed up by employee committees and action groups resulting in public-relations exercises that spin around and around until they are finally flushed down the drain and everything is as it was before.

What is apparent is that change is easier to implement within organizational cultures that support people and foster enlightened leadership and management structures than in toxic cultures. Healthy organizational cultures usually create positive organizational climatic conditions, which, while still somewhat resistant to change, are far more adaptable to new ways of doing things due to heightened levels of trust and effective communications. Conversely, within an unhealthy organizational culture, there are high levels of mistrust, poor communications, and strong resistance to the unknown. That's all obvious, but here's a twist you might not be ready for.

Many people prefer a slipshod, grouchy corporate personality that treats them badly from time to time within a sick system to something a lot nicer but new and unproven. This is because simple human nature prefers the imperfect predictable to the perfect unpredictable. Over time, we learn to adjust to even the most toxic of corporate environments. We learn how to duck, weave, and hide and how to be out of town when we know the organizational personality is in a particularly bad mood. Soon we find a comfortable consistency to the organizational *discomfort*. It's this "devil you know versus the devil you don't" mindset that makes even the most positive change difficult to implement.

We often hear that the goal of an organization's change-management initiative is to "change the culture." What folks (particularly managers and helpful consultants) usually mean by that phrase is that they want people to think more positively, work harder and more efficiently, stop complaining, and get on with a brave new world of doing things. However, what employees *really* hear is that all those things that have made them feel safe, given them a sense of predictability, and provided an environment of trust are on the chopping block. In other words, everything they've been doing is either wrong or useless. They suspect that changing the culture means messing with tried and true traditions, ignoring all those years of positive lessons learned. No wonder people facing change freak out.

The reason many change processes are met with strong resistance, and sometimes downright fear and anger, is that what's seen as changing is not everyday actions associated with organizational climate but the strongly entrenched anchors of security found in the culture. ("We've *never* been open on weekends! Not in one hundred years! We've *always* respected family time!") By contrast, changing actions that are very specific to the organizational climate is a heck of a lot easier, and over time, changes in the climate *may* change the culture.

What makes all of this very challenging is that organizational life is never static and that adaptability to changing environments is a necessary condition of survival. The tricky part is to remain adaptable and to make the necessary changes to organizational climate while not severing ties with those very important stabilizers found in organizational culture.

For change initiatives to succeed, there must be an awareness of the major organizational culture *and* climate factors, especially those seen as having both a continuing negative and positive influence on the organization. Healthy organizations find this out by talking to you directly as well as to many others at all levels of the organization. The goal in such qualitative research (actually talking to you and not just having you fill out a survey) is to find out what long-established organizational behaviors and actions are giving you comfort in the workplace, which instill a sense of security and provide safe boundaries, and which continue to impede adaptability and positive change.

You can get a good idea of how organizational culture and climate is affecting an organization with a simple little questionnaire. The answers will give you a good idea of an organization's operational environment and especially what from the deep past is driving behavior today.

I call this little probe into protective corporate bark the *Organizational Environment Index*. The index, which is a derivative of the Organization Personality Index found in chapter 1, uses a simple 1–5 scale to measure ten factors commonly associated with organizational culture and ten factors commonly associated with organizational climate. Besides being linked to culture and climate, the factors are also related to what creates trust within organizations.

ORGANIZATIONAL ENVIRONMENT INDEX

CULTURE FACTORS

☐ Personal rights and values are respected
☐ Personnel feel safe to express their views
☐ Everyone is treated fairly
☐ Mistakes are seen as learning not failure
☐ New ideas are often encouraged
☐ Management decision making is trusted
☐ There is clear accountability for actions
☐ Lessons learned are part of new action
☐ Personnel feel hopeful about their future
☐ Authority over actions is easily delegated

Low 1...2...3...4...5 high

CLIMATE FACTORS

☐ The organization values individual feedback
☐ Employees can make independent decisions
☐ Exceptional performance is acknowledged
☐ The organization encourages teamwork
☐ Continuous training is a top priority
☐ Help/support for individuals is easily available
☐ Organizational actions live up to promises
☐ Important information is openly shared
☐ There is clear responsibility for actions
☐ Personnel understand organizational goals

I've used the index (and variations of it) with organizations ranging from the Royal Canadian Mounted Police to a regional medical association, and from an international coffee company to a national bank to various mining and forestry companies. But for them to be meaningful to you, you must see the results of the index as just the first step in exploring the culture and climate of an organization. Think of it as doing an anthropological dig. Take the basic results of the index and then start talking to people—start turning over organizational soil, explore the roots, find out where nourishment comes from, and see where the dirt is deep.

My experience with the index shows that if you score the "culture factors" low, there's a very good chance you'll also score the associated "climate factors" low. The reason for this, as you now know, is that organizational *culture* shapes *climate*.

For example, if you think your personal rights and values are not well respected, if you don't think the organization incorporates lessons learned into new actions, and if you think there are low levels of trust (culture factors), then it's very likely you aren't in a position to act independently, teamwork is not being encouraged, and important information is not being openly shared with you (climate factors).

But it's not all gloom and doom. The Organizational Environment Index can also reveal where a corporate culture is strongest and therefore contributes to a sense of trust, security, and positive self-image. In such cases, it's also likely that you've scored many "climate factors" high on the index. Healthy corporate environments generally score high on both the culture and climate factors, while unhealthy organizations score low on the scales. So what's the state of *your* environment?

My experience with the index is that it can prove to be a useful guide in helping manage or positively contribute to a change process. For example, in a department of the Royal Canadian Mounted Police (RCMP), Pacific Region, I first surveyed employees to get their rating of culture and climate and then, through a series of discussions with employees, focused heavily on where quick wins could be achieved in a number of climate factors, many of which are directly linked to effective communications such as "important information is openly shared," "personnel understand organizational goals," "exceptional performance is rewarded," and "the organization values individual feedback."

The next steps included recommendations that involved enhanced teamwork between different work units, greater communication between supervisors and their personnel, and a system of exemplary-work recognition. These and other recommendations regarding "climate factors" were easy to implement and produced positive early results. But as well as addressing some climate changes, the process also made a priority of recognizing the organizational culture.

In particular, personnel were asked to identify positive elements within the RCMP culture. What they identified was the organization's long history as a trusted Canadian icon and the many varied international, national, and regional experiences gained over the years. This information was gleaned not just from the index but also from interviews with personnel. Over time, organizational climate changes may also create positive changes to elements of the overarching culture that employees saw as less than productive in a rapidly changing world. The key words are "over time."

It's time to treat the *corporate* personality much as we would a *human* personality in need of help. In my training as a counselor, I studied cognitive restructuring therapy, which has the patient break away from deeply embedded negative thought processes by positively reframing her emotions and viewpoint. Organizations can also benefit from a reframed perspective.

WHY WE HAVE A CODEPENDENCY WITH NASTY ORGANIZATIONS

Many people are involved with or know an organizational personality that's self-absorbed, is cold and unfeeling, has trouble accepting emotions, and very often can't be trusted. Now, if they had this dysfunctional relationship with a *human* instead of an *organizational* personality, they might have long ago separated. They might have packed their bags, or not bothered to call back, or shown that loutish personality the door. Or maybe not. Maybe because of the children, or the big car payments and mortgage—or because of *all* of that—they feel trapped and making the quick break isn't as easy as it sounds.

Or maybe they think—*just know deep down*—that this mean human personality who really doesn't care for them will change their behavior and treat them with respect if they just keep their head down and hide, don't make eye contact, don't speak up or say the wrong word, and make sure dinner is always ready and the dishes are perfectly washed.

It's the same with organizations. But breaking off an involvement with the *organizational* personality is tough to do. The organizational personality may be dysfunctional, and it may suffer from corporate personality disorder, but it also pays our bills, keeps us warm and fed, and ensures health benefits. Worst of all, many of us have been conditioned from birth to accept dysfunctional organizational personality behavior as normal. We've been conditioned to believe that if we've got a problem with bad organizational behavior, *we* are the problem, not the organization. And that's why it's a lot easier to walk away from a mean *human* personality than a mean *organizational* personality.

We all know that humans are inherently flawed, full of messy, unpredictable emotions, and that it's just a matter of time until we screw up and disappoint others. But organizational personalities, well, that's a different thing altogether. We are programmed to believe that organizations, especially corporate and institutional personalities, are neat and tidy machine works governed by cold, straight-ahead logic that's never wrong. And so it's easy to end up in a codependency with an organizational personality. We keep our head down, don't rock the boat or buck the system, learn how to read rank and just do what's asked, finding comfort in dreams of spending the weekend with the kids, getting drunk on Saturday night, or eventually having our two-week holiday in Mexico.

Often, adults with troubling emotional conditions are the product of a childhood with repressive or abusive family members and/or congenital conditions that manifest as clinical behavioral problems. It's the same with *corporate* personality disorder and the reason many organizations behave badly.

MUTATIONS IN THE ORGANIZATIONAL FAMILY TREE

Understanding the bizarre behavior of an organization requires digging way back into the longest roots of the Organizational Family Tree. Formal organizational system structures were created by Sumarian society over five thousand years ago. For thousands of years, the ancient Sumarians, Egyptians, Greeks, Romans, and other civilizations followed an organizational system philosophy that balanced the demands of the natural environment against human emotional needs and technical knowledge. This organizational structure was far more *organic* than the ones we have today. Emotional factors were especially important in designing system structures that paid homage to nature and later in building secure relationships between nation-states and segments of feudal and agrarian existence. What changed—like the sudden mutation of a cell's structure—was the balance of two essential nutrients within the Organizational Family Tree, human emotional needs and organizational knowledge.

Prior to the Industrial Revolution, emotion factors played a major role in the agrarian-based organizational system structure. Family life and community networking played a major role, and there was a tight affinity with nature. The Industrial Revolution brought a major shift in organizational culture and system structure priorities, with corporate knowledge, especially technology, taking a dominant role over human emotional needs. Nature was seen as a resource to be exploited and savaged, workplace conditions were brutal, and family life took a backseat to the demands of the factory floor. This shift also brought on the first major symptoms of corporate personality disorder, with examples being the Luddite Rebellion against industrialization in Britain and the street riots in London and other major European cities.

Today, many organizational cultures and structures have a direct historical link to the oppressive factories of yesteryear. Their model of organizational life, which places a heavy emphasis on technical knowledge and command-and-control actions, is replicated in many of our institutions, corporations, and organizations. Sterile system structures replete with layered organization charts, carved-in-stone mission statements, and the tasteless fruits of strategic planning exercises are the talisman that some managers hang onto, giving little thought to the fact that all organizations are comprised of *people* with raw emotions, needs, and feelings.

Organizational life is about what I call "the 3Ps"—personal *power, pride,* and *profit,* with all three fueled by raw human emotion, often fear. All of us, no matter how esteemed the name stenciled into the brass plaque on the door or what shape the broom we push, are consumed with our personal power, pride, and profit. In this case the "profit" is not just how much money we make but also the richness gained through job satisfaction or through some other measure of personal value.

The good news is that there are many organizations that do a good job on recognizing the value of both human emotion and knowledge. They're often the ones that genuinely believe in employee empowerment, corporate social responsibility, and a work/life balance for employees. Such places are often strong financial performers as well, proving that it is indeed possible to "do well by doing good." But, sadly, many other organizations don't do a good job in finding such balance.

Power, pride, and profit shape our self-image. When we look around, we find that it's our personal self-image that many corporations, organizations, and institutions often threaten; we are viewed as interchangeable and disposable cogs in a wheel, as issues to be managed, and as damage to be controlled.

Once our self-image is damaged, once our sense of self is brought into question, then so too is our sense of personal power eroded, which invariably leads us to believe that there is little to gain from being in such a workplace. In such stormy environments, we feel battered and emasculated, and we either quit or simply withdraw into ourselves, doing only what's necessary to make it through the day.

HOW TO PREDICT A CORPORATE PERSONALITY CLASH

Sick organizational systems are very easy to spot because they push our emotional hot buttons. I once had college students use the Organization Personality Index to diagnose the personality of places they had a relationship with either currently or in the past.

One student, a recent employee of Wal-Mart, gave the giant retailer a 20 out of 50 score on the emotion factor scale and a 21 out of 50 score for knowledge factors. The ex-employee said in his personality profile of Wal-Mart (Sopow, 2004),

> I look back now and realize that while Wal-Mart was one of the best places to work in terms of employee incentives, financial standing, and training, they had a tendency to pick on those they felt didn't fit into their ideal image of how an employee should act.

In assessing how his *human personality* fit with Wal-Mart's *organizational personality*, the ex-employee had this to say (Sopow, 2004):

> There is an analogy I'd like to use to describe my relationship with Wal-Mart. It's like a fast and furious love affair. I felt like I was cheating on McDonald's, my former employer, and that Wal-Mart knew it and treated me accordingly. But that, by itself, doesn't really explain it. I would also liken the relationship as the self-centered older brother, full of himself and uncaring what his younger, annoying, slow and less-learned sibling—me—has to say and feel on the matter.

In another example, a student used the index to diagnose the relationship between her and her bank—a major national institution called the Royal Bank. The student, who had been a loyal customer for ten years, had this to say:

The index indicates that, as in all personal relationships, my relationship with the Royal Bank should fulfill my needs and match my personality. Unfortunately, regardless of what their advertisements say, the Royal Bank's personality is old-fashioned and does not complement what I require from an organization. They do not ask for my opinion, they certainly do not admit mistakes, they do not treat everyone fairly, and they do not create strong connections with all of their stakeholders.

Using the index, this student realized the following:

The impact of the index is that it illustrates precisely how unsatisfied I am with the Royal Bank. I was initially surprised that it fell into the suspicious-defensive category as I did not realize the degree of my dissatisfaction with them. However, I had never considered many of the items listed in the emotional and knowledge ingredients of the index.

Families are also organizations, as Bowen's *Family Systems Theory* points out. Keeping this in mind, one student used the index to discover what relationship gaps might be in his basic nuclear family. Ben, in his mid-forties and the father of three older children, had recently left a career in the military to pursue a public relations diploma. He said,

The family "organization" has been under significant transitional stress for the last 18 months, including a long distance move and change of residence, complete career transitions for the parents, new schools for all children, and the boomerang return of the oldest child to the family home after two years on her own.

Ben looked at his immediate family through an organizational lens. First he reflected upon the family structure by measuring both the emotion and knowledge factors found in the index. Then he asked his children and wife to do the same.

Application of the index to my role as a family member was an interesting exercise. Like most families we have disagreements, arguments, and periods of darkness. But overall I have always felt that our interpersonal relationships are open, honest, supportive and reaffirming.

What surprised Ben was that the index uncovered some hidden turbulence in the usually calm waters of his family structure. When Ben and his older teenage children applied the index to their family structure, they found an organizational personality that was visionary-adaptive. But when the mother applied the index from her perspective, she came out with a total score showing an organizational personality that was suspicious-defensive. What created such a gap in personality perceptions? As Ben concluded in his diagnosis,

> An open and frank review of her responses indicated that while she is not pleased with the amount of time I dedicate to schoolwork, her major concern is that she feels that our boomerang eldest daughter is not pulling her weight in the family, taking hospitality for granted and behaving at times like Shakespeare's "thankless child."

The index unearthed some very revealing results for Ben's family and at the same time confirmed many long-standing concepts.

> The index confirmed what I largely knew—that as an organization, our family might have a slight temperature but it is not a "sick system"—at least not yet! Reviewing the results revealed the areas of interpersonal relationships that need attention. But the assessment does not provide the solutions—that is left to us. What the index does however indicate is where expectations can be managed more effectively and where communication can be enhanced.

In a final example, the index provided insights into the professional relationship between a member of a national football team's dance group (sometimes called cheerleaders) and the team's management. As the woman wrote in her assessment of index scores, "Even though I have been a member of the dance team for a while, I didn't feel I had a strong relationship with the organization. I often wondered what the reason for this was. It wasn't until I used the *Index* that I began to understand why I feel so unconnected." As the woman explained,

> My communication with the management is very limited and restricted. Our practices are held at a separate facility from the team and we are never required to visit the main office. In fact, the only connection we have to management is the Dance Team Coordinator who briefs us for 10 minutes every two weeks.
>
> This is very disconcerting to me because the Dance Team is viewed and expected to be ambassadors for the team. Not having any knowledge about the organization makes it very difficult to fulfill the responsibilities of that role.

The student dancer gave the football team's organizational structure a 32 out of 50 on the index's Emotion Factor scale and 26 out of 50 on the Knowledge Factor scale. This meant the organizational personality was collaborative-supportive but teetering on suspicious-defensive. The student observed, "They are always open to finding a solution yet they never seem to follow through on their promises." And as she concluded in her assessment of the index scores,

> I often wonder why I keep coming back to the Dance Team each year (an unpaid position). If it wasn't for my love of dancing and performing I probably wouldn't. Being such an important stakeholder to this organization, I find this tragic!

"Tragic" is a good description of workplaces where people give it their all, sacrifice their spare time, and offer steadfast loyalty just to have the organization treat them like a cog on a wheel that can be replaced or relocated at will.

The good news is that many organizations are also waking up to the fact that the emotional well-being of all their stakeholders—employees, customers, partners—is critical to a well-performing organizational structure. As Anat Rafaeli and Monica Worline wrote in a 2001 article in *Social Science Information*, "Emotion cannot be and is not kept out of modern-day social organization, because organizations are composed of people and people have emotion."

While some organizations see the importance of emotions and workplace balance, many other places see emotional content in the workplace structure as just another way to gain a competitive edge over the competition. The idea that employees who show the "right" emotions can be a plus to the organization is especially prevalent in the service sector, where a happy face and a pleasant tone—called *emotional labor*—are believed to produce a greater number of contented customers.

In their assessment, Rafaeli and Worline note that organizations have finally realized that emotions can't be summarily dismissed, discouraged, or ordered away, and managers are now finding ways to capitalize on that fact in their overarching structures. What's happening, they say, is that "future management entails coordination of how people feel as well as how people act."

The danger, of course, is that when human emotion is framed as *emotional labor*—or, even more to the point, *emotional capital*—the next step for organizations is to ensure that employees are trained to appreciate that some emotions are "good" while others are "bad." This determination won't likely be made because of how the emotions relate to societal ethics, values, or just plain consideration for you while you're cooling your heels in a checkout line. Rather, the primary goal will be to ensure a fat financial bottom line. ("That's a really cool dental bridge you're wearing, ma'am. Can I interest you in a frozen chicken to go with that pair of socks?")

TRIANGLE OF TRUST: THE CORE OF THE ORGANIZATIONAL FAMILY TREE

At the core of the Organizational Family Tree is the Triangle of Trust, which combines authority, responsibility, and accountability through a harmonious balance of communications, cooperation, and connectivity to others. How these six factors combine determines the organizational *climate*, which is the here and now, the systems of rewards and punishment, and the importance given to both emotion and knowledge factors.

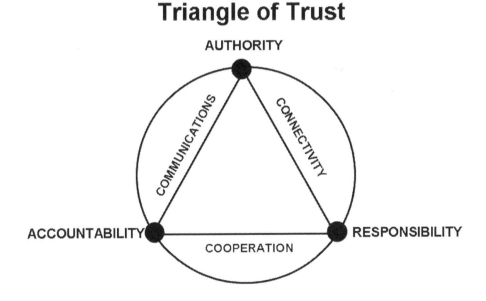

Eli Sopow Ph.D.

When we look closely at the Triangle of Trust we see that it's a simple enough model. But as we look at it more closely and imagine how the different parts connect, it becomes clear that there's a huge range of possibilities. The good news for me is that I'm not some hermit in the forest trying to sell you a snake oil formula. Some of the linkages within my Triangle of Trust were spotted years ago by minds brighter than mine.

The linkage between authority, accountability, and responsibility was first recognized in 1976 by management scholars Harold Koontz and Cyril O'Donnell, who argued that people need to have enough authority to carry out the duties they are being held responsible for and that authority and responsibility should have equal footing—that a superior can't escape accountability by blaming subordinates for not being responsible.

Since then, much debate has occurred within academic circles about the balance of authority, accountability, and responsibility, with some arguing that the higher a person climbs up the organizational ladder, the greater the gap between responsibility and authority.

I remember, in my years as a senior bureaucrat, going to weekly meetings of a provincial government's cabinet and watching the political machinations of those with a great deal of responsibility to create not only a healthy economy but also a healthy, well-educated, and safe society. While the responsibility of the cabinet (driven in large part by the expectations of voters) was enormous, the actual *authority* of the cabinet ministers and the premier was far more limited than any voter or lobby group realized.

Certainly those gathered around the giant oval oak table every week reached many decisions and ordered government policy makers to design all manner of stupefying legislation, complete with incomprehensible rules and regulations. But this authority to make laws wasn't without boundaries. Cabinet ministers were constrained by human rights legislation, by the national constitution protecting citizens, and by dozens of other institutional checks and balances, including the division of federal and provincial powers. Politicians in all democracies carry enormous responsibility and are held continually accountable by voters and supporters, but their authority does have limits, despite the occasional political buffoon who tries to push his weight around.

Yet cabinet ministers are also accountable to the political machinery that gives them access to big, plush offices and expensive cars with drivers. Government decision making is about public administration principles, political realities, and public opinion. Each presents a different level of fear to politicians, usually depending on the size of the government majority and how close the next election is. But having said that, the biggest fear usually stems from the politician's perception of public opinion, which is usually based on the latest headlines.

In examining the roles of accountability, responsibility, and authority, management expert Stephen Bushart (1991) states that when performance is poor in an organization, the accountability for bad performance tends to slide down the hierarchy to the lowest level of accountability. Outside of the rarefied world of academia this principle has long been recognized as "passing the buck."

The notion of "passing the buck" is rampant in organizations suffering from corporate personality disorder. In such organizations, particularly governments and large corporations, the responsibility for disastrous outcomes rarely rests with those with the greatest level of formal authority. There are dozens of such examples, but the following is sadly typical.

In early 2006, in a small Canadian community, Fanny Albo, age ninety-one, was dying of heart failure. Local health officials, despite pleadings from her husband of seventy years, decided to send the elderly woman to a nursing home over one hundred miles away. Hospital officials refused to give the couple time to say their good-byes, refusing even a simple last handholding. Two days later, Fanny died, and her distraught husband, Al, followed soon after. The inevitable news media outage followed, as well as an internal inquiry and the equally inevitable "passing of the buck." As Vancouver *Province* columnist Michael Smyth (2006) wrote,

> When something goes wrong, the government is never to blame.… The Gordon Campbell government has perfected the first rule of thumb, consistently offloading responsibility for gaffes and screw-ups … while the Health Minister was busy acting large and in charge, no individual in any rank of government was actually accepting accountability for what happened. No one was fired, no one was suspended or disciplined.

Over the past several years I've asked many employee and management groups to give me their opinion of what should be listed under each category of the Triangle of Trust. Here's just a partial list of what they've told me:

CRITICAL SUCCESS FACTORS OF AUTHORITY

- Authority is the creation of role clarity
- Authority is sharing power with others
- Authority is having input into planning and goal setting
- Authority is the power to make independent decisions

- Authority is the right to be creative
- Authority is the power to muster resources as needed
- Authority is the creation of clear expectations
- Authority is the creation and preservation of trust
- Authority is the ability to offer both rewards and penalties
- Authority is asking for help without feeling "weak"

CRITICAL SUCCESS FACTORS OF ACCOUNTABILITY

- Accountability needs clear measurements of success
- Accountability needs regular reporting back on progress
- Accountability needs self-awareness of knowledge, skills, and abilities
- Accountability needs clarity of roles
- Accountability needs quick consequences for poor performance
- Accountability needs realistic expectations
- Accountability needs budgets that are efficient and effective
- Accountability needs a clear rationale for decision making
- Accountability needs transparency and open scrutiny
- Accountability needs wide-ranging input into decision-making

CRITICAL SUCCESS FACTORS OF RESPONSIBILITY

- Responsibility means timely and accurate communications
- Responsibility means knowing your gaps in knowledge and abilities
- Responsibility means early identification and resolution of conflicts
- Responsibility means knowing precisely what is expected of you

- Responsibility means practicing fairness in all relationships
- Responsibility means continually striving to be the best you can
- Responsibility means ensuring others know what you expect of them
- Responsibility means being both sympathetic and empathetic of others
- Responsibility means knowing how your job fits into bigger goals
- Responsibility means knowing when and who to ask for help

CRITICAL SUCCESS FACTORS OF COMMUNICATIONS

- Communications should be ongoing
- Communications should be useful
- Communications should be meaningful
- Communications should establish shared goals and values
- Communications should be respectful
- Communications should be inclusive
- Communications should avoid "gate-keepers"
- Communications should be meaningful and relevant
- Communications should be honest
- Communications should be collaborative

CRITICAL SUCCESS FACTORS OF CONNECTIVITY

- Connectivity requires mutual trust
- Connectivity requires sharing with many others
- Connectivity requires cross-training opportunities
- Connectivity requires collaboration

- Connectivity requires a respect for the values of others
- Connectivity requires networks, not silos of activity
- Connectivity requires ongoing communications
- Connectivity requires common goals and objectives
- Connectivity requires "open door" management
- Connectivity requires honesty

CRITICAL SUCCESS FACTORS OF COOPERATION

- Cooperation means others know what you are doing
- Cooperation means knowing what others are doing
- Cooperation means helping the weakest link on the team
- Cooperation means respecting the feelings of others
- Cooperation means trusting others
- Cooperation means listening carefully to others
- Cooperation means "walking the talk"
- Cooperation means sharing a vision
- Cooperation means ongoing communications
- Cooperation means treating others fairly

The above examples are typical of the continuing feedback from leaders, managers, and personnel at all levels of an organization—and I know that you've got a few ideas of your own to add. The answers you see here are typical responses produced in the safety of seminars, but they are *not* typical of what I hear in the actual workplace after the participants get back to cold reality. What I hear in the workplace is, "This is what *should* happen." When I ask why it's *not* happening, the answers are almost always linked to organizational culture—the deep roots of historical and developmental factors that shape today's climate and behavior. And what I hear is the same song with the familiar chorus: too many levels of bureaucratic second-guessing, too many people that say, "We've always done it this way," and too much micro-managing by those without a clue of what needs to be done.

What the Organizational Family Tree emphasizes is that similar to our personality, the way an organization behaves today—its *organizational personality*—is a product of early historical and developmental factors. It's tough to effect climate change without first understanding the influence of culture—the factors that combine to create the climate.

Edgar Schein of the Massachusetts Institute of Technology says in his book *Organizational Culture and Leadership* (2004), "Culture is hard to change because group members value stability in that it provides meaning and predictability." When change is seen as a threat to such stability within the Organizational Family Tree, when power sources and connections are seen as short-circuiting, then two vital components of the tree become especially critical: human energy *resistors* and energy *conductors*. We will explore these in the next chapter.

4

RESISTORS, CONDUCTORS, AND TURBULENT CHANGE

Kevin started off as an energy *conductor* within the Organizational Family Tree. He was gung-ho in singing the praises of his organization, he was enthusiastic, and he was fiercely loyal. That was twenty-three years ago, when he first started his profession as an idealistic young man, freshly trained with a newly minted university degree and plenty of hope. Over the years, sacrifices were made, promotions came, and then the compromises started—first small ones and then bigger. Then, mostly in the past five years, the treatment from one supervisor in particular made it harder for Kevin to get out of bed in the morning.

Today Kevin is an energy *resistor*. He is jaded, has few positive expectations of the workplace, has very little trust in senior management, and is all too willing to share his scar-tissue wisdom with others, especially younger and newer employees who are still powered up to conduct positive energy. Kevin switched from being an organizational energy conductor to an energy resistor because of a series of actions and inactions by managers, but one action in particular stands out.

Kevin asked his boss for permission to attend the funeral of a colleague's young son who died suddenly and violently. The colleague worked in a different department but was well known and highly regarded by everyone in Kevin's department. His boss said "no," the department could not give him a day off for such a thing. It wasn't in the official policy. Kevin then said he would use his holiday time to attend the funeral. Again, the boss said "no." The department could not spare him. Things were too busy. So Kevin said he was going anyway. The boss said if he did, he would be subject to disciplinary action.

By now Kevin was worn down; he had been for many months. He simply didn't have the energy, the will, the fire in the belly to fight yet another losing battle, and so instead of going to the funeral for his colleague's son, he dutifully came to the office and moved through the soulless day as if in a suffocating fog of despair.

Today, Kevin views any efforts at organizational change with deep cynicism. He has learned how to survive—even thrive at times—by staying low, by bending the rules, by creating short-term and long-term marriages of convenience with other employees, and by knowing the minimum expected of him to make it through the day. Even when the organization recently brought in a number of very positive new measures, even when such steps would have significantly enhanced Kevin's workplace environment, he continued to resist. Such is the nature of change—although it is constant, we still fear it, even if the change is good for us.

In human relationships, the actions of a person are a complex amalgam of historical, developmental, and personality factors that embrace both emotional and cognitive-knowledge elements. Often people are unaware of how others see their individual behavior, and when told they have trouble changing that behavior because it's deeply rooted in the past. The Organizational Family Tree suggests the same dynamic unfolds with an organization.

When organizations initiate major change, they can send ripples of uncertainty—even fear—through people. A significant change in the *actions* of an organization signals that either the *system structure* has changed in some way or the new actions are inconsistent with what the structure intends. Organizational structures reflect the organization's "personality," which in turn is shaped by emotion and knowledge factors that can be traced to historical and developmental factors—the foundations of organizational culture.

A sudden difference in organizational action may be positive or negative, a sign of adaptability or regression. But either way, such new behavior creates uncertainty among those affected. Just like the relationship between you and that special somebody, the relationship between you and the organizational personality involves an investment of time and energy, a history of occasional compromise, and established patterns of how problems are solved and how questions are answered.

Such relationships can also involve what management scholar Ralph Stacey (1992) calls *shadow systems*. A shadow system means we have learned how to achieve our goals by "cutting through red tape" or building informal alliances and networks. In time, such a relationship with the organizational personality provides predictability and a level of comfort. This even happens within dysfunctional organizations, where the mindset is one of "the devil I know versus the devil I don't know."

Because all parts of the Organizational Family Tree are connected, a change to organizational *structure* signals that the entire place is affected to some degree. It means that what were once familiar patterns of behavior are no longer the same and that well-known emotion and knowledge factors within the Organizational Family Tree may no longer be there or their role may be very different.

THE ROLE OF CHANGE RESISTORS AND CONDUCTORS

In many ways the Organizational Family Tree is like our own human family tree. The power and energy sources we apply to everyday actions, our viewpoints, and our ability to adapt and react to a changing world are in large part influenced by our historical and developmental factors, our perceptions of the world, and how our brain responds to the various stimuli around us. We both *resist* and we *conduct*. We resist what we don't like and we easily act as a conductor of what we do like by sharing it with others, telling our friends about it over coffee, or sending an e-mail about it.

In his book *Flawless Consulting* (1999), Peter Block states, "Resistance is a predictable, natural, emotional reaction against the process of being helped and against the process of having to face difficult organizational problems." The concept of *resistance* is a popular one within management literature, and it often refers to those who put up roadblocks against change. Too often, resistors are seen as malcontents who refuse to be team players. I think that's a bad rap for a very natural and often healthy reaction.

Resistance to change, and organizational change in particular, can be a far more complicated dynamic than some realize. The circuitry of our brain is buzzing with biochemical electrical power, and this human energy is also what lights up (or darkens) the Organizational Family Tree, which involves both emotion and knowledge circuits. Because it's *all* about the flow of human energy, the Organizational Family Tree is comprised of numerous *resistors* and *conductors*, just as in actual electrical networks.

In the electrical world, a resistor limits the amount of power passing throughout the line in order to prevent an electrical overload. Electrical resistors are engineered to maintain a stable value over a wide range of environmental conditions, producing heat as they dissipate the electrical power moving through them. It's the same with human resistors within the Organizational Family Tree.

Imagine you're a human resistor. The first thing that often happens is that senior management will see you as a negative power source, when in fact you think your role, like the role of the resistor in electronics, is to maintain balance and to prevent what you see as short circuits and power flare-ups within the organization. A human resistor in the Organizational Family Tree, just like an electrical resistor, is also capable of generating heat. In this case, the heat is caused by an emotional reaction to what you see as misplaced power surges in the system, caused by people abusing their power and meltdowns in the system's structure.

Organizational heat really starts to bubble when we get together with others to do what's necessary to protect the status quo—our comfort zones. Defensive actions can include overt and covert resistance (ignoring e-mails, stalling, hiding under a desk), disinformation campaigns ("Did you hear the latest rumor? The company's moving to Brazil"), and communication gatekeepers restricting the flow of information ("Nope. There's nothing new"). But let's not bring out the black paint too quickly. In many cases organization resistors, rather than being a *negative* force, are in fact a *positive* voice of reason and sober second thought. They ask what management scholar Brenda Zimmerman calls the "wicked questions" ("Why *exactly* are we doing this? Why now? And by the way, who's *really* benefiting?"), and they often aren't afraid to say the emperor has no clothes ("This decision will destroy morale").

Occasionally, as with electrical resistors, *human* organizational resistors overheat. Rather than serve to moderate surges of power through thoughtful questioning and constructive criticism, the overheating resistor blocks or diverts new sources of positive organizational energy. They do this through a steadfast refusal to acknowledge that change is inevitable, and they refuse to relinquish, even for a moment, closely embraced notions of organizational power, pride, and personal profit—whether the gain is financial or otherwise. Who are these people, and what are they thinking?

Overheating resistors are rarely young or new to the job. They're usually those who have been with the organization for many years, who have attained a comfortable position of authority and scope of control, and whose leadership style is often of the command-and-control variety. They're what I call the "2 percenters"—the two percent of people who really dig in their heels and aggressively resist change. Why would they do this?

What I've found is that unlike other organizational resistors, the *overheating* resistors have huge difficulty moving even an inch away from their long-held position. Their resistance is deeply embedded within their unconscious psyche, buried deep within historical and developmental factors, enmeshed within an entrenched sense of self and, in particular, their fear.

The fear within an overheating resistor is often grounded in a self-image that has come to equate one's sense of self and worth—one's total personality—with one's job or profession. Being told to change activities or scope of control, no matter how small, is no longer a matter of an organizational process changing. Such "demands" for change are internalized by overheating resistors as efforts to alter not a *process* but that person's very *personality*. Such individuals often have made their work or professional life their only life. They often are—or have been—the hardest workers but also the individuals with the least balanced lives, with few interests outside of work, and who take even the smallest work-related criticism or even question as a personal affront requiring an angry response.

To reconnect an overheating resistor to the natural flow of healthy organizational energy takes time, understanding, and compassion. It requires a leader or manager to have a collaborative nature but also the willingness to quickly enforce accountability measures with overheating resistors before their heat spreads to others. It may require some compromise on carved-in-stone plans for change, the source of concern for positive resistors. It may also, in extreme cases, require the removal of overheating resistors who, regardless of what efforts are made to recognize their needs and concerns, simply increase blockages of positive energy flow and, at worst, infect others with their attitude.

Removing overheating resistors from the workplace by transferring them elsewhere or even laying them off is the quick and easy way out and should be seen as a last resort. Such action is in many ways an admission of personal failure by leaders and managers, who themselves do not have the skills necessary for self-reflection and awareness or for thoughtful connectivity, cooperation, and communication.

It's for this reason that they take the easy path. They believe the only option to prevent what they imagine are ever-escalating negative short circuits within the evolving Organizational Family Tree is to quickly remove overheating organizational resistors through transfers, severance packages, or demotions. It's the Fredrick Taylor culture of management, which sees employees not as people with complex emotions but as interchangeable, displaceable cogs on a wheel that can be discarded at will.

It's not a simple or small task to help others understand why change is occurring. This is the role for organizational energy *conductors*. As with actual electrical systems, *organizational* energy conductors facilitate the smooth transmission of power from one point to another within the Organizational Family Tree. As with actual electrical conductors, they do so with minimal generation of heat and with minimum disruption to the constant, uninterrupted flow of energy. How do organizational energy conductors do this incredible thing? More importantly, how can *you* be a positive energy conductor within the Organizational Family Tree?

Well, for starters, an organizational energy conductor doesn't need a fancy and formal title associated with leadership or management. You can be the president of a corporation, a middle manager, or any one of many thousands of people who show up for work everyday with the hope that your hours unfold with interest, that your job has some meaning to your life, and that you're treated with the same respect and collegiality you give to others.

As an organizational energy conductor, you view the system structure holistically rather than through a compartmentalized view. You understand the importance of communication, cooperation, and connectivity to others. And you know that positive energy is magnified when there's a harmonious balance of authority, accountability, and responsibility.

But a word of caution is also needed here. Even enlightened approaches to change management often focus on the specific new actions and what's happening to the structure and the *immediate* climate. It's easy to fall back into the knee-jerk, mechanistic model of how organizations are *supposed* to run. During change, communications, connectivity, and cooperation with others usually follow the cookie-cutter formula from other organizational "best practices," with a specific focus on "selling" you on the reasons why the changes are going to benefit *the organization*, with far lesser emphasis on why the changes are going to be good *for you*.

What's missing in such boxed-in change-management strategies is an appreciation of *all* factors in the Organizational Family Tree, not just the system's structure or immediate actions. What you, as an organizational change conductor, can do is take some time to understand the powerful role of emotion and knowledge factors within the system's structure (climate), and especially the enduring attributes found in early historical and developmental factors (culture). As an organizational change conductor, you'll especially know how to successfully marry culture to climate, creating through that process a healthy and flourishing corporate environment.

The Organizational Family Tree is a dynamic, living system with very deep roots. It stresses that successful emergence or organizational change comes by intertwining the best of historical and developmental factors (culture) with the need for innovative and adaptive ways of dealing with a rapidly changing environment (climate). As scholars Manfred deVries and Katharina Balazs (1999) point out regarding organizational change, "Leaders need to create pride in the organization's history but also point out how this pride in tradition can anchor the organization to the past ... leaders should build on aspects of the existing culture that are appropriate for the new organization."

Organizational change, regardless of how turbulent it is, requires a solid thread of connectivity to long-established and successful patterns of behavior based on historical and developmental influences, as well as a connection to the organizational personality, comprised of well-established emotion and knowledge factors. But just as important as maintaining a common thread to the best of the past and to what works well now is acknowledging the detrimental influences within the Organizational Family Tree and what *not* to maintain.

The phrases "We've always done it this way" and "The more things change the more they stay the same" are symptoms of stultifying organizational historical factors that shape how the organizational personality acts today. They are signs of an organization (like a person) being "stuck" in an early developmental period and afraid of moving forward. Before any meaningful change can occur, before there's a true improvement in relationships, there must be a deep understanding of how the organization's past affects its behavior today, why such historical traits persist, and what interventions can occur to break from the past and change both attitudes and behavior.

This is difficult ground to reseed, because organizational historical and developmental factors constitute organizational culture. As we've seen, organizational culture is deeply embedded and involves well-established values, beliefs, and a way of looking at the world that has persisted for decades if not longer. To question organizational culture is to question the heart and soul of the organization itself. It's far easier to change organizational *climate*—the here and now, including rules and regulations, ways of cooperating and connecting to others, and communications.

Effective communications is the lifeblood of the Organizational Family Tree and connects everything that's important within the system. However, in many organizations, healthy arteries of communication get blocked or clogged with information gatekeepers, top-down models of communication, ingenuous statements that don't "walk the talk," and a protective "need to know" attitude from those who equate information with power. My definition of fear is a lack of power and knowledge. So, getting rid of or reducing fear within an organization requires that you, as an organizational energy conductor, take actions that create a sense of personal empowerment and knowledge in those affected by change. Here are a few ways this can be done.

When organizations do change out of necessity, communications to those directly affected must include (1) a status report on the past influence and current role of historical and developmental factors, (2) an assessment of what has happened, if anything, to the known personality traits of the organization, and (3) the current status of emotion and knowledge factors. Providing such key information is the job of an organizational energy conductor. Not only do you share information often and openly; you're also open to hearing feedback—*really* open to it, not just nodding your head and thinking, "Yeah, yeah, whatever."

What an organizational energy conductor conveys through ongoing communication is that the new change is still true to old values and to the positive and long established emotion and knowledge factors. Just as in relations between people, the *organizational* personality's message must be, "Although I'm doing things differently, what you like about me hasn't changed."

As an organizational energy conductor, you use communications to build connectivity and cooperation among individuals and groups. Through this process you positively align the *organizational* personality with *human* personalities, producing a powerful harmony of authority, accountability, and responsibility. This isn't a simple task, as is evident in many public-and private-sector groups affected by changing circumstances.

THE NOTION OF "POWER PACKING" DURING ORGANIZATIONAL CHANGE

We react in a split second when we sense a physical threat to our existence. Fear is our first reaction, triggered by neurotransmitters in our brain's amygdala—home to the fight, flight, or freeze response. This is exactly the same brain chemistry that's triggered when we face a threat to our sense of self from organizational change. We may turn our fear into anger and try to protect ourselves, attempting to stop change. We may "freeze," doing nothing beyond the basics and keeping our head down. Or we may turn to flight, looking for a new job or in some cases retreating into private depression and even physical illness.

During this turbulence, there's often a natural tendency to seek out a group of like-minded individuals. I call this process *power packing*. I'm sure you've either seen it happening or been part of it happening. Power packing happens when we feel an organizational threat and then look for others who have something in common with us, such as the same job interests, maybe a personality close to ours, or shared roles such as those found in specialized units or branches within an organization. But here's something you may not have noticed. In many cases of organizational change, the nature of a power pack mutates as change accelerates, as human energy builds, and especially if the organization is having a tough time with the change process.

At first, when we were just beginning to feel threatened by organizational change, we looked for others who had something in common with us, folks that shared our fears and maybe even our anger. But now things are *really* getting nasty. The organizational personality just isn't letting up, and the changes feel more threatening than ever. So we start looking for very specific allies, those who are also freaked out by what they see as threats to their self-image, power, and position. For example, if we've got little job security, or we're at the bottom of the organization chart, or we have very little power, we feel comfortable with others in the same position, because they have plenty of reason to share our fears and anger. The same is true if we're higher up the organization chart, pull in a six-figure salary, and have a corner office.

I've watched senior managers, when facing resistance from employees, power pack together and very quickly use typecasting and pejorative language to dismiss criticism leveled against them. Most often in the privacy of their leather-chaired offices, they describe organizational resistors as "crazy," "trouble-makers," "not team players." In many cases, the private criticism of employees by their managers takes on a very personal tone, with references to physical appearance, gender, and education.

This power-packing turbulence is a critical time in the change process. Sloppy efforts at cooperation, connectivity, and communication (or a total absence of effort) have created a flurry of activity, almost all of it divisive and destructive. Not only are disinformation and rumor campaigns under way, not only are communication gatekeepers thwarting the change process, but entire new clusters of resistor employees are being formed who quickly become infected with the contagion of negativity that grows exponentially in such a Petri dish of discord.

Hearing all this, you might be wondering how you, someone who clearly sees that change has to come to your organization, can actually accomplish anything. After all, change is something fiercely resisted by both organizational and human personalities, who have been brainwashed into thinking that the status quo is the ticket to everlasting happiness. So, how do you as a positive energy conductor try to make your organization a healthier place? A place where *you're* going to be a lot happier?

First off, introducing change works a lot better when we use respectful communications to connect our ideas of change to what is both already comfortable and trusted within the Organizational Family Tree, including historical, developmental, emotion, and knowledge factors. Our communications also need to be ongoing (even when there's supposedly nothing happening), open to others' opinions (even really angry ones), empathetic to the emotional needs of others, and quickly responsive to both questions and to the obvious need for understanding and support.

Leadership by organizational energy conductors requires not a draconian, benevolent-dictator approach that attempts to control the apparent chaos but a transformational approach where deep listening and careful attention to emotional factors is at the forefront, as you'll see in greater deal in the closing chapters. It also takes time, transparency, and honesty. Cooperation comes from adaptation, from questioning assumptions, from looking inward for answers before demanding them from others, and from finding commonalities that ultimately serve to rebuild or sustain trust.

We often hear certain misguided folks saying, "Don't take it personally." That's total nonsense, of course, a loose nut from the machine metaphor of organizational life. It's impossible for us *not* to take life personally. We are, after all, sentient beings who embrace life through our senses, who react to stimuli first through our brain's emotional center and then through our cognitive appraisals, and who ultimately create a sense of self through how we *feel* as much as what we *know*.

ORGANIZATIONAL FAMILY TREE ACTIONS AND IMPACTS

There's no escaping the organizational personality. It's everywhere. It's at the place we work, the school we send our kids to (or attend), the government agency we have to argue with, the phone company that puts us on hold, and our corner grocery store. It can be compassionate or cruel, supportive or a real pain in our butt, but one thing is certain: the organizational personality affects us every day and in every way.

Just as *our* personality reacts in all manner of ways and takes all kinds of actions, ranging from how we politely respond to that idiot driver who just cut us off to how we deal with that officious bureaucrat on the third floor, the *organiza-*

tional personality also takes actions based on the influences of its Organizational Family Tree.

To recap, in the Organizational Family Tree energy is generated and flows through the structure based on the influence of historical factors, developmental factors, the organization's core structure (including the Triangle of Trust), and attention to emotion and knowledge factors.

Organizational system structures influence *system actions*. These actions, driven in large part by the system structure, include:

- The specifics of how we do our work every day, including the type and level of support from management and colleagues;

- The way relationships are built and carried out with those that have expectations of us;

- The style, frequency, and nature of communications;

- The way the organization learns and incorporates experiences into new actions;

- The way the organization stays accountable to those who need to judge its actions;

- The way the organization responds to crises, criticism, and opportunity.

Organizational actions lead to *impacts*, including the impact on people within the organization as well as customers, clients, students, parents, patients, and others who have expectations of the organization or who just happen to be bystanders. System impacts include levels of efficiency and effectiveness ("I've been waiting all day for that cable guy"), levels of creativity and adaptability ("We'd better not do that. It's never been done before"), and the state of individual psychological and physical health ("This place is driving me nuts!").

System impacts also include the organization's affect on the social, economic, political, communications, and ecological environment it lives within. This can include impacts on markets, on community well-being, on workplace conditions, and on the natural environment, including air, soil, water, plant life, and wildlife conditions. (A chemical plant that's making the river turn dark green, a local hardware store that's donated new sweaters to the peewee hockey team, and a multinational corporation that's just paid off a shady politician are all examples.)

Many organizations expend huge amounts of time, effort, resources, and energy on designing impersonal system *structures* that look a lot like the machine works envisioned by the engineer Frederick Taylor, who designed the impersonal model of scientific management in 1911. Well, why not? That's what's *always* been done, because managers have been led to believe that's what's comfortable and safe and perfectly measurable. So what if many organizations end up reacting to change like frightened monkeys in a cage?

The "so what" is this. When things finally start falling apart in the mechanical organization, when the nuts and bolts start getting loose, when organizations start exhibiting signs of corporate personality disorder, many people get very excited about the immediate *actions* of the organization and *not* the organizational *structure* that's causing the actions. This is perfectly normal, for two reasons: First, we have a natural tendency to focus more on the *here and now* than the *then and there*. This is because our natural survival instincts are honed to spot and deal with immediate threats. Second, we've been led to believe from early childhood that it's *normal* for organizational personalities to behave the way they do and that this is actually a *good* thing for us. Most of us have been taught not to question authority, to make sure our printing is neat and within the margins, to memorize facts and regurgitate them by rote on final exams, to do what we're told (regardless of whether it makes sense), and to always park our car in the right spot.

If you've been led to believe throughout your life that the behavior of organizational personalities is always right, then it's obvious when things go wrong that it's not *their* fault but *yours*. This is one of the reasons that when things go wrong and trouble happens, as it always does, folks tend to blame system *actions* and not the system *structure*. This is because actions are the here and now. Actions are easy to associate with a human—like you—and that means it's also easy to find a scapegoat. But a system *structure* is another thing altogether. A *structure* is a creation of organizational culture (historical and developmental factors). It's all about an entrenched way of doing things—a way of doing things that a lot of people have invested power, pride, and profit in.

The above differences between a system's *structure* and its everyday *actions* are often the reason that our first *re*action to a really bad organizational action (such as poor medical care, high crime rates, or a sloppy education system) is to demand something be done to fix the immediate and obvious problem. Usually this demand involves more resources, including more money or more personnel. What this logic concludes is that it's not the overarching structure that's at fault, not the deeply rooted *culture* within the Organizational Family Tree, but rather it's the *climate* that needs changing, including everyday human actions. It's around this point that a tap on the shoulder (and a $300 an hour invoice) comes from a well-intentioned organizational psychologist, human resource manager, consultant, or counselor who fervently believes that changing individual behavior within a dysfunctional organization will produce the cure for the structure itself. ("You need to do some attitude adjustment around here. Get everybody on the same page. Let's do a team-building workshop using toothpicks and orange marmalade.")

None of this ameliorates the *real* reason organizational actions are causing trouble. Until the system *structure* is identified as the real source of the problem, throwing more money at bad actions or introducing all manner of leadership, management, and wellness programs and workshops is a waste of time and resources. It's like squeezing a rubber ball because we don't like its shape. The moment we let go, the ball springs back to its original offending appearance.

OUR HUMAN PERSONALITY IS AFFECTED BY THE ORGANIZATIONAL PERSONALITY

If we wake up one morning and our stomach's plumbing is gurgling like a volcano, if our head is spinning, and if we just want to pull up the covers and disappear, there are things we can do. The first is to diagnose the symptoms and consider remedies. Maladies of body and mind manifest in a variety of recognizable ways, including fever, rashes, unusual forms of behavior and ideation, physiological disorders, and increasingly dysfunctional relationships with others.

The same holds true for the *organizational* body, which, just like our human body, is susceptible to system sicknesses. Corporate personality disorder, like human personality disorders, can be measured and probed, quantified and treated, once we fully understand the organization's culture and climate and how human energy is created and flows through the Organizational Family Tree.

Just like mental illness in human personalities, corporate personality disorder causes an organization to manifest a number of particular traits. The organization appears reactive, controlling, defensive, ultra-conservative, and uncommunicative. A dysfunctional and untrustworthy organizational personality, when in conflict with our personality, can create very real health problems for us, including anxiety, depression, fear, and anger. The fact is our human personality and the organizational personality are inextricably intertwined—they are tied up in a tight knot. Sometimes this intertwining is compatible and everybody is mostly happy, but often it's no bed of flowers. There's a really good reason for this. Our human system is organic and holistic in design (we have lots of messy emotions and a need for other people) while the organizational system is mechanistic and reductionist (cold, unfeeling, and definitely a real neatnik).

In most cases, the design of an organizational structure is not a natural, holistic, evolutionary, and adaptive process that works to fit into a changing environment. In most cases, it's a design that seeks to change the environment to meets *its* needs. The mechanistic design of today's organization is the lasting heritage of a few individuals who, as you'll see later, created what they did in large part because of their own sack full of personality disorders. In other words, the basic Organizational Family Tree has a few big skeletons in its closet. Unfortunately for us, those skeletons keep rattling around, and their ghosts show up in everything from a company's organization chart to the uptight behavior of a boss.

The behavior of an organizational personality can affect our emotional makeup and—as Matt Ridley points out in his book *Genome* (2006)—can actually affect your genes. "Genes need to be switched on," he says, "and external events—or free-willed behavior—can switch on genes. Far from us lying at the mercy of our omnipotent genes, it is our genes that lie at the mercy of us." What this means is that organizational actions such as how we're treated by a company can, through a neurobiological process, switch on DNA-based determinants of behavior that influence both our actions and our physical condition.

From a clinical perspective, organizations with corporate personality disorder that subject us to a psychologically abusive relationship may be switching on genetically imbedded human reactions that make it easier for us to be nasty to others or to ourselves. In addition, dysfunctional and downright mean organizational personalities can deeply stress us out. It's a very well documented medical and neurological fact that stress increases our bodies' level of the hormone cortisol, which in turn suppresses the manufacture of white blood cells, which are essential to a healthy immune system.

Levels of cortisol are so sensitive to stress that just *thinking* about a stressful situation can increase our cortisol levels, making us more susceptible to viral infections and disease. So when we think, "I'm really sick of this stupid job and that mean boss," there's a very good chance we really *are* physiologically sick. And that's why corporations pay out billions of dollars a year in stress pay.

There's a direct correlation between the *personal* psychological meltdown we feel at work and the *organizational* meltdown the corporation is going through as it manifests all the signs of corporate personality disorder. Here are a few clues as to whether or not we're heading for trouble. The Boston-based human rights group Peace at Home, Inc. has come up with what it calls the Warning List, comprising eleven factors that indicate emotional abuse in human relationships. Those factors are

- Destructive criticism/verbal abuse
- Abuse of authority
- Disrespect
- Abuse of trust
- Emotional withholding
- Breaking promises
- Minimizing, denying, and blaming
- Pressure tactics
- Intimidation
- Destruction
- Threats

Many, and often all, of those eleven factors manifest in an organizational environment with corporate personality disorder. And as in abusive human relationships, organizational emotional abuse causes the sufferers of abuse to display many of the following physical ailments—intense headaches, painful stomach troubles, a feeling of constant tension and stress, heart palpitations, fatigue, back and neck problems, and melancholy. The statement "I'm sick of this job" likely indicates there's more going on than a mere bad mood.

An example of the above was reported in late 2004 by the Public Health Agency of Canada, which found that the downsizing strategies employed by financially squeezed public and private sector organizations in the 1990s burdened Canada's health care system with up to $14 billion a year in extra costs. The agency's report, *Exploring the Link between Work-Life Conflict and Demands on Canada's Health Care System*, stated that one in four Canadians believed the demands of their job interfered with their responsibilities at home and that 58 percent of Canadians experienced high levels of work overload. The study also found that 10 percent of employees had seen a mental health professional in the six months prior to the study and that employees who felt work pressures along with the pressure of family life saw physicians at a 25 percent higher rate than those who did not feel such pressure.

So if you're thinking, "I'm sick of my job" or "This place is driving me nuts!" take those thoughts very, very seriously. They are the flashing red lights and wailing siren of a meltdown in your personal energy system. They are warning messages being transmitted from your *emotional brain*, which has been programmed over tens of thousands of years to warn you of imminent danger. The reason many of us are *not* listening is because our *logical brain* is programmed with tight, machine-like thinking to see all emotions as bad and the *Organizational* Family Tree as more important to our survival than our *human* family tree.

CORPORATE PERSONALITY DISORDER IS EVERYWHERE

We find corporate personality disorder as easily in the British Parliament as we do at the White House. We find it within well-intentioned nonprofit groups like Greenpeace and in the most profit-plundering multinational corporations. The big deal here is that there's a good chance *you* are threatened by decaying Organizational Family Trees, manifesting corporate personality disorder, in many parts of your life, whether it's at your job or in dealing with that insensitive jerk at a utility company.

Every day, the Industrial Revolution-based cookie-cutter formula used in designing organizational and social institution structures inflicts physical and emotional harm on thousands of employees and their families, causing burnout, anxiety, depression, violent attacks, and in many cases death by suicide or homicide.

According to the American Foundation for Suicide Prevention (2007), a person dies by suicide about every 16 minutes, while there's an attempt at suicide once every minute. Corporate personality disorder is a major contributor to suicide. When we dig deep into the causes of the abject depression, we often find a huge disconnect between the emotional needs of those individuals and the rigid, mechanistic offerings of the system structures they were grappling with—be it the organizational structure of a school, religion, workplace, or government agency.

Clients of worker compensation boards are some of the saddest examples of this phenomenon. These government agencies are supposedly structured to assist workers injured on the job with rehabilitation and insurance claims. Elected government politicians tell us that their most frequent constituent complaints concern insurance claims involving the workplace. An example of such a claim was my niece Julie, a hospital nurse who, until she was injured on the job in her early thirties, had enjoyed a full life with a husband and two young girls. The despair of dealing with years of physical and emotional pain—kept fresh by bureaucratic red tape and faceless, stone-walled system structures—led first to the death of Julie's self-image, then to the death of her hope, and finally one cold weekend to her physical death as she took her own life.

Corporate personality disorder is a debilitating condition affecting hundreds of thousands of North Americans. But while it is still largely unrecognized as a direct cause of human misfortune, thousands of physicians continue to treat it in the only way they know how—prescribing a magic pill. For example, according to the National Mental Health Association, eighteen million Americans are suffering from clinical depression and thirty million Americans are taking the "wonder drug" Prozac. Why not?

Whether we're talking about school systems that will not put up with active children with too many questions or multinational corporations that will not bear squeaky wheels, the assumption in these organizations is that the system is just fine—it's the cogs on the wheel that are not meshing and therefore need chemical realignment.

In reality, it's often the *organizational personality* that needs a magic green and cream-colored pill, not us. However, the nature of the modern organization is to point the finger of blame at noisy and squeaky cogs on the wheel, not to question whether there should be cogs and wheels and a machine works of human management in the first place.

The actions of many organizational system structures are hurting more than humans—they're also destroying many aspects of Earth's environment. When corporations downplay human emotion needs and emphasize technical benefits and financial profits, a number of things occur. Instead of respect for the natural environment, the focus is on short-term monetary gain and corporate marketplace dominance. And instead of corporate social responsibility and recognition of gender, workplace, and community needs, there's a blind allegiance to return on investment and maximization of shareholder value.

What's frighteningly different about corporate personality disorder is how the organization behaves *in exactly the opposite manner* to the patterns of behavior found in all natural organisms, which successfully adapt to their environment and evolve based on patterns of communications, connectivity, and cooperation. What *natural* systems have perfected over 3.8 billion years of evolution, *organizational* systems are destroying in a comparative blink of an eye—in less than 300 years.

In naturally occurring systems, *apoptosis*, or the "suicide cell," is triggered when an organism is deemed redundant to the efficient operation of the overall network of existence or when its qualities either take away from or hinder genetic improvement. The writer Howard Bloom and many neuroscientists have studied how this self-destruct process is also evident in entire organisms, both animals and humans. Bloom says,

> The immune systems of creatures with few or no friends and intimate kin shut down, while the immunological resistance of those who are part of a social web remain more vigorous. In other words, isolated individuals undergo a strictly involuntary surrender to disease and body dissolution.

However with corporate personality disorder, something quite *unnatural* occurs. The system structure, rather than encouraging healthy evolution by rewarding the most innovative and imaginative parts of the system, actually *destroys* efforts at such contribution. When we work within such a structure, we quickly learn that our initial zeal to *make a difference* is precisely what the organization rebels against. Differences, after all, run against the grain of the status quo and the sense of equilibrium that senior management, held hostage by their Industrial Age mentality, deems essential to survival.

Making a difference means rocking the boat, and rocking the boat is not what command-and-control systems encourage. What is left then, within an organization suffering from corporate personality disorder, is fear-based mediocrity, a creeping dysfunctionalism, and people who feel burned out, bummed out, and sold out.

Corporate personality disorder displays what I call *contra-apoptosis*. Remember, in every *natural* system on the planet, including our own body, the process of apoptosis destroys that which offers up little or nothing for survival. Get rid of the useless stuff and you live on. But it's the opposite in a decaying Organizational Family Tree. In such a place, the actions of the organization actually destroy the things that are good for it and can keep it evolving. The "things" I'm talking about are positive suggestions, change, new ideas, and other actions that support innovation, re-birth, and renewal. And guess what? Often those positive ideas and actions come from people trying to revive a sick system. But instead of being seen as positive contributors, they're branded boat rockers. And so they shut up, put their heads down, and struggle on.

As if this were not bad enough, corporate personality disorder is also destroying thousands of animal, plant, and other natural systems sharing the planet.

There may be up to thirty million species of life on the planet, but only one displays the propensity to destroy not only itself but all other living species. This aberrant, seemingly irrational, and frightening behavior of course belongs to humans, who through organizational system structures and system actions have helped speed the extinguishment of more than six thousand species of life, including plants, animals, fish, and insects, all in the name of industrial progress.

Peter Raven, director of the Missouri Botanical Garden, believes species are becoming extinct at the rate of one hundred per day, or one every fifteen minutes. At this rate, the effects of corporate personality disorder will have destroyed one-half of all existing species on Earth within fifty years. This is a phenomenal achievement for a species that first stood upright just two million years ago, built the first city 5,500 years ago, and created the first corporation less than 300 years ago.

5

THE PATHOLOGY OF CORPORATE PERSONALITY DISORDER

We have choices about how we behave. When we finally decide to reflect on why we're acting like a bull in the china shop of human relationships, we can start by questioning why we do what we do—looking at our histories, seeking patterns, and asking some hard questions. It's the same with the organizational personality. In this chapter, you'll see that the mindset of the modern organization isn't based on a long family history of behavior. In fact, the behavior of many organizations today is a recent and dramatic departure from what was once a more organic, easy going, natural, and healthier way of thinking.

Like many counselors, my wife, Lindsay, were she to counsel you, would explore your historical traits, the influences you were born with as well as your history of early growth—the developmental factors that shape the person you are today. In addition, Lindsay might discuss your family patterns over past generations using what's called a *family genogram.*

The family genogram maps out trends in generational relationships and behavior, which in turn can spill over into how you are coping with your current environment. Just as it's important for us to be aware of our past if we're going to deal with our current behavior, it's also important for us to know an organization's roots if we're going to understand—or affect—its behavior. With that in mind, let's do a little time traveling to see if we can figure out why the organizational personality we're dealing with is behaving the way it is.

Despite the flavor-of-the-year management systems being embraced and then discarded by many organizations, the underlying reason why organizations do what they do was seeded thousands of years ago. Since then, there have been only a few, yet very profound changes. In the blink of an eye (in terms of the earth's evolution), humans created artificial systems of control and certainty. We clever humans have done this in order to assuage our primordial fear of clinical death, deal with our vulnerable self-image, and especially overcome natural systems found in our natural environment. But it seems that every human, mechanistic system of control that has been created has led to somebody or something losing out.

The first organizational system appeared about fifteen thousand years ago during the upper Paleolithic period, when Cro-Magnon society used a rudimentary yet structured approach to hunting and hiding from wild beasts. The human-centric efficiency of that early structure led to a concomitant decline in wildlife, which fell to the deadly tools of hunting and killing. As Ronald Wright in his book *A Short History of Progress* (2004) points out, the system structures of hunting were close to industrial in scope, with up to one thousand mammoths and more than one hundred thousand horse carcasses found in different burial sites.

The first major change to human and organizational systems didn't occur until five thousand years later. It happened about ten thousand years ago, caused by mankind's excesses, specifically the over-hunting of wild animals, which necessitated a shift in food sources to an agricultural and domestic animal base. A pattern was starting to form: build a system that's geared to meet mankind's needs, and when that approach creates devastation and destruction, move on to another system.

Small tribes of settlements in four regions of the world simultaneously turned their attention to growing food and herding rather than hunting, and the Neolithic Revolution was born. The prevailing organizational structure, specifically the knowledge factors, now favored human skills geared to planting, growing, and harvesting rather than hunting and killing, and new system structures were born. But wait, what good is an organizational structure without bureaucracy and red tape?

Bureaucratically layered organizational systems complete with reporting lines and other frustrations of the modern organizational structure started with the Sumerians and their nature-centered religion in 3,500 B.C. These ancient folk knew the potential power of wind, rain, sun, heat, and cold. Mother Nature in her generosity offered the Sumerians the ability to survive as a culture, to gain and retain personal power, pride, and profit, and to contemplate how they could combine their strong emotional connectivity to nature with organizational knowledge. In time, the clever Sumerians created elaborate systems of public administration, organized education, contract law, and the beginning of theology.

Feeling an understandable sense of powerlessness and the unknown (the chief ingredients of fear) in the presence of natural forces like winds and floods, the

Sumerians created a religion that promised control and certainty (the promise of all religions and corporate mission statements in centuries to come). This was the very first formalized approach to system structures—one that for the first time used knowledge-centric bureaucracy to mitigate human emotions, especially fear. By 2,250 B.C., the Sumerians had created a neatly ordered pantheon of gods representing the strongest emotional impulses of mankind and the most powerful elements of nature.

There were separate gods of air and water, a goddess of love and procreation, a god of war, a god of wisdom, and a god of the plough. If you flip back to chapter 1, you'll see that the organizational personality of Sumerian culture could best be described as Collaborative-Supportive, particularly in regard to how that personality coexisted with nature. But it was also the first example of how formal systems were structured to not only control the uncontrollable but also lessen humankind's fear of death. As historian John Roberts says in his book *A Short History of the World* (1997), "One of the great demands which men came to make of religion was that it should help them deal with the inevitable horror of death."

The Sumerians were first to develop bureaucratic system structures, but soon to follow were the early Egyptians, who also created elaborate organizational models that tried to offset unpredictable emotional needs with predictable nuts-and-bolts knowledge. For example, in order to harmonize farming practices with the powerful tides of the Nile River, the Egyptians invented the 365¼-day calendar. In addition, the methodical Egyptians created a bureaucratic system of viziers, provincial governors, and senior civil servants who oversaw laws, legal reforms, weights and measures, and huge public works projects like the building of tourist-drawing pyramids. Roberts writes,

> The supreme change threatening men was death, the greatest expression of the meltdown and flux which was their common experience. Egyptian religion seems from the start obsessed with it: its most familiar embodiments, after all, are the mummy and the grave-goods from funeral chambers preserved in our museums.

Next stop, Ancient Greece, where hard-core knowledge factors grew so influential that they still show up in how we think organizations should behave.

How system structures were designed, especially the weight given to both the emotion and knowledge factors required for action, shifted dramatically in early Greece during the fifth and fourth centuries B.C. as the hard sciences of physics and astronomy gained prominence. This period marked the second great change in the Organizational Family Tree's structure—some six thousand years after the first.

ANCIENT GREEKS AND THE ORGANIZATIONAL FAMILY TREE

The first systems diagram was drawn up about thirty-two thousand years ago. It wasn't really called that, but it made a lot more sense than many current "decision trees," "logic maps," and "SWOT" exercises that you see. Our Paleolithic ancestor-artists used cave walls to bring to their fellow cave dwellers a lasting image of the fears, intrigues, and panoply of emotions in their stark environment. Far more gripping (and more useful) than many boardroom PowerPoint presentations, the paintings portrayed animals that were hunted for food and dangerous beasts to be avoided. Thirty-two thousand years later, the lasting messages still intrigue us, found today on the cave walls at Chauvet-Pont-d'Arc in France.

If you venture into the caves today (or into the nearby replica), you'll see how the drawings combine strong emotion factors with organizational knowledge, leaving a clear message of recommended action to members of the group. ("This beast is big and hairy and has sharp teeth and can chase you down in a prehistoric minute.") Caves, it turns out, tell us a lot about the deep roots of the Organizational Family Tree. (Anybody working in an inside office or cubicle with no windows can easily relate.) Besides the expressive "systems diagrams" of our cave ancestors, the cave wall also gave meaning to human existence in ancient Greek society, but in the form of allegory, in the artful words of Plato.

In his *Republic*, Plato depicts mankind as sitting in an underground cave, capable of only looking straight ahead. Behind mankind is a bonfire that casts silhouettes on the wall ahead of deity animals carried by puppeteers. Because the shadows constitute the only reality humans know, they are seen as alive and real by the squatting cave dwellers.

In time, a member of the group escapes. Invariably he discovers the truth: there is far more to life than the shadows. But for his efforts he is stoned to death, because those in the cave don't want to believe there can be more. They are comforted by *what is*, even if the reality is false, because the thought of something more is simply too frightening and incomprehensible to contemplate.

Today's organizational environment has much in common with the unfortunate member of the cave group. Those long entrenched in the status quo of organizational life are like Plato's cave dwellers, staring transfixed at but shadows of what is real. When invariably new realities are introduced, when the idea of change enters their insular lives, they do not embrace the news as enriching or empowering but as a frightening assault on what's comfortable, controlled, and contained.

The general lesson from Plato's *Republic* is that there's much to be gained by having a questioning mind, but such questioning is not without peril. Nevertheless, despite the apparent downside, the ancient Greeks excelled at asking tough, detailed questions and through that process fundamentally redefined what is important within the Organizational Family Tree.

Initially, Greek thinkers saw a connection between mankind and nature using mythology as a touchstone of understanding, and through this connection, they balanced emotion and knowledge factors. In analyzing the epics penned by Homer in the eighth century, historian Richard Tarnas (1993) says the universe was "an ordered whole, a cosmos rather than chaos. The natural world and the human world were not indistinguishable domains in the archaic Greek universe, for a fundamental order structured both nature and society...."

But then the idea of *duality* took root. Mythic dramas staged at Dionysian religious festivals balanced the Greek sense of the heroic—rich in emotional factors of courage, cunning, strength, and nobility—against the inevitability of mankind's mortality. Plato wrote about the human soul being divided into the immortal rational species and the lustful and irascible mortal subspecies. It was the first bad rap against the power and importance of messy, hard-to-contain human emotions.

The idea of duality created the first imbalance between emotion and knowledge factors within the Organizational Family Tree, with knowledge factors now gaining a significant upper hand over emotions. In order to preserve harmony, bring control, and have certainty, people needed education, philosophy, mathematics, music, and gymnastics. Science became far more important than tough-to-quantify and impossible-to-calibrate human emotion. What occurred was a major and lasting realignment of what was important within the Organizational Family Tree.

Continuing with the trend of using hard science to override soft and squishy emotions, the Greek scientists Leucippus and Democritus developed the notion of *atomism* in the fifth century B.C., saying the world was comprised of immutable material atoms—a changeless substance. They argued that all human knowledge was derived simply from the impact of the material atoms on the senses. It was straightforward, logical, and linear thinking not too unlike what goes on in many corporate strategic planning sessions today.

But there's more. The notion of human perception was also put into a little box of thinking by the influential Parmenides, who used rigorous deductive logic to conclude, as Tarnas says, "Things cannot be as they appear to the senses; the familiar world of change, motion, and multiplicity must be mere opinion, for the true reality by logical necessity is changeless and unitary." This logic, from the very deep and early roots of the Organizational Family Tree, still prevails within many modern organizations, whose leaders and managers strive desperately to keep the workplace "changeless and unitary."

So now you know that the ancient Greeks spliced into the Organizational Family Tree's root structure the idea of *dualism* and, from that, the idea that human senses were an impediment to action—that true reality was only accessible to the soul. "Big deal" and "So what?" you might say. Well, here's what. It's because of those curly-bearded Greek big thinkers that we have an environmental activist movement today—that we have Greenpeace, Earth First, and the Sierra Club. We see devastation of the natural environment by industry because thousands of years ago, they seeded into the root structure of the Organizational Family Tree the idea that humankind through science could and *should* control nature.

The ancient Greeks and their obsession with science certainly produced many lasting legacies that serve us well today. But they also created an Organizational Family Tree historical root structure that has managers acting more like robots than thinking like humans. For example, Pythagoras, in the middle of the sixth century, popularized the notion that mathematics was the basis of all things and that numbers defined reality. This concept is seen today in the mindset of newly minted MBAs and corporate chief financial officers, who narrowly focus on minutely measurable *outputs* while totally disregarding *outcomes*. As a friend of mine, a CEO of a large organization, put it, "Counting how many times a day you brush your teeth is a dumb way to measure the overall condition of your oral hygiene."

The move by the Greeks to embrace the hard logic of the sciences meant a significant shift in human consciousness, how we think about things. But the biggest lasting historical factor in the Organizational Family Tree was the move away from a collaborative, worshipful, and respectful embrace of nature. This was the beginning of the dehumanization of "Mother" nature and the abandonment of the biomorphic qualities associated with "her."

Once people rejected the notion of there being a life force in nature and instead accepted that the environment was a collection of scientific elements comprised of earth, air, water, and fire ready for manipulation, then anything was possible. Unfortunately for nature, these possibilities, including the wholesale slaughter of living species, destruction of wide swaths of forest, and pollution of both air and water, were often achieved through system structures where the primary goal was fulfillment of egocentric human needs.

The ancient Greeks introduced a major change within the Organizational Family Tree, dramatically shifting the balance of emotion and knowledge factors. It's an influence you see today in many organizations—more than 2,600 years later—where modern system structures give short shrift to emotions and focus intently on the caliber of individual knowledge, skills, and abilities—the technical things needed to make the organizational machine hum along predictably and profitably.

FROM THE FRENCH TO THE TECHNOLOGICAL REVOLUTION

By embracing "logical" and highly structured organizational systems that ignored the emotional needs of people, the Greeks not only broke away from but actually *attacked* nature, which seeded the symptoms of root rot and decay in the Organizational Family Tree. A glaring example was the structure of Western religion, which quickly manifested all the worst symptoms of a sick organizational system. At its most basic level, the structure of organized Western religion was designed to shame, blame, diminish, and ultimately use as a weapon the strong emotions felt by individuals, particularly fear. (There's nothing like the fear of God to snap us back into line.)

Religion played a major role in the continued restructuring of priorities within the Organizational Family Tree during the Middle Ages. This was a time of huge conflict and controversy, of power struggles and the creation of system structures and actions designed to protect the power, pride, and profit of those in strong positions. As historian Barbara Tuchman says in her 1985 book *The March of Folly*,

> Over a period of 60 years, from roughly 1470 to 1530, the secular spirit of the age was exemplified in a succession of six popes—five Italians and a Spaniard—who carried it to an excess of venality, amorality, avarice, and spectacularly calamitous power struggles. Their governance dismayed the faithful, brought the Holy See into disrepute, left unanswered the cry for reform, ignored all protests, warnings and signs of rising revolt, and ended up break-

ing apart the unity of Christendom and losing half the papal constituency to the Protestant succession.

Dysfunctional structures beget dysfunctional system actions, which in turn can leave us frustrated, fearful, and angry. When a sick system takes root, manifesting as corporate personality disorder and really bad organizational behavior, there's often a natural, protective counteraction from those suffering from the impact. Like a nuclear power plant in meltdown, organizations in meltdown create a toxic environment with the potential for explosive release of energy—in this case human energy. Now, this is a *good* thing, contrary to the mechanistic mindset that preaches to us the gospel that the status quo is the way things should be and change is freaky and dangerous.

And so it was when corporate personality disorder appeared in the Catholic Church in the sixteenth century. German Augustinian monk Martin Luther looked at the symptoms of a sick system running through the Roman Catholic Church, with its crass commercial practices, its privileged clergy, and its role in military struggles. He concluded, in his rather reflective manner, that the institution had become "the seat of the antichrist."

The Catholic Church in Luther's day was in deep meltdown, with trust at an all-time low due to the church's iron grip on authority along with its complete abdication of both responsibility and accountability to those it was meant to serve.

In an organizational meltdown, tremendous energy is created and transferred, usually resulting in dramatic change. Nothing is ever the same again. And so it was with Catholicism. Single-handedly, with the help of the early printing press, Luther ushered in the Protestant Reformation and a permanent shattering of Western Christendom despite all the damage control, counter-spin, and heavy-handed tactics of the Roman Catholic Church.

Western religion was wildly successful at using its iron grip of authority to imbue people with fear, guilt, shame, and blame and, through that system structure, at making them reliant upon the church for protection, predictability, and order. Such codependency, built upon notions of subservience and fear of retribution, was also the hallmark of the institutional and organizational system structures created during the Industrial Revolution, as we are now about to explore.

While revolts and wars, particularly religious wars, were a common feature prior to the eighteenth century, two major events symbolize the repercussions of organizational meltdown—the French revolutions of 1798 and 1848 and the overlapping Industrial Revolution that spread from Britain to the United States and Europe between the early eighteenth and late nineteenth century.

The Industrial Revolution represents the third major contribution to the Organizational Family Tree's historical roots, coming some 2,100 years after the early Greeks' contribution. This third mutation brought major changes to all manner of Western social, economic, and political system structures. Manufacturing and industrialization concentrated jobs and power in large urban centers, and the rhythm of life was forcibly changed for many. For thousands of years, mankind had lived in a certain intimacy with nature, guided by its ebb and flow, its seasons, and even its unpredictability.

You've heard the expressions "stovepipe organizations" or "silos" to describe organizations that have structured themselves into neat, separate, isolated departments that never talk to one another or share ideas. Now you know where these accurate and rightfully negative descriptions of the modern organization come from—the literal stinky smokestacks of the Industrial Age.

The Industrial Age imposed a machine-works existence on men, women, and children, reflected in the patterns and hours of work and the diminished personal freedoms. Authority resided solely in the "upper class" and with industrialists who showed neither accountability nor responsibility to those they affected. Sharp disparities in "classes" of people invariably led to negative energy surges and system meltdown, as historian J. R. Roberts (1992) describes:

> Cities were regarded suspiciously as likely nests of revolution. This is hardly surprising; conditions in many of the new metropolitan centres were often harsh and terrible for the poor. The East End of London could present appalling evidence of poverty, filth, disease and deprivation.

In France, the revolutions of 1789 and 1848 were examples of a major meltdown in the Organizational Family Tree. The social action and public protest at that time redefined sources of power and how energy was both created and conducted. In June of 1788, in the marketplace within the city of Grenoble, citizens organized and acted out what is now seen as the first networked urban insurrection in French history (and likely in all history to that time). This action would be replicated in part not only during the revolution of 1789 but in numerous protest events to come, including the "Battle of Seattle" in 1999, as members of the World Trade Organization tried to meet.

Combining strong emotional energy with technical knowledge, the tactics in France were direct, issue focused, and physical at the start. In Grenoble, government troops were showered with roof tiles. During the French uprisings, barricades became a common feature, including chains pulled across roads. But there were also less confrontational forms of protest. By the 1790s, launched primarily by the Manchester anti-slavery movement, signed petitions, formerly the tool of a single complainer to the British Parliament, had become a broad-based instrument of social change. As historian Sidney Tarrow (1998) points out, the petition was also the progenitor of the peaceful rally:

> By the 1830s, the decorous presentation of mass petitions had been combined by the Chartists with the collective use of public space to demonstrate the movement's strength. In presenting their "people's petitions" to Parliament, they brought thousands of people into the streets.

Organizational Family Trees that are decaying with root rot and creating dysfunctional organizational behavior can set off alarm bells in our emotional brain that can spur us to action. Those actions in turn can have a major impact on the climate and then the culture of the organization in decay, ultimately creating a new environment. What's fascinating to observe is how this new growth—these radical offshoots from the conservative old root structure—gets enmeshed into the overall Organizational Family Tree.

When we follow the history of many protest movements, and even rebellions, we see that after a while a certain pattern forms. System structures can indeed change when we start digging around the root structure and pruning away some decay. But the change won't usually be as dramatic as we had first envisioned. In fact, what often happens as a result of a serious attack on an organizational structure is that the system sways and bends but rarely snaps and breaks. In the process, synergy occurs—our radical and sensational ideas get quickly enmeshed within the organizational climate and over time affect the deeply rooted culture, in turn creating a new organizational environment that is now seen as the status quo. Here's an example of what I mean.

In the nineteenth century, unique and radical actions to change the structure of badly behaving organizations didn't take long to become institutionalized. Things *did* change within the organizational structure, as its developmental growth reflected the influence of those who were mad as hell and not willing to take it anymore. But what began as a dramatic aberration soon became commonplace. Radical and dramatic offshoots to the Organizational Family Tree became embedded into the dominant root structure. As Tarrow (1998) observes,

The strike became an institution of collective bargaining; the demonstration was covered by a body of law that both regulated and distinguished it from political activity; and the sit-in and building occupation were treated with greater leniency than ordinary delinquency.

So what's the deal? Am I saying that social movements and protest groups have their own unique Organizational Family Tree in the forest of human and organizational systems? That the Activist Oak you see swaying wildly in the winds of change is hugely different from that Industrial Cactus squatting in a desert of creativity? Well, yes. And no. Social activism definitely has a culture (historical and developmental factors) very different from that of the Solid Steel Corporation. There are also very different climatic factors with activist groups, usually giving emotional needs far more importance than technical knowledge necessities.

But (to the horror of most activist groups) there's also much in common between the structure of grassroots social movement groups and that of greedy corporations squinting intently at their financial bottom line. The reason for this is very simple. In most cases, those at the sharp point of activism, those with the fiercest fire in their belly, those with the greatest disdain for all the ugliness wrought by mean and nasty corporations, share the same general mindset of the captains of industry when it comes to thinking about what makes for an orderly organizational structure. And so, throughout the Industrial Revolution and beyond, social movements, labor unions, and activist groups adopted formal structures that most polluting steel conglomerates would be proud to accept as their own. These "advancements" included well-defined organization charts, detailed delineation of duties, and plenty of rules and regulations.

In lockstep with advancements in social protest organization came a major change to the system structure of the military, with the chief architect being Helmuth von Moltke, who commanded the Prussian army in 1857. Von Moltke introduced major changes to how large armies were managed—or mostly mismanaged. What he designed was a system structure that produced highly trained officers who could be dispatched to lead and manage standardized units, called divisions, which in turn were comprised of tightly coordinated separate functions, including cavalry, infantry, and artillery.

Von Moltke's military structure called for not only highly trained but easily interchangeable staff officers, standardization right down to the number of cooking utensils allowed in each division, and tightly administered central command and control. Planning and scenario building, including mock battles, were constantly undertaken and refined. It was a brilliant solution to managing huge groups of personnel in a consistent and effective fashion—one that was soon copied by all countries and which later served as a model for managing larges industries. Today, you can see examples of von Moltke's genius in how McDonald's serves Big Macs and manages its employees as well as in dozens of other one-size-fits-all, do-it-this-way-or-else organizations.

The birth of the twentieth century heralded continued growth in industrialization and an expansion of American global influence. But with this came an increasing need by those in power to find ways to deal with what seemed like a never-ending stream of independent-thinking folks who could see corporate personality disorder for what it was—a threat to not only their emotional and economic state but the health of the natural environment. There clearly was a problem with the machine-works design of organizational life: The gears didn't mesh quite right. Screws kept coming loose. And instead of things humming along smoothly and profitably, there was this damn incessant whining and screaming as public protests increased in both magnitude and impact.

From the middle to the end of the twentieth century, our power to cope with and react to corporate personality disorder received a huge boost. Three interlocking factors contributed to this power surge: a far better informed populace with easy access to information; rising public disenchantment and sense of disempowerment related to a wide swath of economic, social, and political structures; and the advent of the Internet—a communications technology that gave otherwise disparate groups instantaneous, relatively inexpensive, and phenomenally efficient abilities to connect and cooperate globally. Here's little story illustrating just how powerful the Internet is.

In 1995, a forest company owned by a nice old man hired me to help them chase away a corporate giant that had just made a very unwelcome and threatening $100 million attack on the old man. (In business language, it's called a hostile takeover bid. Suddenly one company says it's going to try to buy enough shares of another company to end up owning it—despite the other company opposing such a shotgun wedding.) This was 1995, not that long ago. My idea was simply to provide the nice old man with an e-mail address (there were very few Web sites then, and the company didn't have one) where he would be available to anyone who wanted to know why the takeover was bad. We issued a news release with the e-mail address and pointed out that this was the first time in history that the Internet (a new technology) was being used as a communications tool in a hostile takeover bid.

The reaction was incredible. The news story made international headlines. Journalists from Canada, the United States, Germany, Britain, and numerous other global financial hotspots wanted an interview with this technology-savvy old president. Positive and wildly supportive e-mails poured into his address from employees, shareholders, ordinary folks, union activists, and environmentalists. His company was portrayed as "cutting edge" and "modern," while the giant forest company trying to buy him out was painted as a stodgy, conservative ogre. It was a public relations miracle. In short order, the hostile takeover fizzled out, the old man held on to his forest company, and I was invited to address groups around North America on the magic of the Internet.

That was 1995. This is 2007 as I tap away on a cool Toshiba laptop, sitting in a college cafeteria, sipping a tasty vanilla latte while connected remotely to the Internet through a Sierra Wireless AirCard. At the tap of my finger I have access to millions of Web sites and millions of blogs, and I am part of the over fifty *billion* e-mails being sent *a day* throughout the world (many, it seems, arriving on my computer in the morning promising me a larger penis or instant cash). The structure of the Internet is in fact a lot like the evolved structure of many social movement organizations (and terrorist networks). There is plenty of decentralization, personal empowerment, and adaptability.

What we are seeing now, thanks to massively enhanced communications, connectivity, and cooperation, is a profound divergence from the old mechanical mindset of how organizations should be structured. But this adaptive thinking is happening—for now—on the margins. It's happening with groups and organizations that understand there's a lot of root rot in the traditional Organizational Family Tree. But it's *not* happening with many staid organizations, institutions, and corporations. Places that are so choked with the old weeds of culture that they have trouble feeling the sunlight.

Why are these places so stubborn? Because they still believe and continue to preach that the puppet shadows in their cave are real. The ancient Greeks may have been the first to significantly mutate the deepest part of the Organizational Family Tree root structure (historical factors), but it was modern society that ensured those inflexible, nonadaptive roots kept growing (developmental factors).

LAYING THE BLAME FOR UNHEALTHY ORGANIZATIONAL TREES

There's a broad level of agreement among many philosophers that the seventeenth century marked a major turning point in how mankind viewed its relationship with Mother Nature. This shift resulted in a collective consciousness that still permeates every aspect of Western life. The result is the mechanistic model of human and organizational development, which sees you as a cog in a machine—a deterministic, cause-and-effect, predictable, and controllable life.

Francis Bacon, born in 1561 in London, was one of the major influences on how people in the sixteenth century viewed organizational systems. Historian Richard Tarnas provides this revealing description of Bacon:

> While Socrates had equated knowledge with virtue, Bacon equated knowledge with power.... With Bacon, science took on a new role—utilitarian, utopian, the material and human counterpart to God's plan of spiritual salvation. Man was created by God to hold dominion over nature.

The emotions of fear and anger when combined with knowledge can create an intensity of action so great that it can change the very structure of an organizational system. Throughout his life, Bacon was plagued with personal misfortune, including rejection by relatives, mistrust by those in power, and imprisonment for accepting a bribe. So what's a guy to do? Bacon, not being one to sit around, combined the energy of his emotions with his prodigious scientific knowledge to forever change the system of scientific discovery and research. His inductive methodology was comforting, reassuring, and stable—a great counterbalance to the chaos of his personal life.

But Bacon's fear, anger, and need for action also needed a specific victim—he needed to blame and shame another in retribution for the troubles in his life. And that other was Mother Nature. As Fritjof Capra (1982) writes,

> The terms in which Bacon advocated his new empirical method of investigation were not only passionate but outright vicious. Nature, in his view, had to be "hounded in her wanderings," "bound into service," and made a "slave." She was to be "put in constraint," and the aim of the scientist was to "torture nature's secrets from her."
>
> The ancient concept of the earth as a nurturing mother was radically transformed in Bacon's writings, and it disappeared completely as the Scientific Revolution proceeded to replace the organic view of nature with the metaphor of the world as a machine.

And so it was that the formation of scientific research had a major, lasting historical influence on the modern Organizational Family Tree and became an underlying cause of corporate personality disorder. This shift in thinking carries the stamp of sexism, racism, and anti-ecology that often surfaces today in the behavior of the corporate personality. But cold scientific precision was just the beginning of the problems. As Bacon was establishing the linear model for scientific thought, another major shift in thought was occurring in France that would have a lasting impact on the historical factors of most Organizational Family Trees.

Rene Descartes was a brilliant mathematician who devised analytic geometry, a branch of mathematics still used today. His *scientific* work heavily influenced his *philosophic* view of the world—a world he saw as an extremely disorderly place driven by messy and intangible human emotions. Known as the "Father of Philosophy," Descartes is most celebrated for his statement "*Cogito, ergo sum*," meaning, "I think therefore I am." Descartes believed that our emotions should have no role in our decision making, and when it came to coexistence with nature, he wrote, "The Laws of Mechanics are identical with those of nature."

Through his rigid, mathematics-based scientific thought, Descartes brought the promise of control and certainty to an age full of fear—fear of new discoveries, crumbling institutions, and mistrusted authority figures. In so doing, he also provided a precise organizational system structure that allowed people to exploit with immunity the one remaining mysterious and uncontrollable force in their lives—Mother Nature. As Capra (1982) says in reflecting upon Descartes' huge influence on how systems are structured,

> The drastic change in the image of nature from organism to machine had a strong effect on people's attitudes toward the natural environment. The organic worldview of the Middle Ages had implied a value system conducive to ecological behavior.... These cultural constraints disappeared as the mechanization of science took place. The Cartesian view of the universe as a mechanical system provided a "scientific" sanction for the manipulation and exploitation of nature that has become typical of Western culture.

To get a sense of how Descartes' mechanical thinking rolled out, it's useful to consider his ideas about animals, including humans: "I consider the human body as a machine ... my thought ... compares a sick man and an ill-made clock with my idea of a healthy man and a well-made clock" (Capra, 1982).

To Descartes, everything in the world fit together in a neat machine-like model, where the sum of all the parts always added up to the whole. This view of the world is called *reductionist thinking*, and it is still very evident in many modern organizations. When is the last time you heard the word "machine" used in favorable tones to describe how efficiently and effectively an organizational unit or team was operating? What about "reengineering" to describe how an organization had been restructured? Now you know whom to blame—the same guy who thought your pet cat is really a cold assembly of springs, nuts, and bolts.

Bacon, Descartes, and others of like mind succeeded in changing how powerful people perceived the world—from a view that saw humans existing in unity and harmony with Mother Earth to one where humans were elevated above nature. This is the bedrock of the modern Organizational Family Tree, which shows up in all manner of corporate thinking today. But there are more skeletons in the closet. Descartes' mechanistic notion of how organizations should be structured took deep root during the Industrial Revolution. Along came machine-based factories, production lines, regulated efficiency, predictable outputs, and the use of "human capital," which perfectly blended Cartesian thinking into a mechanical paradigm of how the world should exist.

And so we come to Frederick Winslow Taylor, an engineer who needed precision in his life more than a junkie needs crack cocaine. In 1911, he introduced scientific management—the blueprint for micromanaging organizational structures that still haunts many of us today. In describing scientific management, Taylor once said,

> In the past the man has been first; in the future the system must be first.... In our scheme, we do not ask for the initiative of our men. We do not want any initiative. All we want of them is to obey the orders we give them, do what we say, and do it quick.

Wow. When's the last time you heard a manager say that? Yesterday? Today? In my case it was just a few weeks ago, as I was counseling a friend who had just received a gobbledygook bureaucratic edict from his head office that completely ignored the fact that there was life on Earth.

Today the majority of Organizational Family Trees, including system structures and daily corporate actions, show the continuing historical and developmental influences of Granddaddy Taylor. If something goes wrong (as it always does), then it's the immediate *actions* that are blamed (and often individual behavior) rather than the *structure*, even when the latter is imbued with unhealthy behavioral patterns.

To deal with corporate personality disorder is to ask, "Why are we still doing this?" and "why not another way?" It is to continually challenge assumptions and to have the courage to sometimes say no. Why would we not do this? The answer is because we've been conditioned to deal with immediate actions and offer simple remedies instead of challenging the continuing necessity of certain historical and developmental factors within an organization. After all, challenging the deeply embedded root structure of an Organizational Family Tree is akin to challenging creation itself.

The striking thing about the cold, clinical, machine-like thinking that Taylor brought to organizational system structure design is that it was driven by the very emotions he despised, his lasting personal fears resulting from a strict family upbringing, horrible nightmares, and insomnia.

In describing Taylor, Gareth Morgan (1997) cites "an obsessive, compulsive character, driven by a relentless need to tie down and master almost every aspect of his life." This included the strictest of rules in his home life, his leisure activities, and even his playtime. Everything he did was micromanaged in the tightest of detail and the most precise of schedules—nothing was left to chance, and everything rigidly followed.

Now this sounds like a really fun guy. Kids in his neighborhood didn't like playing with Taylor because he insisted on rigorously measuring everything, including the distance between bases on a dirty field. Grown-ups hated working with him because he had the infuriating habit of counting, calculating, and cross-verifying everything, including the number of steps he took between buildings. As one might expect, workers vilified Taylor and feared the impact his scientific management would have on their lives. But his thinking had huge appeal among those in power, who also feared that their power, pride, and profit hinged on their ability to keep workers contained and controlled. Again, to cite Morgan,

> It is clear that his whole theory of scientific management was the product of the inner struggles of a disturbed and neurotic personality. His attempt to organize and control the world, whether in childhood games or in systems of scientific management, was really an attempt to organize and control himself.

Have another look at that organizational personality you're dealing with. Recognize any Taylorisms? Have a look at yourself. Do you think that effective and efficient management means having everything precisely in its place, *people in their place*, and everything predictable, neat, and tidy? I don't blame you if you do, because that's what we've been conditioned to think since grade one, in every management-training program we've taken, and by the organizational personality that tells us what to do.

THE BIZARRE NEED TO STUFF OUR BEHAVIOR INTO A NEAT, SMALL BOX

I often stick a song called "Little Boxes" into my car's CD player and turn up the volume until the windows of my Mini Cooper threaten to burst. The song was written by Malvina Reynolds and sung by folk singer Pete Seger. It tells of Western society's penchant for control and containment and for preserving a bland status quo. The lyrics include this perfect description of today's mechanistic approach to management:

> *Little boxes on the hillside,*
> *Little boxes made of tickytacky*
> *Little boxes on the hillside,*
> *Little boxes all the same.*

The song was a big hit in the 1960s, when many in society were taking a hard look at the sick system structures prevalent in corporations, government, and the military. But in many ways not a great deal has changed with organizations.

In the 2001 movie *Traffic*, Michael Douglas plays the role of the U.S. government's drug czar, heading up a frustrating and unsuccessful "war on drugs." One day he's on a flight in his executive jet, surrounded by bureaucratic lackeys. He looks at his assembled staff and asks desperately for "some out-of-the-box thinking, anything at all, any idea" on how to deal with the crisis before the nation. He's greeted with a long silence and blank stares from the young, perfectly tailored staff members in their white shirts and dark ties. There's nothing. No ideas, fresh or otherwise.

For a while, the term "out-of-the-box thinking" was in vogue among management, the idea being that we should show creativity and original thinking in the way we approach our daily tasks. Of course, most of the corporations encouraging "out of the box thinking" have us tightly locked *in* a very small box, as illustrated in their boxy organization charts.

Always at the top of the organization chart are those with the greatest power, pride, and profit. They not only dwell at the top of the paper pyramid but also, in almost all cases, occupy the biggest corner office perched at the highest reaches of their building, fly first class while we jam our knees into our jaws in steerage class, and have salaries many times greater than those residing at "the bottom." While organization charts symbolize control and containment, loyalty to the status quo, and a defense against change, company newsletters and CEO pep talks are often laced with cognitively dissonant happy talk like "out-of-the-box thinking" and "empowerment." The climate, driven by organizational culture, is "Do as I say, not as I do."

So you might wonder: Where did the idea of box-like organization charts come from? In their 2002 book *The Boundaryless Organization*, Ron Ashkenas, Dave Ulrich, Todd Jick, and Steve Kerr explain that so-called silo organizations—those with neat rows of specialty functions and nice square boxes describing who does what—can be traced to classical economist Adam Smith and his 1776 book *The Wealth of Nations*. Smith was a big fan of delegating piecemeal work to employees who would specialize at doing one simple job rather than learn how to do many things.

The idea, of course, was to maximize productivity and profits for factory owners, not to enrich workers with greater knowledge, skill sets, or emotional job satisfaction. The authors also point to technology as a major contributor to today's box-driven organization chart, offering as an example Henry Ford's moving assembly line, which brought factory owners huge efficiencies and maximized profits.

Alfred Chandler tells us in his Pulitzer Prize-winning book *The Visible Hand: The Managerial Revolution in American Business* (1977) that the first large-scale, highly detailed corporate organization chart was drawn up in 1846 by the Baltimore and Ohio Railroad Company. There were two reasons that such a plan was needed. Railways had become incredibly complex infrastructures by the 1800s, with rapid growth in traffic and a great need to coordinate and manage both the daily working of trains (including scheduling) and the collection and distribution of revenues.

But the other reason was rooted in a crisis—the most common trigger to organizational change. On October 5, 1841, a head-on collision involving passenger trains run by the Western Railway killed a conductor and one passenger and injured seventeen other passengers. As Chandler writes, "The resulting outcry helped bring into being the first modern, carefully defined, internal organizational structure used by an American business enterprise."

An even more refined version of the organization chart was designed by Daniel C. McCallum of the Erie Railroad Company, who built upon the work of the Western Railway and the Baltimore and Ohio Railroad Company. McCallum's design was so effective that the editor of the *American Railroad Journal* had McCallum's organization chart lithographed and sold it to the public for $1. Again, it was the pursuit of corporate efficiency, centralized authority, and maximization of profits, and not concern for the employee's or customer's emotional needs, that led to the mechanistic streamlining of America's railroad system.

Ashkenas, Ulrich, Jick, and Kerr say that organizations have both vertical and horizontal boundaries, with vertical boundaries defining status and career progression and horizontal boundaries defining functional specialties as well as separating hourly from salaried employees and union from non-union workers.

While they agree all organizations require some degree of both vertical and horizontal boundaries, they stress that most organizations can also benefit from a more open and flexible approach and that today's box-like structure is creating more harm than good in many cases. As they say, "Mazes of functional boxes inevitably create delay, indecision, uncoordinated action, and least-common-denominator products and services." What the authors show is that such system structures manifest what they call "five typical dysfunctions," including "slow, sequential times; protected turf; sub-optimization of organizational goals; the enemy-within syndrome; and customers doing their own integration."

There's plenty of other expert opinion in the field of management theory and strategic planning related to the failure of mechanistic, box-like-thinking approaches to organizational systems. In their book *The Strategy Focused Organization* (2001), Robert Kaplan of Harvard Business School and David Norton talk about the modern organization's need to deal with strategy—not just tactics—in managing change. As they point out,

> Many organizations, even until the end of the 1970s, operated under central control, through large functional departments. Strategy could be developed at the top and implemented through a centralized command-and-control culture. Change was incremental, so managers could use slow-reacting and tactical management control systems such as the budget. Such systems however were designed for 19th century and early 20th century industrial companies and are inadequate for today's dynamic, rapidly changing environment.

A GLARING ABSENCE OF EMOTION IN ORGANIZATIONAL PLANNING

If you want to see just how mechanistic most organizational behavior is, just sit in on a corporate planning session. The first thing you'll notice (after the pricey lunch being served) is what's *not* there. Glaringly absent from most strategic planning exercises is any reference to or acknowledgement of the emotional factors inherent within all corporations, institutions, and organizations. At the very most, superficial references to internal and external communications might recognize that organizations are actually comprised of *people*. But even in such references, minimal thought is extended to what emotions are at play, what our expectations are at work, and what makes us angry or afraid (or full of hope or joy).

Colin Eden and Fran Ackermann point out in their book *Making Strategy* (1998) that the most overlooked consideration in developing organizational strategy is political feasibility—in other words, "the social processes of delivering, discovering, and negotiating the data, determining and manipulating its meaning, and agreeing on the strategic direction." Eden and Ackermann go on to say that it's impossible to understand strategic issues within an organization "without an understanding of the issues of politics, power, personalities, and personal style.… There is no separation between the work of the rational analyst and the work of the social process facilitator." This is similar to my idea that all organizational issues come down to what I call the "3 Ps"—*power, pride, and profit*.

We need a sense of empowerment to keep fear at bay; we need a sense of pride to secure our self-image; and we need to profit from our experiences in either a monetary, experiential, or emotional way. All organizational life is really about individual people who are part of the corporation, association, institution, or team. Ignoring the huge emotional component of organizational action—ignoring human needs—is one reason why many sterile, technical-knowledge-laden strategic planning exercises fail.

For example, Henry Mintzberg, Bruce Ahlstrand, and Joseph Lampel, in their book *Strategy Safari* (1998), cite a study showing that not one company that did traditional planning with a SWOT (strengths, weaknesses, opportunities, threats) model actually used the information later. In addition, Kaplan and Norton (2001) cite a survey of management consultants showing that fewer than 10 percent of their strategies were effectively implemented.

Kaplan and Norton also point out that 85 percent of corporate management teams spend less than an hour a month discussing strategy, instead getting bogged down in the minutia of budgets, tactics, and other details. Senior executives in organizations may spend less than an hour a month on high-level strategy, but it often appears that most spend less than an hour *a year* discussing the emotional impact of their decision making on us.

Cultural historians will some day look back at the ubiquitous "org chart" and recognize it as the quintessential symptom of corporate personality disorder. The skeletal, connect-the-boxes design of a modern org chart is in fact a blueprint for organizational meltdown. In some ways, today's org chart is like the design of a

medieval chastity belt—both are mechanistic designs intended to stop the naturally inevitable, a futile attempt at control and containment brought about
because of fear of what human emotions can lead to.

In the last few years, managers feeling the dysfunctional results of their system
structures have attempted such refinements as flattening the organization chart,
turning it upside down, and lacing it with a lattice of dotted lines (representing
reporting relationships) and solid lines (representing foundational relationships).
But in the end, small boxes are still small boxes no matter how they are stitched
together.

One of the world's freshest thinkers about how organizations are designed is
Karen Stephenson, a New Yorker who combines her background in quantum
chemistry with anthropology to dig deep into organizational culture. Over her
many years of extensive work in the field, including building the largest database
of information in the world about corporate networks, she's come to many
insightful conclusions about how corporations are structured. For example, in a
2004 interview with Bob Rosner, who hosts the *Working Wounded* Web site, she
said,

> I used to call the organizational chart the "corporate lie." I don't say it any-
> more because the organizational chart is a map of formal procedures and pro-
> cesses and does work in times of organizational stress. But humans are
> cantankerous, don't follow the rules, are naturally creative, and tend to step
> outside the lines. When they do, they create processes, behaviors, and habits
> that don't follow the organizational chart.

What Stephenson figured out is that while formal organization charts may
provide us with a one-dimensional view of how a company looks, the daily flow
of energy and power within the Organizational Family Tree is determined by
relationships between the people in the company. As a colleague of hers, futurist
Thornton May, said a couple of years ago about her work, "The organization
chart basically shows you the formal rules. But the ropes of the organization, how
it actually works, is the human network. Karen, more than anyone else, knows
how to make it visible."

So what would happen if a company did away with organization charts?
That's exactly what Ricardo Semler, chief executive officer of Brazil-based Semco,
did—after first collapsing on a factory floor, suffering from stress caused by an
old sick system organizational structure. His near heart attack changed Semler.
For the next twenty-five years, Semler fostered an organizational climate where
employees set their own hours and wages, chose their own technologies, and

operated through systems of flextime and open communications. It was an Organizational Family Tree with wide open flows of communications, connectivity between groups, and cooperation, bound together through broadly diffused authority, accountability, and responsibility.

As described in the April 2004 version of the online journal *CIO Insight*, "He did away with dedicated receptionists, org charts, even the central office. He encouraged employees to suggest what they should be paid, to evaluate their bosses, to learn each other's job, and to tolerate dissent—even when divisive. He set up a profit-sharing system and insisted that the company's financials be published internally, so that everyone could see how the company was doing."

Is Semler's approach pie in the sky? The results say otherwise. In his book *Maverick: The Success Story Behind the World's Most Unusual Workplace* (1993), he talks about the absence of a dress code, voluntary meetings, and mandatory vacation time. But he also points out that the corporation is extremely successful from a financial perspective. Looking back from 2004, we see that Semco's revenue's jumped $35 million to $212 million in just six years, and the company has grown to three thousand employees from just a few hundred.

There is indeed a cure for sick systems, and that cure can not only benefit you and others affected by the organization's behavior but also the financial profitability of the company. "All" the organizational personality has to do is break away from some of the worst influences of its deeply rooted culture, particularly its penchant for control. As Semler states, "The desire for uniformity is a major problem … but it is a by-product of the same problems that plague management, which is the need to feel in control."

So the solution is to stretch our thinking. To get out of the small box of logic created by organizational cultures rooted in a mechanistic past. The solution is to ask "Why?" and "Why not?" Tear down the walls of small-box thinking by challenging stuck-in-the-mud assumptions and saying no when necessary. Start doing this and soon we'll create *bigger-box thinking*, a place where there are indeed safe boundaries ("out of the box" leaves you vulnerable and unprotected), where there's room to do jumping-jacks of creativity, where there's plenty of elbow room to move ideas around, and where we can actually breathe.

6

DEATH, EMOTIONS, AND ORGANIZATIONAL MELTDOWN

One day as I was quietly sitting at my very important executive desk in a large corner suite office with a view of the city, the chief executive officer walked in carrying a letter-sized manila envelope. He was dressed in an undertaker-style shiny black suit and bright white shirt, monogrammed on the pocket and cuffs, with a somber dark silk tie.

"How are you?" I jovially asked.

"No too good," he said without returning a smile, motioning for me to sit with him at my executive office meeting table. (Actually, he was *very* good—that good feeling that comes when you finally pull a burr out of your butt.) Within seventeen minutes, with the precision of a medical examiner dissecting a corpse, the unsmiling CEO notified me I was being "constructively dismissed"—corporate speak for being fired without a cause—and I was told to gather up my things and immediately leave the office. My computer was suddenly frozen, my telephone disconnected by some mysterious outside hand.

The manila envelope contained a severance package offering money in return for my silence, and the CEO suggested I fabricate a story to explain my departure. The exact moment of my professional death is indelibly branded in my mind's eye, although it occurred many years ago. The feelings of shock, panic, fear, and emotional collapse have permanently wormed into a corner of my consciousness and unconsciousness, reappearing at unexpected times when least invited.

Over many months, my sudden death of self-image was followed by my death of hope and, for a while, thoughts of suicide—the final death. Today, many years later, I continue to be visited at times of emotional distress by those ghosts from my past—ghosts named the Death of Sense of Self and the Death of Hope, who replay in perfect detail their white-hot seventeen-minute performance from years ago. The fear is gone, but the anger remains, as it does with many who have become human sacrifices on the organizational battleground, where "make a killing" can take on many meanings.

The phrase "make a killing" describes what many corporations strive to accomplish in their steadfast pursuit of profit. Indeed, battle metaphors invade all corners of an organization in meltdown, where technical proficiency and ruthless efficiency often supersede the unpredictable and messy demands of human emotion. But, like it or not, organizations are inhabited by people whose actions are driven by emotion—particularly the emotion of fear.

When organizations are in meltdown, the core of the Organizational Family Tree—the Triangle of Trust—is badly out of alignment. Communications, cooperation, and connectivity to others are dangerously absent, and there's a huge imbalance among the core connectors of authority, accountability, and responsibility. In a particularly advanced state of meltdown are vital emotion factors (key nutrients within the Organizational Family Tree), their demise creating a strong sense of fear.

Lift your eyes from this page for a minute and think about the organizational personalities you know. I bet most of them are in various states of meltdown. The result can easily be the death of a corporation or institution, but then this should come as no surprise, since most organizations are rife with metaphors of destruction, such as "battlefield," "combat," "take no hostages," "to the victor go the spoils," and "making a killing," just to cite a few.

THE DEADLY LANGUAGE OF SICK ORGANIZATIONS

The phrase "make a killing" says a lot about the organizational personality, and it says a lot about managers who use such combative language. Do you ever wonder why all this talk about "battlefields" and "killing" is so easily woven into the language of organizations? It's there because organizations are full of humans with emotional brain structures that have been wired for hundreds of thousands of years to think about survival (despite the anti-emotion nature of the mechanistic *organizational* personality). Unlike any other species, we have an early awareness of our mortality, which also means we think a lot about staying alive. Here's what English philosopher Thomas Hobbes has to say about the matter, as cited in Becker (1973):

> Man is the mortal being who is aware that he is such. The consequence of this awareness is constant anxiety … the fundamental desire of the human animal is the unlimited desire for self-preservation.

Self-preservation is a natural instinct embedded in our DNA structure and our conscious and unconscious self. We're genetically programmed to avoid death, and when death invariably and inevitably comes there's a sense of fracture, a breaking away from what up to that point has been whole and comfortable and often secure. The presence of death brings a sense of incompleteness, of loss. All this death talk can be a bit morbid, but it's a key to understanding why the organizational personality behaves the way it does, why you react to the organizational personality the way you do, and how things can be adjusted for the better.

A fractured self-image can be the result of a messy divorce or separation from a loved one, changing circumstances at work, the impact of disease or accident, or a failure to make the grade or meet an expectation. We are constantly striving to feed our image of self, to validate (with ourselves and with others) that we meet expectations of behavior, physical appearance and prowess, intelligence and cunning, trustworthiness, sensuality and sexuality, and a litany of other traits and attributes. Such self-expectations are wired into our brain at a very young age and by the messages we are bombarded with by consumer marketing, TV shows, peers, and organizational structures. These messages can be implicit or explicit and can come from corporate, social, or religious sources.

The environment of the Organizational Family Tree, particularly the influence of both emotion and knowledge factors found in the everyday climate, plays a major role in the state of our personality and our sense of self. If you're like me and many others, you're consumed, both consciously and unconsciously, by self-image; you constantly engage in self-talk (too often critical); you catch and hold your reflection in plate glass windows as you quickly stride down a sidewalk; and you spend considerable time contemplating both your physical and emotional presence in bathroom mirrors.

We keep a multibillion-dollar brand image industry alive by attaching labels like Coke, the Gap, McDonald's, IBM, BMW, and hundreds of others to our lives, and we collectively spend hundreds of millions of dollars a year on activities and actions targeted at our self-esteem and self-image, including everything from diet pills and fad exercise programs to weekend meditation and spirituality retreats.

One of the many manifestations of corporate personality disorder is this: the more important the job title or public perception of a particular profession, the more traumatic the death of self-image will be when it comes. I recall being asked to facilitate a session at a management conference in San Francisco a few years back, one of those one-size-fits-all, vanilla-flavored workshops on leadership, filled with good intentions and a bevy of buzzwords. I particularly remember how participants, mostly middle-aged men, answered when I invited the obligatory round-the-room introductions. "Hi, I'm Bob Roberts, vice-president at Omnipresent Corporation." "I'm Kevin Krueger, director of corporate planning at Mountain Pacific." "Hello, I'm Michael Svensen, executive director of marketing at Crescent Industrials." And so it went, each person providing a hyphenated version of their identity, linking *who* they *were* to *what* they *did*.

It's true that you can get so caught up in *what you do* that you forget *who you are* as a human. My friend, Staff Sergeant John Ward of the Royal Canadian Mounted Police, likes to start his communication workshops by asking participants not who they *are* but what's important to them in life. It's always interesting to observe how men and women stumble over that deceivingly simple question. I've often thought that we should not ask people *what they do* but *why* they do what they do (and in fact, that's what I now do in workshops and in casual conversations). The answers you'll get will be a lot richer with meaning (once you get past the first look of suspicion).

What you'll be probing for is that person's emotional basis—what really makes them tick and what's important to their self-image. This is why I'm suggesting you also ask the *organizational* personality not *what* it's doing but *why*. In other words, ask committee heads, managers, directors, and others making decisions just why are they taking the action they are. What you'll often get is an insight into what makes *that* personality tick—where *its* self-image comes from.

For example, I often ask executives why they want to quickly run out and publicly respond to a negative news media story about them or their company. They often say that the public is anxious for a response from their company and that "everybody" is looking for a comment. The reality in most cases is that very few people have even noticed the news story. What's driving the executives to action is that they think everyone else feels like they do—under attack, and so they must fight back. In such cases my advice to the executives is take a big breathe, relax, and understand that very few, if any, people are as concerned as they are.

What my above example of freaked-out executives is meant to show is that all of us are very deeply absorbed with our self-image. Psychologist Daniel Goleman, who popularized the notion of emotional intelligence, says this about the vital importance of sense of self and self-image in his book *Emotional Intelligence*, updated in 2005:

Communication that threatens the self—that does not support the story one tells oneself about oneself—threatens self-esteem. Such threats are a major source of anxiety. For animals, stress is most often in the form of a threat to life or limb. For humans though, a challenge to self-esteem is enough to brew anxiety.

The theme I'm developing here is this: human personalities and organizational personalities both have a self-image. Ours is based on our personal culture and climate, while the *organizational* personality has a way of doing things and seeing itself based on its Organizational Family Tree. If what we do or say threatens the organizational personality, there can be trouble. Conversely, the actions of a mean and nasty organizational personality can also cut our self-image to the core, and again there will be trouble. The ramifications of an attack on self-image are starkly portrayed by sociologist Terrell Northrup:

Identity is conceived of as more than a psychological sense of self; it encompasses a sense that one is safe in the world physically, psychologically, socially, even spiritually. Events which threaten to invalidate the core sense of identity will elicit defensive responses aimed at avoiding psychic and/or physical annihilation. (As cited in *Intractable Conflicts and Their Transformation*, 1989, p. 55)

"Annihilation" is a pretty strong word to describe how we might feel. But it's also right on target, especially when we think about how people respond to change. The very phrase "change management" is, to me, a curious oxymoron. The phrase suggests that events in flux and naturally morphing and self-adapting must be constrained and contained through *management*, which guarantees control and certainty (as if *that* will happen).

The reality is that such a soulless exercise religiously avoids any thought, reference, or reverence to the human emotions attached to our self-image, particularly the emotion of fear. And yet it's personalized *emotion*, not structural and systems logic and cognition, that will determine how change eventually rolls out.

WHEN MEDICAL DOCTORS GET ILL FROM SICK SYSTEMS

Earlier I told you about a research study I did on the organizational well-being of a health care system. That study showed an environment deeply affected by corporate personality disorder. The Triangle of Trust that forms the core of the

Organizational Family Tree was a pool of toxic liquid. Communications were dysfunctional, cooperation among many groups was nonexistent, and connectivity among key professions and administrators was threadbare at best. Authority was a concept to be grabbed, hoarded, and defended. Responsibility and accountability were lackluster and poorly defined.

Expectations were not being met through performance, and system structures mandated actions that consistently had a negative impact on patients, nurses, doctors, and even administrators. I found that both historical and developmental factors in the Organizational Family Tree had led to a very rigid organizational structure rife with protective administrative silos and professional jealousies. In a series of community forums, patients, community residents, and various medical professionals were asked to describe the organizational personality of their health care system. Their immediate characterization was "overloaded," "worried," "caring," "deceptive," "starving," "depressed," "competent," and "unaware."

Those in what I named *community conversation* sessions admitted they would certainly be uncomfortable working for or living with a human exhibiting such traits. The remedy offered by physicians in the sessions was to attack the system's actions and not to question the organizational structure. It was quite the opposite reaction from that of nurses and naturopaths (and other practitioners of nontraditional medicine), who saw a rigid Organizational Family Tree as the problem.

It's far easier to attack system *actions* than system *structures,* because to attack an organizational structure means to challenge our conditioned belief that structure brings control and certainty. How can we possibly attack something that protects our sense of self from our atavistic fear of death—including the death of self-image? The good doctors couldn't. What they couldn't do was heal themselves by moving away from obvious symptoms and looking at the deeply ingrained causes. Instead, the medical doctors in my research study took great comfort in the historical structure of health care—the *culture* of being a physician.

The doctors fondly recalled both historical and developmental factors in a health care system that placed physicians on a pedestal of unquestioned authority, well above other medical professions in status and power. But the reality was that the environment of health care was changing. Organizational systems don't remain frozen in time but are continually buffeted by the winds of change. But how much they're willing to bend and adapt depends on the rigidity of the Organizational Family Tree. In this case, the turbulent nature of health care delivery was seriously challenging the traditional role of medical doctors. Fear of a dying self-image was clearly present in the comments the physicians in the study provided (Sopow, 2000).

- I feel I have no control of my working life. I'm totally fed up with it. If I could get out of this now I would retire. I would never agree to my children being a doctor.

- I hate my job and I hate my hours. I hate it because it takes me away from my family, my hobbies and my leisure time. But the quagmire of medicine is such that I am on this virtual treadmill. If I get off, then I will be in relative financial ruin and I'd definitely have no family, no hobbies, and no leisure.

- I work much harder, have less time for my family and have less disposable income. It is getting progressively worse. I feel terrible. I am overweight, out of shape, and about to lose another relationship.

When our need for control is certainly high in both our work and our personal life, when such control is essential to our sense of self, then loss of such control can be devastating. The physicians, affected by the caustic impact of corporate personality disorder, were dying on many levels. There was death of self-image, the death of hope, and even clinical death, as physicians, seemingly with everything to live for, committed suicide using their easy access to the right drugs.

The many medical doctors I spoke with had lost power, pride, and profit (in finances and reputation, traditionally awarded their profession). Their reaction was fear, depression, and anger—a buildup of negative energy and a *personal* meltdown in the face of an organizational meltdown. But remember what's next? Fearful, angry people will respond according to the defensive programming of their emotional brain, which screams out, "Fight back. You're under attack!" The physicians' collective anger eventually led to a protective reaction—a public relations *war* against a government they saw as responsible for their plight (and I have to fess up here that as a consultant I helped design that battle strategy).

By using sensational news media coverage, staged events, and carefully scripted quotes for the 6 PM TV news, the doctors created a campaign of fear that struck at the deepest emotional core of patients and the public. The government was cleverly framed as being responsible for the atmosphere of public fear—for playing with patients' lives with its intransigent policies, specifically those related to physician incomes. Fear, remember, triggers a protective reaction in humans. And that's precisely what the politicians did.

In short order, politicians, panicked by the news headlines and negative news coverage, bent to pressure and changed the health care system's *actions*. They were worried about their public image and about getting reelected. The result was not better care for patients but more money for physicians. Left untouched was the Organizational Family Tree's original root structure—one of inefficiency, ineffectiveness, and misaligned authority, accountability, and responsibility. Especially left untouched were the dismal communications, cooperation, and connectivity between the various groups involved in the health care system.

Throwing more money at medical doctors was a classic case of knee-jerk public policy targeting the most high profile and sensational elements of organizational *climate*—what basic political lobbying is all about. The physicians gladly took a pay raise, but the victory was hollow, since the significant structural problems caused by the *culture* of health care administration remained—problems that were the root cause of physicians' death of self-image and death of hope. Predictably, within three years, more meltdown occurred in the system, creating even more devastating impacts on patients, doctors, nurses, support staff, and administrators.

By April 2006, it was clear that simply dealing with the impacts and actions of the health care system—and not dealing with the deeply rooted structural issues—had done nothing to help patients in pain. As the screaming headline of the largest regional newspaper read, "Overcrowded ER Killing Patients at Royal Columbian Hospital, Reports Says."

The lesson from the above is that old Organizational Family Trees are not easy to renourish, just as human personalities are not easy to change. Historical and developmental factors, which comprise a deep-rooted culture, can present powerful sources of power that shape the organizational structure, including the priorities afforded to emotion factors as well as to the critical components within the Triangle of Trust.

But there is another lesson: once an organization goes into meltdown, the tremendous human energy and power generated is impossible to contain. Once in meltdown, an organization invariably changes due to the forces being released. How that change occurs, including the level of positive versus negative energy being released, depends on how adroit managers and leaders are at harnessing the power surges and overheating resistors within the organization.

REIGNITING ENERGY WITHIN THE ORGANIZATIONAL FAMILY TREE

When an organization is in meltdown, when it shows signs of corporate personality disorder, there's often a widespread release of negativity that in turn dilutes any positive energy within the work environment. This condition is often referred to as a *toxic workplace*. There's absolutely no scientific doubt that organizational meltdown negatively affects both our psychological and our physical health.

In such toxic environments you can "die" on the job, figuratively and sometimes literally. Yet people can be incredibly resilient when dealing with the constant haranguing of a badly behaving organizational personality. My wife Lindsay, a grief counselor, has noticed parallels between work in a hospice setting, where people are physically dying, and in an organizational setting, where people are dying emotionally.

When attending to those who are physically dying, it becomes obvious that the concept of time is different for them—it's more condensed. Those dying often work harder at attaining self-understanding than at any other time of their life. They come to accept that before they can acknowledge their mortality, they must first accept life without any clever disguises, to see it for what it is. Dying people seem to grant themselves permission to make choices based on their desire to complete themselves. It's as if they have more power than ever, and can manage their anxiety with a sense of freedom that comes from wanting to make decisions based on living a life of significance rather than following the lead of others. Ironically, their looming death motivates them to live a fuller life. Dying people seem to stay cognizant of the needs of those around them, largely because they are immersed in the tenderness of their own essential being, which encompasses the drive to touch and be touched by grace and good counsel.

Counseling the dying can be challenging, since we want them to see their goodness and to acknowledge that it's not too late to make amends with oneself and others. We feel agitated at times when people remain stuck in guilt or victimhood—maybe because we've entertained those immobilizing anxieties ourselves at times. We struggle with projecting our need for them to claim responsibility, because we believe it will help them, even though we understand that each person gains insight and growth when the time is right for that person.

Even though we understand that this inherent pull to self-actualization has been our own life-long experience (or at least our *desired* experience), and as such can vouch for its power to heal, we can't push a person to see more than he is ready for. Being human means being involved in a continual process of *becoming*—becoming as honest with oneself now, moment to moment, as one was when life began.

You may be wondering how the way we deal with death, specifically physical death, has to do with badly behaving organizations. Well, it has everything to do with it, actually. That's because death of self-image and death of hope can be as frightening and devastating to us as the thought of real-life clinical death. And it's these last two forms of death that are now rampant within organizations suffering from corporate personality disorder.

The death of self-image can be as traumatic and frightening as clinical death, but there's more trouble ahead, because the death of self-image easily beckons the death of hope. By death of hope, I mean losing hope that things will work out and losing faith in our abilities. Many of us have *experienced* love and laughter and warm days at the beach. But the death of self-identity and the death of hope are states of mind deeper than the word "experience" can ever hope to capture.

Felt deeply, the death of self-image and the death of hope are akin to burning—pain that induces bodily responses such as headaches and flashes of white-hot anger. Death in this form is a constantly knotted stomach with the accompanying digestive ramifications; it's the opiate of planned suicide and imagined homicide and nightmares that come so constantly and vividly that soon they are intertwined and indistinguishable from waking consciousness. It's a constant state of tiredness, where one awakens not to a refreshed state of renewal but to an even deeper fatigue and a dread of getting out of bed.

You may have been there. I know many who have and who are today. I've been there, and it's not a pretty place. (The really weird thing, of course, is that if you stay bummed out long enough, you start to think it's normal, and that's when you're really in a downward crash cycle.) But here's the thing. The death of hope is not uncommon within the standard species Organizational Family Tree. It just happens to be one of the more devastating symptoms of organizational meltdown.

By not catching ourselves early and quickly enough, by not looking in the mirror and recognizing our true reflection, we're in danger of allowing the death of hope to envelope us completely—to wrap us in a dark, suffocating blanket. When we become afflicted with the death of hope, we start feeling a deep and ongoing sadness about our daily existence, a joylessness that's far more than "giving up."

Giving up requires an act of "giving," which in turn requires a source of personal energy, a directional thought, and action. But there's no such energy left when the death of hope settles slowly into our consciousness, one heavy layer stacked upon another in a succession of trapped emotional turmoil, desperation, and personal diminishment. Suffering from the earlier blunt-force trauma of the death of self-image, we now have simply nothing to give—up, across, or down. And so we just *are*—neither here, nor there, nor anywhere. We might, in our darkest moments, even think about the sweet escape of clinical death. But we lack the energy even for that. This is very heavy stuff but not uncommon within a sick organizational system. This is why it's important to think about how such a black cloud can engulf us. How can we avoid sinking into this murky quicksand?

To stop ourselves from getting sucked into the vortex of an organizational sick system, it's important to appreciate that the death of identity, of self-image, can hit us like a kick-in-the-chest heart attack when who we *are* becomes inextricably entwined with what we *do* at our daily work life. In such a place, when we no longer *do* what we've always done and been known for (such as after a demotion, firing, layoff, quitting, retiring, or even promotion), we no longer *are*. This is a very common condition for those working within a typical Organizational Family Tree, and the reason for it is simple: the mechanistic culture of most organizations, with its heavy emphasis on *outputs* rather than *outcomes* ("I don't care if nobody is aware of our product! Did you reach our goal of issuing twenty-seven news releases?") and micro-measurement ("How many times did you answer the phone today?") means there's little left for attention to human emotional needs, to asking "Why?" and "Why not?" and to saying "No."

HOPING FOR THE BEST IS A NATURAL SURVIVAL MECHANISM

Why do we often stay so optimistic that a dysfunctional situation will improve, despite all manner of evidence to the contrary? The answer is pure neurobiology. There are natural, primordial survival instincts buried deep in the recesses of our brain—a region called the limbic system, which carries code from millions of years ago. This ancient part of our emotional brain can trigger actions and responses that can have us clawing back, reframing and reinventing our situation in an effort to breathe new strength into our spirit.

Like the pilot light in a gas furnace that continues to flicker small but alive in the dark when the system is cold, we'll find or invent sparks of light in the far distance; we'll line our clouds with silver; and we'll see friendship where none existed. When an organizational personality treats us badly and abuses us, we may end up doing what many victims of personal abuse do—we'll blame ourselves and be convinced that things will get better.

This common pattern of abuse by the organizational personality is frequently evident in abusive human relationships, such as when a husband continually inflicts physical and/or emotional abuse upon his wife. The wife, her self-image and self-worth debased, nevertheless continues to stay in the relationship, fueled by hope. As Yale University professor Maggie Scarf says in her book *Secrets, Lies, Betrayals: The Body/Mind Connection* (2004),

> This periodic positive reinforcement serves to keep her hopes alive, and during those times when things are going well, she will often indulge in the fantasy that their problems have been settled and the rewarding parts of the attachment are here to stay.

It's the same with victims of abuse by organizations with corporate personality disorder. No matter how vicious or uncaring the actions of the organization against us seem, we will likely look for the bright side, thinking that *our* actions and behavior are to blame and hoping that things will get better and that the organizational personality will accept us again.

We are naturally inclined to see the upside to life. In fact, our genetically encoded proclivity for hope is even reflected in our religious beliefs. As a World Values Survey of North Americans found, 90 percent believe in God, but a significantly fewer 70 percent believe in the devil. And while 81 percent believe in heaven, a fewer 70 percent believe in hell. The simple reason for this is our genetic programming—a "hopefulness gene" in our brain that strives to find silver linings in dark clouds and keeps us clawing our way upward despite the harshest of conditions and setbacks. This is indeed a good thing, and the examples range from amazing cases of survival at Nazi concentration camps to individuals who have beat seemingly impossible odds—whether fighting disease, devastation, gender inequality, or the sudden loss of a job.

Scientists recently found a neurochemical basis to our hopefulness—the pilot light that flickers deep in our soul. Actually, the seventeenth-century philosopher Spinoza made first reference to our obsession with feeling good, describing this pursuit with the Latin word *conatus*, meaning a striving, an endeavor, and the tendency for human life to preserve itself. Neuroscientist and author Antonio Damasio, combining his reflections on Spinoza's philosophies with his own recent work involving brain circuitry, has this to say in his 1994 book *Looking for Spinoza*:

> Spinoza's notion implies that the living organism is constructed so as to maintain the coherence of its structures and functions against numerous life-threatening odds.... What is Spinoza's *conatus* in current biological terms? It is the aggregate of dispositions laid down in brain circuitry that, once engaged by internal or environmental conditions, seeks both survival and well-being.... This is accomplished by chemical molecules transported in the bloodstream, as well as by electrochemical signals transmitted along nerve pathways.

So here is the good news (after all that doom and gloom we've been discussing): *you are a survivor!* You are genetically encoded to be optimistic, to think positively, and to wear those rose-colored glasses. Still, it takes work on our part to keep from falling down the dark rabbit hole of negative thinking. It especially takes the ability to know that it's not *our* personality that's the problem in most cases; it's the uptight *organizational* personality, with its small-box tight thinking, that's the problem. The timid organizational personality that's afraid of challenging assumptions, that's afraid of asking, "Why are we doing this?" and afraid of change.

Because of what we've been taught about organizational life, it's hard *not* to think like a machine, to believe that it's essential to mesh perfectly and obediently into the mechanics of everyday organizational existence. But of course, being a cog on a wheel is very *unhealthy*. After a while our pilot light, our flame of human energy, struggles to flicker, doing so intermittently, close to extinguishment. This is where it's urgent to catch ourselves. Here is where we must scream "NO!" to the clear symptoms of corporate personality disorder. But we're going to need help, because without help from others who also see the organizational personality for what it is, our death of self-image can melt into the death of hope as inevitably as deep darkness follows dusk.

This dark existence is harder on some than on others. It all depends on a complex interweaving of genetic traits and a lifetime of developmental influences, the strength and prevalence of networks of supportive friends and family, and the depth of emotional suffering, which your perception paints as a unique and often deeply secretive reality.

To keep from spiraling downward requires us to ask bold and tough questions ("Why are we doing this?" "Why not do it another way?") and to say no to demands that are unreasonable, unethical, or, most importantly, against our gut instinct of what is right and wrong, and what is safe for us and for others.

Even if we're not directly affected by corporate personality disorder, we can end up feeling bad and in despair simply knowing those who are, such as family and friends. We may want to help them, but we don't know what to say or do. We might offer small talk and platitudes, but we also know that such meager offerings evaporate as soon as they are given. And so we either avoid that person or react with silly comic bravado. ("So you lost your job? Boy, you'll do anything for a holiday!")

Because of how we've been conditioned throughout our lives, we often automatically pick the side of the *organizational* personality and not the *human* personality. ("You got fired? Oh brother! What did you do wrong?") So if we really want to help others, it's important to start with a very simple premise: it's the *organizational* personality that's usually the bad guy, not our friend or acquaintance.

Because of our conditioning, it's very easy to see a meltdown in others as mere human weakness or fear. But the reality is that we hate seeing others weakened because it can remind us of our own pain, fear, and vulnerability. It can remind us of the dark feelings and doubts that we've been working so hard at suppressing. We don't want to think about that—we don't want to feel the sense of powerlessness and unknown that constitutes human fear. And so we bring out a first-aid kit of positive platitudes. We wrap others' pain in the sanitized verbal gauze of "I know how you feel" and "It's going to be okay. Just hang in there."

Of course, it's *not* going to be okay—at the very least it will never be the same again—and we really *don't* know how the other person is *exactly* feeling, because no matter how similar our experiences are, it's impossible for any two people to perceive something in exactly the same manner. In thinking about those hollow Band-Aid words, I was moved to write the following:

Authenticity

you want me to say
"I know how you feel."
that magic thread of words
applied like sterile gauze
over your open wound.

clean, clinical words are easily packaged
and arranged in neat important rows.

it is much safer to say the words to you
than feel the fear, the anger, the hatred, the love.

you want me to say
"I know how you feel."
the word "I" suggests a journey completed inward
where layers were peeled back
exposing that secret place within.

the word "Know" delivers knowledge,
but is knowledge the same as wisdom?
the same as consciousness?
does knowledge share a room with spirituality?

the word "How" offers a prescription.
deterministic, unquestioning,
mechanical, inorganic.

the word "You" confers an image of intimacy,
recognition, brotherhood, sisterhood,
a validation of self.

the word "Feel" promises connectivity,
an alliance of intimacy and love
and a promise of soulfulness.

you want me to say
"I know how you feel."

I know I have seen a sunrise in Shanghai
felt the morning rain in Caracas
danced drunk under the northern lights.

I know I have been fired from jobs and fired others
married and divorced, then married and divorced.
I have been stabbed once and saw friends die too early
a sister die too early
my nephew die too early

a niece, my friend, die too early
my cousin the police officer die too early.

you want me to say
"I know how you feel"
to apply the healing thread of words
like clinical sterile gauze
over your open wound.

but I know of no such medicine
I know not how you feel
I know only that to feel
to honestly feel
is the true beginning of healing.

You have a chance, this very moment, to start a process of rescue and recovery. Are you thinking of someone who is clearly the victim of corporate personality disorder and in personal meltdown? If so, then reach out to that person. Communicate, connect, and build bonds of cooperation to save him or her from being sucked down the drain of mechanistic mind control. How do you do this? Start with genuine empathy and understanding, and with honesty. It may start with a conversation over a cup of coffee. Merely taking the time to set aside the busy work of the day and reach out can make a critical difference.

Just the act of quiet listening on our part can reignite the pilot light of human energy in others. It can give them the confidence to find their own voice, to find that solid emotional footing to stand up to a badly behaving organizational personality. Because when we *don't* stand up to the organizational personality, when we make excuses like "I can read rank," "That's the way we've always done it," "That's not for me to say," "I know my place," or "That's not my job," then we are directly responsible for extinguishing our own flame of humanity and hope. It's healthy for us to be human, to feel and express deep human emotion, and to allow the fire in our belly to guide our actions—not just rules, regulations, and red tape. But it's very easy to take the easy way out. It's easy to allow our inner energy to be extinguished by corporate personality disorder and to lose our soul to the machine.

Writer and poet David Whyte (1994) has a remarkable ability to see, through a poet's eyes, how life and work can be diluted by the actions of others and how the death of hope can arrive at our doorstep. He writes,

> Our refusal to stand up to those who harass us on a daily basis becomes, in effect, a lack of faith in our own voice, and the nature that that voice bestows on us. A vicious circle begins in which our refusal to speak out confirms our vulnerability and increases our invisibility. We feel certain that we will lose our job, our position, our career, and no one will ever look at us again.

David goes on, drawing into the discussion that most powerful of all emotion, fear. "Sometimes we are rightly quiet in the face of dire consequences for our career or our families, but more often than not we are simply living in the shadow of our own fears."

It's important for us to reach out to others in need, but it's also vital for us to recognize our own needs and to reach out to those we trust when the days seem darker than others. Death of hope brought about by exposure to corporate personality disorder, like the death of self-image, is not restricted to any age, income, race, gender, or religion. Some time ago, a fifteen-year-old boy by the name of Kip Kinkel walked into his Springfield, Oregon, high school carrying a fully loaded semiautomatic rifle. Within minutes, he shot and killed two students and wounded twenty-two others. Later, as police looked through his private journal, they read, "Everyone is against me.... As soon as my hope is gone, people die."

SICK SYSTEMS AS A WEAPON OF MASS DESTRUCTION

The human devastation caused by badly behaving organizations has spawned an entire industry dealing specifically with system *actions*, as opposed to the causative elements inherent within system *structures*. This is akin to focusing exclusively on why one needle on the pine tree looks off color instead of dealing with the tree's systemic root rot. This industry, sometimes called "the grief industry" by professionals in the field, typically draws in the disciplines of psychology and sociology, as well as those plying their trade as management consultants and human resource specialists.

Let me share a snippet of how this thinking works: About a year ago I watched a television news reporter giving viewers advice about what to do when they lose their job. I can't recall the reporter's name, but I made a note of what she said, which was, "Above all else, experts say, 'Don't take a layoff personally. Remember that everyone goes through it at some point or another.' The old adage that it takes a lot of no to get to yes was never truer than when you're looking for a job."

The reporter might as well have been describing a case of dandruff. There is little in life as personal as losing one's job. The experts in the news story claimed that losing a job brings out emotions similar to those of losing a loved one. Well, they were right: losing a job can be like death, but it's not like losing a loved one. It is like losing *you*—who you are, who you hoped you'd be, who you need to be.

Years ago, psychologist Elisabeth Kübler-Ross (1969) described the emotions following the death of a loved one: denial, anger, bargaining, depression, and acceptance. All of those powerful emotions are present when you lose your job (or receive a demotion). But here's the big mistake employment counselors and psychologists make: they say that given enough time and counseling, people adjust and recuperate. That is just not the case in many instances, and the pain and memories are only a matter of degree, depending on how deeply that person was entrenched in the job he lost.

The fact is, if we fall victim to organizational action, if we lose our job or have our job downgraded, it's hard to regard the superficial in a positive light. In such situations, we're often consumed with guilt, shame, and self-blame for the death of our self-image, which was defined by what we did and the title on our business card rather than by the person we really are. Happy talk geared toward simple acceptance of our demise will not likely be productive, because while we may in time accept *another's* death, it's very, very tough for us—biologically, neurologically, and psychologically—to accept *our own*.

So, what can you do to help yourself or others when things get bleak? First, you must do away with the notion that the individual is at fault. It's important at this time to fully understand what makes the organizational personality tick, to understand its Organizational Family Tree and especially the roots of its culture. Consider the six points of the Triangle of Trust and think about just how well they come together within the organization.

It should be remembered that dealing with an organization's immediate climate alone won't bring new vitality to the overall structure. What's needed is a major revitalization and careful pruning of the Organizational Family Tree, a review of the impact of both culture and climate, and an honest look at the impact of historical and developmental factors on the actions of today. Finally, the will to change organizational behavior is needed.

How can this be done? We start with *you*, because your well-being is what this journey into the corporate psyche is all about. It's vital for you to fess up to the powerful yet debilitating emotions that have exploded from your inner core to the surface—emotions such as fear and anger and shame. Until you locate and label those often deeply buried and frequently unconscious negative emotions and memories, until you diminish their power by shining a bright light of understanding upon them, they'll continue to unconsciously control your temperament, identity, and hope.

You can turn emotion (and the energy it brings) into positive action by using the six key elements in the Triangle of Trust, together with an awareness of the historical and developmental factors (culture) influencing system structures. In natural systems, where adaptability and mutations are common (like real trees and fish in the sea), we commonly see intertwined forces at play—*communication* among the various elements in the system, *connectivity* between often disparate parts of a holistic system, and *cooperation* among various parts and subparts in the natural system. All of this coming together results in evolution. But not everybody sees it this way.

The common refrain from those who have a job, especially outplacement and career services professionals, is don't let your shock and anger lead to an outburst of emotions, including speaking out about the work conditions you are leaving. The fact is, we *must* speak out. It's not about launching tirades about people's personal traits or mannerisms (which is *not* the thing to do). It's about respectfully challenging the behavior of system structures and their influence on organizational behavior.

Many people will advise us against listening to our instincts and our emotional brain. A corporate job-placement consultant once counseled readers of a major news magazine to "try to funnel your anger into more positive avenues. Do an aggressive job search, when you can channel anger that way, it's really terrific!" What such experts, who are in fact symptoms of corporate personality disorder, fail to accept is that losing a job is not like losing someone *close to you*—it is in fact losing *you*.

7

EVEN HEALTHY ORGANIZATIONS GET SICK AT TIMES

The Organizational Family Tree of Starbucks Coffee Company might seem like a great example of healthy commingling of corporate and human personalities. Since its inception in Seattle, the company has focused on the emotion *and* knowledge factors key to its employees and the communities where it sports the distinctive green awnings and trademark mermaid logo. Not only do employees receive very competitive wages, but even part-time employees—called "partners"—enjoy both profit sharing ("Beanstocks") and a dental plan. Not a bad deal for a twenty-year-old going to college full time or plying a musician's trade part time.

In the late 1990s I provided consulting services to Starbucks Coffee Company, which for the first time in its global experience would see a store become unionized (in Vancouver, Canada). How could such a thing happen to a company providing the best employee benefits in the industry and with a well-deserved reputation for social responsibility?

The answer was a mild form of corporate personality disorder, which one could diagnose by applying the Triangle of Trust model to the company's operations—how communications, cooperation, and connectivity to others were channeled through a harmonious balance of authority, responsibility, and accountability. In applying a very efficient, standardized approach to opening coffee outlets, Starbucks ignored that individual geographic regions have unique social, economic, and political environments based on a combination of culture and climate.

Internal communication structures failed to hear the voice of Starbucks employees in Vancouver, who valued job security and predictable scheduling over many of the other perks offered by the company. The company provided ongoing training to ensure important knowledge factors were being instilled in employees, but it paid far less attention to its employees' emotional needs—specifically those related to issues of personal life balance, to being heard, and to having an optimistic attitude about one's future. Besides communications, both connectivity to others and cooperation were short-circuiting.

Starbucks was not providing a secure sense of self to employees, but the workers found a source that could—the Canadian Auto Workers (CAW) Union. What on earth did a union from the production lines of Ford Motor Company have in common with a Starbucks barista? Plenty, as it turned out. The slow deindustrialization and modernization of smokestack industries in North America and the rapid acceleration of the service and technology industries had endangered the power base of many traditional trade unions. With the structural realignment of their Organizational Family Tree evolving, trade unions were scrambling to find new membership, and a ripe new recruiting ground was the service sector.

The CAW union was a victim of its own organizational meltdown. In this case, the meltdown related to an organizational culture and climate including power and energy flows first designed in the Industrial Revolution. The CAW was reacting to its organizational meltdown by reenergizing—by creating new power and energy sources through communications, connectivity, and cooperation with employees in the service sector, who had never felt the need to be unionized before.

The move to unionize the service sector was a reenergizing of the Organizational Family Tree as it applied to the Canadian Auto Workers union. To Starbucks employees, the opportunity to build personal energy and empowerment through a formal connection to the big union was just what their emotional needs demanded.

To their credit, Starbucks senior management in Seattle reviewed their corporate system structures, particularly those related to internal communications and the company's ability to not just listen to employees, but to actually *hear* what those employees were saying and how their concerns linked to their emotional needs. This was possible because Starbucks' corporate culture is characterized by a willingness to adapt and to consider human emotion factors in its relationships with both employees and communities. The company reached out through improved communications and through new system structures that saw a revamping of authority, accountability, and responsibility.

For client confidentiality reasons I can't go into detail about what Starbucks did, but the result was that some employees ended up voting to legally discontinue their attachment to the CAW. But in other cases the connection continued, particularly when employees felt the CAW culture and climate gave them what Starbucks could not—a sense of not only being an important part of the Organizational Family Tree (of having both emotion and knowledge needs addressed) but feeling safe, secure, and protected.

TRIMMING GREENPEACE'S ORGANIZATIONAL FAMILY TREE

My first acquaintance with Greenpeace was back in 1970. Of course it wasn't called Greenpeace then—it was an idealistic gaggle of West Coast anti-nuclear protesters opposed to the American military's plans to test a bomb near Alaska. The group was called the Don't Make a Wave Committee and I was one of many members who blockaded the Canadian-U.S. border as a small expression of our dissent. The following year the Vancouver, Canada-based group changed its name to Greenpeace and the rest is history.

Over the decades, Greenpeace became an international powerhouse of activism with offices around the world, including an international head office in Europe. The social movement organization became layered with committees, bureaucracies, multimillion-dollar budgets, and a reporting structure with neat boxes connected with dark lines and dotted lines. Although fighting for grassroots issues, over the years, Greenpeace seemed to be organizing those battles from the corporate stratosphere. In other words, there were major power and energy shifts in the Greenpeace Organizational Family Tree as its operational climate became increasingly distant from its core culture.

I was hired by Greenpeace Canada's executive members in 1999 to do an action research study on how it had strayed from its grassroots and collectivism, becoming in some people's minds just another globetrotting multinational corporation. A deep examination of the key components of Greenpeace's Organizational Family Tree revealed that the operational system structure of the giant environmentalist group was not reflecting the most positive historical and developmental factors in its culture.

In addition, Greenpeace was paying a lot less attention to the emotion factors within the network, which gave it the huge grassroots support it once had. The problem was that Greenpeace, due to its phenomenal growth and multinational presence, started using Industrial Age models of management and leadership, learning not from its naturalistic past and its culture but from the mechanical structures of organizations it was dealing with.

My research showed that many of the environmentalist organization's original supporters now saw Greenpeace through a nostalgic lens. While they still respected the organization's goals, many also agreed with the comment by one supporter who said in a focus group I was conducting, "Greenpeace has got too big. It's just another corporation with a slick marketing campaign." As another supporter confided to the focus group, "I'm tired of the confrontational tactics. It's so easy to see right through all the posturing and slick phrases. I just want the facts so I can make up my own mind."

The leadership of Greenpeace was horrified to see how deeply they were afflicted by corporate personality disorder. One senior staff member told me they had only the faintest idea how deep they had become enmeshed in bureaucracy, box-like system structures, and nasty office politics. Their positioning was now light years from the grassroots origins of the organization, founded in 1972 with a dream, a pot of coffee, and a rebellious spirit. The strategist, a very pleasant man with thinning hair, a wide girth, and a salt and pepper beard, pondered how things so easily changed in this anti-capitalistic, anti-big company, pro-consensus organization.

> It's completely invisible and deadly silent. Just like a buried, growing cancer. One day you're fighting big companies, the next day you're meeting with them, and then, quite unconsciously, you're mimicking their mannerisms, language, and God help us, even their values!
>
> It all starts on the margins, a little bit at a time, until pretty soon the margins are the entire page and you stand back one day and wonder just what the hell you've created.

The staff at Greenpeace took the action research results to heart, blended their own self-reflective insights into the findings, and soon emerged with a new strategic approach to protecting old growth forests from destruction. What Greenpeace did was find the true and sustainable power sources within its Organizational Family Tree, particularly the key historical and early developmental factors (its culture) that created the organizational personality so many people fondly remembered.

By doing this, by understanding its energy and power flows, Greenpeace in Canada was able to quickly adopt behaviors and actions that reflected a system structure that was organic—not mechanistic—and rebalance the Triangle of Trust so that its structure of authority, responsibility, and accountability facilitated a healthy flow of communications, connectivity to others, and cooperation.

On the West Coast, Greenpeace moved away from blockades and confrontational language and embraced community consciousness, focusing on how out-of-work loggers, savaged by declining revenues in the forest industry, could create sustainable jobs through more value-added manufacturing practices. Simultaneously, they applied international pressure to corporations buying raw timber products cut from endangered trees on the West Coast rainforest.

In time, this more organic model of organization and system structure produced dividends for Greenpeace. One early morning, my friend the environmental strategist called and excitedly urged me to look at the morning's *Vancouver Sun*. The headline read, "From Global Pariah to Eco-hero in One Day." The front-page story opened with these words:

> The province of British Columbia moved to end the war in the woods Wednesday with a landmark deal to protect a vast swath of the central coast.... The historic agreement between loggers, environmentalists, Native Indians, and government immediately prompted Greenpeace to call off its campaign against forest products from the rain forest.

The Greenpeace example shows that using the Organizational Family Tree can revitalize an organization and create positive power. But this takes work and deep reflection—getting beyond the surface actions and digging deep into the embedded factors influencing system structures.

Those within such a structure may experience an organizational version of the Stockholm syndrome, having become so enamored with their philosophic captors that they are now one and the same, not recognizing the debilitating effect on human relations and the incremental death of their self-image and their hope for something better.

But here's the good news. It doesn't take a huge amount of energy on our part to escape this small-box philosophy of how things are *supposed* to work. What it takes is looking at the world through a different mindset. It's just like that optical illusion—the picture of a woman who can appear both young and old. Depending on your mindset, your perceptions, you'll initially see either an old woman with a big nose or a young woman looking sideways. But soon enough, with a little concentration, you'll be able to switch back and forth between the two.

It's the same with our view of organizational systems. Up to now, many of us have been convinced to look at the Organizational Family Tree from one narrow perspective. Now it's time to switch that viewpoint—to see the organization from a different perspective, to break away from being held hostage by small-box thinking. Let me share with you an example of how easy this is to do. The example comes from a group of folks who know a lot about hostages.

SICK SYSTEMS AND THE ROYAL CANADIAN MOUNTED POLICE

The scarlet tunic and peaked hat of a Royal Canadian Mounted Police (RCMP) officer in full dress uniform is one of the world's most recognizable and trusted symbols, so much so that at one time, the Disney organization paid for exclusive marketing rights to the symbol of a Mountie in dress uniform. For over 120 years, the RCMP has been Canada's national police force. The Organizational Family Tree of the RCMP is rich with both historical and developmental factors, producing an organizational personality characterized by some police officers as being conservative, brave, honest, and trustworthy but also inflexible, bureaucratic, and dictatorial.

In a command-and-control paramilitary organization like a police force, the issue of authority—who's in charge—is rarely in dispute. The rigid rank structure and culture of following orders is well ingrained. What can be less ingrained is responsibility and accountability.

In my work, I've found that the greater the centralization of authority, the greater the chance that leadership is based on a transactional model of following orders or suffering the consequences, the less responsibility individuals are willing to take on, and the less emphasis there is on accountability. The reason for this is simply that those being told what to do in a top-down, command-and-control structure will wait for orders rather than show initiative, and they will take few risks and show little imagination because of fear of repercussions.

In the Organizational Personality Index, the above description usually places an organization in the Suspicious-Defensive category, in which very little attention is paid to the emotional needs of personnel. This results in low levels of power and energy within the Organizational Family Tree, ultimately leading to organizational decay. As a large national police organization, the Royal Canadian Mounted Police were certainly susceptible to more than a little root rot and systems decay. But it was also willing to examine its environment and to inject some fresh nutrients—at least in this example.

Here's how it all rolled out. I was asked to facilitate a strategic planning session for a group of police officers involved in an integration of their various specialty units and services. The effort at integration followed the terrorist attacks on

America in September of 2001. Senior management wanted to impose an organization chart that would unite various independent units under one command structure. The assumption was that the integrated teams would produce great efficiencies and effectiveness as they went about catching smugglers, terrorists, and organized criminals.

The proposed design completely ignored the human, emotional component, although there was certainly plenty of emotional energy residing within the directly affected personnel. I didn't have to be a seasoned investigator to figure out what was going on in the minds of the expressionless faces of the police officers whom senior management had ordered to attend the workshop—their body language screamed out a confession!

Arms were crossed in cynicism. Some officers slouched back in their chairs, while others looked out the window, while a few just stared at me. To punch a hole in the tension, I said the obvious: "Folks, if we were in your shoes I'd be thinking, 'Who is this civilian know-it-all sent by headquarters to tell us what to do with the latest flavor of the week?'" Honest disclosure can produce interesting results. The icy atmosphere in the room was slowly replaced with laughter, the body language changed, and a connection was formed.

We agreed not to follow blindly headquarters' prescription for integration of specialized teams. Instead, I threw out a challenge. "You're the folks in the field. You know what's happening right and wrong every day—not some planning officer up at headquarters. And I bet that on a regular basis you find a better way to catch the bad guys working outside the formal system. So let's roll up our sleeves and design from scratch what will work for you."

What we did was use the Triangle of Trust model as a basis of new thinking, challenging the specialized security unit to rethink how authority, responsibility, and accountability could be applied to their needs. As part of the process, I divided the police officers into groups to encourage cooperation, communication, and connectivity. As a result, they created new power and energy sources within the Organizational Family Tree.

As the groups discussed senior management's proposed model, complete with neat rows of cascading boxes tied together with solid lines, it became obvious that the front-line police officers regularly operated not so much "out of the box" but in a much *bigger* box, where there was lots of elbow room for creativity and adaptability. It turned out the tight constraints of a traditional command-and-control organization chart simply impeded that adaptability.

The various units of police officers needed a system that could quickly prioritize actions (communications and connectivity), could provide ongoing professional development and experience (authority and responsibility), had excellent cross-functional communications, allowed for cross-unit connectivity and coop-eration, and could help the new integrated unit meet its mandate (accountability and responsibility). They definitely needed structure and clear boundaries, but they also needed breathing room to think for themselves.

So, I asked them, if left to their own devices, what would that organization chart look like? After a day of brainstorming using multiple sheets of flip-chart paper, breaking into groups, regrouping and taking stock of progress, and then brainstorming again, the officers came up with two alternative designs for a sys-tem structure that would operate efficiently for a new integrated unit. In fact, rather than call this design an "organization chart," they called it an "operations map." However in doing so, the officers did not throw the traditional approach out on its ear.

They concluded that there is no one-size-fits-all approach to corporate struc-tures and that in some cases a strict command-and-control approach can have merit. They were in fact maintaining the best from both the historical and devel-opmental factors found in the RCMP's Organizational Family Tree.

The group also said that in their experience, it was the *people*—and especially leaders—within a command-and-control structure who were responsible for effective results and not the formal design of the system structure (which could in fact inhibit cooperation and collaboration). *Authority*, they said—a key point in the Triangle of Trust—was a balance of both emotion and knowledge factors.

In designing their "operations map," the officers literally produced "out of the box" thinking. Rather than cascading boxes joined by neat, straight solid lines, the results included two options: the first included not boxes but four interlocked circles within a larger circle, and the second was two large rectangles joined by a superimposed circle.

The first alternative offered benefits including better communication between units and better coordination (cooperation and connectivity) of activity, with intelligence gathering serving as the overlapping hub of activity. The second alternative also offered better information sharing (connectivity, cooperation, and communication). Each large rectangle was a mirror of the other, including spe-cialized units from drugs, immigration, intelligence, and federal enforcement ser-vices, with both rectangles connected by the overlapping circle representing the enhanced intelligence-gathering services.

To decide which model really met the organizational needs of law-enforce-ment and anti-terrorism activities, the participants in the workshop designed a five-point scale. The scale measured how effective each model was in being accountable, responsible, and having an authority structure that maximized communications, connectivity and cooperation.

The traditional small-box org chart proposed by senior management failed miserably, with 80 percent of workshop participants saying such a design would not do very well. However, 45 percent said the model with two parallel teams connected with a common intelligence function (option 2) would do very well. The clear preference among the men and women on the front line of policing was the org structure with large circles connecting to other overlapping circles (option 1). In fact, the police officers gave the model a 65 percent "very well" approval rating.

We called this new model "bigger box" rather than "out of the box" thinking because organizations and those within them require boundaries, guidance, and a plan of action. But they also need elbow room to think creatively, to self-organize in the face of rapid change, and to feel safe experimenting with new ideas. The idea of "out of the box" was seen as too unstructured, as dismissive of the important role of culture in organizational change.

Why did the far more organic and networked model of system structure appeal to the police officers? The answer was simple. In designing their "bigger box" operational system maps (as opposed to "org charts"), the police officers drew upon their daily operational experience rather than on the bureaucratic mindset of a far-removed planning officer. The members of our group understood where their energy sources were and intuitively knew how to channel that energy into a powerful system structure that acknowledged both emotion and knowledge factors.

The police officers were fortunate to have a section head—a man with a far more organic than mechanistic view of systems—who encouraged this kind of adaptive thinking. But then, as in many tales of organizational meltdown, the section head was transferred to another posting, the fresh thinking from the trenches had lost its champion, and the innovative notions were put on hold.

GOVERNMENT AGENCIES AND ROOT ROT IN THE ORGANIZATIONAL FAMILY TREE

In April of 2004, we witnessed a good example of organizational sickness and corporate personality disorder. The case concerned a government department in the Canadian West Coast province of British Columbia. A newspaper report chronicling the meltdown noted,

> Environment officials are highly stressed, deeply demoralized, and believe science is taking a backseat to the political priorities of the BC Liberal government. A comprehensive survey of 840 Ministry of Water, Land and Air Protection—70 percent of the workforce—suggests a kind of "*institutionalized sickness*" may be hampering environmental protections. The study, commissioned by the government and conducted by two Ontario business schools, says those charged with protecting the environment are disillusioned, distrustful, cynical, stressed and have low job satisfaction.

What the study of employees found within the haggard government department was classic corporate personality disorder, with the vast majority of workers living a lifeless existence, their self-image and hope extinguished. As with all classic cases of corporate personality disorder, the trouble lay with the system structure, which paid little attention to human emotional needs and in turn produced dysfunctional system actions and highly negative impacts. The system structure, as it turned out, was *restructured* with a 30 percent budget cut and the loss of 380 employees.

Typically, the politician in charge of the department, a cabinet minister totally blind to the meltdown within the Organizational Family Tree of his ministry, had this insightful comment to make: "It's news to me. I haven't heard that there is a chronic morale problem. People are working extremely hard in my ministry and things are going quite well." So well that just over a year prior to the public release of the consultant's report, a senior manager with the department, having received sudden notice that he'd been fired, went home to his suburban residence, gathered up his high-powered pistol, drove back to his field office, and murdered his visiting supervisor before shooting himself to death.

Many years before news that the Ministry of Environment was suffering from "institutionalized sickness," a report that professionals working in the health care industry were suffering from "*moral distress*" appeared. Patricia Rodney at the University of British Columbia wrote in the *Canadian Critical Care Nursing Journal* (1988) that health care workers ranging from medical doctors to cleaning staff were being traumatized by the relentless pace of change imposed on them, all in the service of financial models created by politicians whose primary concern was balancing a budget.

Rodney's phrase "moral distress" is a good description of corporate personality disorder—a condition where communications are short-circuiting, where entrenched and isolated organizational silos prevent cooperation and connectivity, and where heavy-handed authority precludes both accountability and responsibility.

"Moral distress" is a symptom of a maladaptive Organizational Family Tree. Describing the impact of organizational meltdown, Rodney stated,

> I am witnessing a level of distress I have not seen in 15 years of doing work in health care ethics. Nurses and other health care providers are anguished by the progressive erosion of resources. Just as important we're seeing skyrocketing levels of stress among health care providers. Many have talked to me about being terrified that a patient in their charge is going to die while waiting in the hall or in a chair.

Elaborating on her notion of "moral distress," Rodney explained, "Moral distress generates feelings of anger, guilt, frustration and powerlessness and these leave a moral residue, the corrosive emotional after-effects that afflict people when they cannot fulfill their ethical obligations." She also added that moral distress has a cumulative effect that can actually be "soul destroying."

Rodney's term "soul destroying" is very accurate. Those feeling the impact of corporate personality disorder are like the victims of any abusive relationship. There is a loss of one's sense of self; there is the death of identity, there is the death of hopefulness, and in very extreme cases physical death or disease may follow.

In his book *The Heart Aroused: Poetry and the Preservation of the Soul in Corporate America* (1996), David Whyte reflects upon employees caught in a world where "Corporate America seems to encompass our whole vision yet refuses to belong or care for any one place or person." In the face of this, Whyte describes how fearful employees begin to make themselves invisible, going on the defensive and trying their best to avoid change:

> The simple innocences of creative urgency are pushed away and, it is hoped, forgotten. Finally we learn how to keep our heads down and endure, hoping the CEO's finger of death will not point to our department as things go slowly but irrevocably wrong.

The impact of corporate personality disorder affects you even when the worst is yet to come. In their study of how workers deal with just the *possibility* of being laid off, psychologists Tahira Probst and Ty Brubaker (2001) found the following:

> Modern workplace realities, including the threat of layoffs and working long stressful hours, may be taking more than just a mental toll on your

body—they could be putting your health and safety at risk. Policies related to job design may be undermining the health and well being of workers. Employees who are worried about losing their jobs show less safety motivation and compliance on the job, which in turn is related to higher levels of workplace injuries and accidents.

THE NEWS MEDIA AS A SICK SYSTEM VIRUS

So far we've looked at internal operating environments created by an Organizational Family Tree's culture and climate. But just like that oak or pine growing in our favorite park, the Organizational Family Tree, including all the folks who are part of the organization, is continually affected by what's in the bigger external environment surrounding it.

We're well aware of the harmful effects of air pollution, solar radiation, and global warming. But I want us to consider expanding our well-entrenched concerns to the *organizational* environment. Bad things can happen to living things when harmful ingredients, such as excessive carbon dioxide, enter our atmosphere. Bad things can also happen to the Organizational Family Tree when harmful pollutants enter its environment—and in this case, the toxic pollutants are in the form of information.

Specifically, I'm saying that the air is not polluted with chemicals but with the content of news media stories that inculcate your human consciousness with bits of disinformation, distortion, and high drama.

Oscar Wilde once wrote, "Most people are other people. Their thoughts are someone's opinions, their lives are a mimicry, their passions a quotation." This is especially true today with the tremendous influence news media stories have on what we are thinking about, how we react to the world about us, and what fears we harbor.

Communications are a critical component of the Organizational Family Tree and especially the core Triangle of Trust. But how communications are shaped, twisted, and baked involves many external influences that we may not have given much thought to. Now is the time to think about it. Here's a little factoid pulled from my past twenty years of doing surveys on the impact of news media stories on public attitudes: most of our general information about the outside world comes from news media stories, not from personal experience, friends and family, or those with specialized expertise. However, the nature of mass media communications within a mechanistic model of organizational design is as harmful to our existence as any deleterious substance being emitted on a smoggy day in Los Angeles. Let me introduce you to my friend George, to make my point.

George is forty-two years old, blond and balding, with a face full of wrinkles from long studies and teaching at a local junior college and a body that clearly shows the metamorphisms of time. We're crouched over a round wooden table in the Bean Around the World coffeehouse, George clutching a touchstone of granite-solid reality in his hand. It's a big-city newspaper that serves as the gospel truth to George, a man with two university degrees and a sensible outlook on life and who therefore should know better.

George uses his daily newspaper—not CNN or the local radio station—as his personal barometer. George tells me he finds CNN (and TV news in general) too fleeting to recall in any specific detail. Like many, he knows the venerable vessel of pure truth in his hand mirrors what the majority of others think. In this way, George is different from most of us, who rely heavily on TV news as our primary source of general information, followed far behind by newspapers, the Internet and even further behind by radio news. But in many other ways, George is very similar to many of us.

Every day, George calibrates his philosophical, spiritual, theological, emotional, and cognitive inner compass according to news stories that line up in neat, evenly distributed gray columns of trust. The newspaper stories, unlike CNN, welcomes his embrace with no pressures of time or demands for sharp sensory attention. George consummates his relationship through tactile flourishes—gentle circles drawn around important paragraphs; strong exclamation mark tattoos applied to the end of a sentence; and occasionally bold, expressive yellow highlighting of key words and phrases.

If the headline and text of the newspaper focuses on anti-globalization, then George knows his own compass must point away from *pro*-globalization, and he feels quite solid voicing his anti-globalization opinion to anyone who will listen because he is, after all, part of the majority. If, on the other hand, the headline and story, especially a story with strong quotes from important people, is about support for gay marriages, then George knows his own ambivalent opinion is totally against the grain of what everyone else thinks and so he keeps his mouth shut.

I often tell George he's spinning in circles—within what communications scholar Elizabeth Noelle-Neumann calls the spiral of silence. Back in the 1970s, she discovered an interesting fact. She found, through her detailed research of news media consumer habits, that most people use the media to check the validity—the public acceptance—of their own thinking. How better to validate whether or not our ideas about global peace, Medicare reform, or sex after midnight is shared by others than to see what's being reported in the news?

Noelle-Neumann found that if our opinion is not supported by what others are saying about the same topic, as reported by the media, we immediately feel alone. Being in the minority means keeping our ideas to ourselves unless we want to be laughed at, thought of as ignorant, or ostracized. But here's what Noelle-Neumann found that was particularly revealing: it turned out that in many cases, what the media was reporting was not a majority view at all—it was simply the view of those who knew how to manipulate the media into getting attention for their cause or viewpoint.

Those who managed to get media attention did that by feeding news reporters what they salivated for—conflict, sensational language, fear, and the impression that many supported a cause when in fact such claims were made of flimsy rice paper. And so those in the majority stayed silent, because the minority was successful at creating the media mirage that their opinion dominated. The more the noisy, sensational, fear-mongering minority created the mirage of magnitude, the more withdrawn the silent majority became. Hence, the "Spiral of Silence" theory developed.

On this day, the smells in Bean Around the World are a collection of coffee and steamed milk and old wood floors. The sounds and sights include couples curled up on small couches sipping big mugs while listening to the café's stereo—an old Dire Straits tune called "Brothers in Arms." There are single men and women lost in thought, reading, or studying the nuances of body language and the quiet confessions found in others' eyes. Each of them possesses a consciousness unique from that of the other, for there is never one single reality shared in exactly the same way among us. But there can be a common outlook, shared values, and shared fears, outrage, and anger. And in many cases, these shared emotions are fueled by the evening TV news or the latest newspaper headline.

Academics, who have lots of time and tenure to think about these things, call our common emotions, values, and opinions "frames" and "schemas." This is important stuff when we're thinking about the behavior of an organizational personality, because we tend to base our opinion on a checklist of things that we think are *supposed* to be right and wrong, not necessarily what our gut instinct says is right. Where did this magic checklist of organizational behavior come from? In large part, it came from what we've absorbed from news media reports. Here's what both my original research and other research shows about media consumption.

For most people, the newspaper headline is the bait, but what really gets us to bite deeply and slowly chew into a story is the personal impact. It's my experience that news stories must meet three basic necessities for being "news." They must be emotional, simple, and personal—an ESP that is mostly perception. It requires nothing extrasensory, and in fact the often subsensory emotion of fear is the king of a good news story. (I know. I created a lot of public fear through my news stories when I was a journalist.)

The national surveys I have conducted and analyzed for many years consistently show that the public relies on the news media for 90 percent of all general information, that the news media is cited in one-third of conversations, and that news stories are believed eight times more than direct communications from a company or an organization. Our adult awareness is shaped by slickly crafted media sound bites that, in ten-second bursts, inculcate both our conscious and unconscious brain with anxiety, discomfort, and fear—the hallmarks of a great news story. As we used to say in the craft, "If it bleeds, it leads."

Each phrase, each comment, and each word has been designed, polished, and targeted to a specific audience by shadowy communication spin doctors, who, with the skill of an Academy Award-winning screen writer, design natural-sounding instant quotes emerging from the mouths but rarely the brains of organizational spokespeople. The spin-doctors, as powerful as any primitive shaman, understand the competitive needs of news reporters and feed the beast accordingly with tasty bites of emotion, simplicity, and conflict.

There are many complaints about journalism, but likely none so elevated and spiritual as that offered in April 2004 by three Nobel Peace Prize winners—the Dalai Lama, Bishop Desmond Tutu, and Shirin Ebadi (the 2003 Peace Prize winner and a human rights activist from Iran). At a gathering in Vancouver, Canada, the three combined with U.S. Rabbi Zalman Schachter-Shalomi to gently admonish the many news media present to intensify their coverage of "hope, truth, and good news" in their media reports. The Dalai Lama reminded reporters through his perpetually beaming, gentle countenance, and soft voice that "too strong a media emphasis on death and violence can lead to despair."

It's unlikely that even the spiritual weight of a figure such as the Dalai Lama will do much to change the system structure of journalism. In some cases, a degenerative disease can be so advanced that no manner of intervention, no matter how spiritual, aggressive, or scientific, can do anything to save the patient. Journalism, more so than many trades (it is not, for the most part, a profession by any acceptable standard), is extremely reluctant to take the first vital step in combating corporate personality disorder—and that is to take a moment to practice self-reflection and to challenge its own assumptions.

MORE THAN NEWS STORIES POLLUTE THE ORGANIZATIONAL ENVIRONMENT

While news reporting has a major influence on how we view the world, it's not the only mass communications influence. Much has been written about the numbing and dumbing impact of mass commercialization, with its attendant multibillion-dollar advertising campaigns that create unattainable images of perfection. Today there's a proliferation of "reality shows" on television in which both women and men undergo major physical and cosmetic "makeovers," where couples gush out their venom toward each other before millions of viewers (e.g., programs like the *Jerry Springer Show*), and where singles and couples play out everything from mating rituals to acts of duplicity and depravity (e.g., shows like *Survival*).

Richard Eckersley is with the National Centre for Epidemiology and Population Health and the Australian National University. He is the author of *Well & Good: How We Feel and Why It Matters* (2005). He says that the contrivance of such artificial realities does little to help you gain a measure of *who* you are, instead placing all the emphasis on *what* you should be. Eckersley uses the term *cultural fraud* to describe "the projection and promotion of cultural images and ideals that do not meet human psychological needs or reflect social realities."

In his review of consumerism, Eckersley pays particular attention to the world of cosmetic surgery, saying that while there may be a place for such actions in the pursuit of a better life, "we need to increase the social pressure against its more excessive and addictive forms." Eckersley cautions you about confusing personal autonomy with independence. As he says, "Defining autonomy—the ability to act according to internalized values and beliefs—as independence means there is a less perceived connection to others, and a greater likelihood that the social forces acting on us are experienced as external and alien."

What mass communications has been doing in the past few years is beyond even the historic objective of marketing and advertising: to create idolized versions of what we should own, eat, look like, work for, and vote for. What Eckersley and others (like Naomi Klein in her book *No Logo*) are seeing is a shift in the nature of materialism and consumerism—from getting you to *have* more to getting you to *be* someone else. Eckersley explains the phenomena: "The goal of marketing becomes not only to make us dissatisfied with what we have, but also with who we are. As consumerism seeks ever more ways to colonize our consciousness, it fosters—and exploits—the restless, insatiable expectation that there has to be more to life."

This phenomenon is not entirely new. Advertising and Hollywood have for decades portrayed the ideal body type acting in the ideal manner, whether it is chiseled, handsome good looks for men or firm-breasted, trim bodies for women.

Most of us long ago figured out the artificiality of ad campaigns and movie star looks. These were, after all, artificial people living fabled lives. The difference today is that reality TV shows offering "complete makeovers" convince us that the "ideal" is not only desirable but also necessary and attainable if we really care about what's important.

The message is that we are a failure for having breasts too small or too large, having a nose too long or too crooked, and a hairline that parts the wrong way or not at all. All this erodes our sense of self, and when a truly deep crisis touches our life, such as a lost job or relationship or a major health setback, our resiliency is already weakened and our capacity to fight back is rock bottom. What we now feel most strongly is fear—fear of our own diminished self-image, fear of not being worthy of friends or networks of support, and fear wrought from mounting powerlessness and uncertainty.

We can't do much to help others and ourselves if we buy into the numbing negativity of mass marketing. So say to hell with those dumb messages. Say, "There is absolutely nothing wrong with me!" And say, "I'm quite okay. But you, over there, that *organizational* personality, well, you're definitely one sick puppy!"

There are giant forests of diseased Organizational Family Trees around, each day killing the hopes of people and debilitating thousands of others. It's rare for us to trace the disease back to its source—back to why system structures are designed the way they are and for whose benefit. Instead, it is easy simply to withdraw and die the deaths of self-image and hope. Or, maybe, propelled by the brain chemicals adrenaline and cortisol plus fear and anger, just like the little gray field mouse fighting the cat in one last futile attempt at survival, we fight back. Unfortunately, as with thousands of others, our spirited fight was probably not against the system structure and culture that was the root cause, but against actions within the organizational climate.

We might have put up a good fight against a mean organizational personality. In return we were likely promised that our grievances and fears would be addressed. Committees were formed, reports were prepared, and surveys were taken. But in the end nothing changed. And so we retreated into a now even more diminished life. Having already died the death of self-image, it's now just a matter of time until the death of hope completely overwhelms us. In the interim, we exist as the walking dead—a reindustrialized zombie. Our productivity decreases, our stress wounds are exposed and raw, we can never get enough sleep, we experience sexual dysfunction, and the travel to and from work seems longer by the day.

The bleak description above is the worst that can happen to us as we face a dysfunctional organization suffering from corporate personality disorder. Unfortunately, it happens all too often, and the only surprise is that human and organizational meltdown is not worse than it already is. But just give it time. It will be. And if we're not impacted today, we will be soon enough.

POST-TRAUMATIC STRESS DISORDER AND CORPORATE PERSONALITY DISORDER

Corporate personality disorders are not just about the here and now. If we're immediately impacted by a badly behaving organization, or even just *anticipating* such an impact, we're susceptible to some very debilitating effects. In fact, those affected end up with symptoms that last well into the future, similar to the symptoms of post-traumatic stress disorder (PTSD).

According to the American Psychiatric Association, PTSD is evident if a patient presents the following classic symptoms a month or more after a tragic or traumatic event: flashbacks, intrusive thoughts, and nightmares; avoidance of activities and places that are reminiscent of the trauma; emotional numbness; and chronic insomnia activities Diagnostic and Statistical Manual of Mental Disorders (DSM-IV-TR, 1994). Those are also the exact symptoms that long-term victims of corporate personality disorder present—a fact that has huge ramifications for workers compensation boards throughout North America. Someday soon, as corporate personality disorder continues to spread, it won't just be employees going on stress leave for a minimum of three months at a time. Soon enough, a legal and medical case will be made that sick organizational systems are as identifiable and preventable as sick building syndrome—and that employers and managers must be held accountable.

If executives and managers are aware that their system structures and actions are likely to create a negative emotional and physiological impact on us, then should not those organizations (and specifically those executives) be held financially liable and legally culpable for their actions? If the top executives of Enron can go to jail because their corporate meltdown bilked hundreds of millions of dollars from investors, then shouldn't corporate executives who knowingly inflict the death of self-image and the death of hope upon us, who subject us to physical and psychological pain, also be subject to severe penalties? I think I hear the cheering, "Yes!"

Helping Others Maintain Their Personal Pilot Light

One day as I was driving to a meeting with a friend, I noticed his body language changing. He appeared paler, tighter, and reticent. I asked if he was okay, to which he replied that the street we were on just happened to be the route he used to take fours years earlier to his old job at a government agency.

He said the job was pure hell. The boss was a monster; he was continually berated and humiliated; he was told he was "deadwood," with no future; and he was generally demeaned in front of his colleagues on a regular basis. Finally, he quit.

"I just couldn't stand it any more. It made me sick to my stomach. I couldn't even get out of bed in the morning knowing that I had to face that witch of a boss again," my friend said.

My friend then confessed that for two years following his retreat from the job from hell, he would suffer heart palpitations and shortness of breath whenever he came within a mile of his old office. Today, four years after the fact, he wasn't feeling much better. Why should he? There had been no closure. The boss was still there despite internal assessments that found incompetence, despite a bevy of complaints and formal grievances, and despite no change in the boss's behavior.

The death of self-image is often sudden, especially when who we *are* becomes confused with what we *do*. The death of hope takes longer, because natural, primordial survival instincts buried deep in the recesses of our brain's hard wiring, like the pilot light flickering tiny but steady within a darkened and cold furnace, can empower us to claw back with renewal and reinvention. We find or invent sparks of light in the far distance, we line our clouds with silver, and we seek friendship in even misty mirages. Our world would become cold and time would become quite meaningless without this pilot light of sustainability, and in the final stages we would simply be drained of all energy and emotion and caring.

It's this pilot light in our soul—this tiny but powerfully meaningful flame of emotional energy—that ultimately sustains us through the darkest and coldest of storms, proving the source of reignition and renewal. But pilot lights need to be lit, and sometimes we need help from others to ignite the flame—from those whom we trust and who see the organizational personality for what it is.

So here's something to think about. If you're feeling pain because of the effects of corporate personality disorder and experiencing both organizational and personal meltdown, just stop what you're doing. Light a candle and think about who you *really* are as a person—not the mechanical creation, but your emotional self—your inner core. Think about what's truly important to you. Not your job, not the organization chart, but your need to really be human—to deeply experience emotions and to be open and honest about those emotions with yourself and others. You need to recognize that in your light-speed life of Blackberries, laptops, cell phones, and pagers, you've become a servant of technology, not the master of it.

The traditional Organizational Family Tree and its sterile system structure has made it very easy for us to be the cog on the wheel. As the wheels in our organizational life spin and whir increasingly faster, the person we knew long ago—our authentic self—is replaced by e-mail addresses and Web sites and business cards with important titles. The glow of comfort we now crave comes not from the warmth of a candle flickering in the night but from the glare of a computer screen or a tiny LCD. It's become very easy for us to become so entwined in the *doing* that we've forgotten not only *who* we are but also *why* we are.

8

WAKING UP TO OUR ECO-ALARM

Listen for a second. Can you hear it? That ringing deep inside your emotional brain, deep inside your instincts? We are now witnessing the greatest level of public activism in global history. This is because a subconscious alarm bell is ringing loudly in our emotional brain, marshaling us back to an early affiliation with natural systems and away from a threatening mechanistic systems structure. The draw of this powerful, natural *eco-alarm* is akin to what chaos theory calls a *strange attractor*—an event or action that occurs unpredictably but serves to pull events in a specific direction.

What I call our *eco-alarm* is biochemical is nature. Its program was written about 3.8 billion years ago and eventually evolved into what is considered our human consciousness. Specifically, this natural alarm bell resides in the two almond-shaped amygdala located in the limbic system within the inner recesses of our emotion-bearing human brain.

My "eco-alarm" theory is not the same as the "devil made me do it" thinking that some associate with human nature—that humans have a genetic disposition to model specific behaviors like war, murder, rape, and even the pursuit of power. This *naturalistic fallacy*, as it's called, suggests that all actions related to natural functioning are inherently right and uncontrollable.

This theory lends itself to persuasive tactics that lawyers love to use in the courtroom, referred to with catchy terms such as Black Rage Syndrome, the Twinkie Defense, and the PMS Defense. But as Harvard neuroscientist Steven Pinker (1997) points out, "Neither adultery nor any other *behavior* can be in our genes. Conceivably a *desire for* adultery can be an indirect product of our genes, but the desire may be overcome by other desires that are also indirect products of our genes, such as the desire for a trusting spouse."

We have a natural disposition to being connected with organic rather than mechanical systems. This is not another rehash of the nature vs. nurture argument but a suggestion that a complex mix of nature and nurture has created a very conscious age of outrage and associated behavior among many alarmed individuals.

As Pinker points out, human brains are still adapted to a Stone Age life of foraging in small nomadic bands. Why not? That's what humans have done for 99 percent of our existence. Or, as Pinker says, "Our minds are designed to generate behavior that would have been adaptive, on average, in our ancestral environment." In other words, the behavior of protest and advocacy groups today is simply a mimicking of our innate predisposition to survive through group action.

Our built-in alliance with nature is why we feel compelled to react to the neural bells ringing away within our eco-alarm, and it's why tens of thousands of people are waking up to the deadly precipice mankind faces. But even to admit that the alarm is ringing is to submit to an incredibly fearful notion—that our current Western values, religions, and machine-emulating organizational structures, indeed our very sense of self, may have recently taken a deadly detour. Where, how, and why did this wrong turn occur? Not all that long ago (in terms of Earth time). It happened in Europe, and it happened for very selfish human-centric reasons.

Before we identify what went wrong, it's important to understand a couple of major implications of the eco-alarm theory. The first implication is that the urgency of the eco-alarm can't be downplayed through slick PR campaigns using "facts" and "logic" to try to convince us otherwise. That's because when we demand a cleaner environment, a restriction on corporate global power, or an end to a senseless war, we're acting this way for two intertwined reasons.

The first reason is partially nurture. We have a cognitive, intelligent, reasoned position for what we think based on our personal values, education, and awareness. The second reason is pure nature. We also have a subconscious, genetically driven, emotional disposition for survival, and right now global survival (which includes you) is not looking very promising, whether we're talking about global warming, pandemics, or escalating military debacles.

Those who oppose our actions and object to our survival instincts are still prisoners of the mechanistic model of how things are *supposed* to work. They're convinced that evolutionary biological imperatives can be controlled and contained in a small, tight-thinking box. Our perceptions and their positions are worlds, if not galaxies, apart.

The second implication of the eco-alarm theory is that tens of thousands of like-minded thinkers are genetically predisposed to protecting humankind and the planet. This doesn't mean that a subconscious, genetic drive for survival is totally responsible when some environmental or anti-globalization protester smashes windows at a McDonald's restaurant. However, the conscious choice to smash windows *has* been influenced by the overarching subconscious, genetically driven need to protect our ability to replicate—to survive as a species and to stop the ravages of organizational meltdown.

MAYBE THE BEE GEES ARE RIGHT

Do you remember the movie *Saturday Night Fever* and its hit opening song by the Bee Gees, "Staying Alive"? John Travolta showed us a lot of great dance moves in his tight white disco suit, but his bumping and grinding is nothing compared to the moves we have to make to survive the dance of life. There's general agreement among social and natural scientists that if any living thing is to reproduce, it has to be able to recognize immediate and future dangers, know how to protect itself from immediate threats, and know how to maximize ongoing survival.

The same principle applies to every corporation or institution where issues of crisis management and business continuity are a fact of everyday life. But just as major corporations have a system of crisis management to deal with situations that pose a threat to their survival, we have a natural neurobiologic crisis-management system to deal with threats to our personal condition. The difference is that our human systems crisis management plan has been around a lot longer than the organizational one. Let's go back in time so I can show you what I mean.

This ability to differentiate, to learn from experience, to adapt and evolve was evident about 3.4 billion years ago, when hydrogen, oxygen, nitrogen, and carbon atoms combined in varying proportions to form nucleic acids and proteins, which in turn formed into an integrated chemical system that succeeded through trial and error in replicating itself as a form of life.

About 250 million years ago, mammal-like reptiles called theraspids roamed the earth. Their primitive brain structures and nervous systems had the same basic components as ours today. The mission statement of theraspids—as well as other fish, fowl, and beasts with rudimentary brain structures—is summed up by the title of that Bee Gees disco song: "staying alive." Neuroscientist Robert Ornstein (1991) explains it this way:

> The mind based its organization on the most important of the ancestral adaptations: those specialized for life and death decisions. Since these circuits were in place early and have enormous consequences for life and death, these same quick processes were recruited for commonplace percepts.

> This works well in life-and-death conditions, but it also sways all the mind's routines, even into perceiving what we read, how we link forms together, and what we hear. The neural underpinnings of the mind evolved in part to select only that which is of use to survival.... The mind needs quick action to help avoid poisons, avoid dangers, and prepare to fight. There is no time for self-understanding, no way—no need.

In other words, the same soup of chemistry that combined to protect very basic living systems millions of years ago from threats in the natural environment still protects us today from threats in the very *unnatural* organizational environment. It also means our *human* Organizational Family Tree predates the *corporate* Organizational Family Tree by over 250 million years. It's no wonder we hear subconscious alarm bells going off as we struggle to fit into the machinery of the modern corporation.

Survival in a broader sense means appreciating the presence of current and future dangers and incorporating defense and long-term procreation measures to stave them off.

An organization experiencing corporate personality disorder signals all manner of danger to us. Despite what Fredrick Taylor and subsequent proponents of mechanistic models of management think, we're *not* cogs on a wheel. We are living, breathing vessels of emotional energy that react to threats to our existence on both a conscious and an unconscious level. This book is a journey inside the corporate psyche, but right now it's important to poke around inside our brain, to demonstrate why we are indeed driven to challenge badly behaving organizations. This little exploration will underscore why there's nothing wrong with our reaction—in fact, it would be unnatural and unhealthy if we did *not* feel like protecting ourselves.

Here's a question: What role, if any, does this thing called "consciousness" play in the Organizational Family Tree—and in our survival? Just what is *consciousness*? And when did it develop in our brain? Neuroscientists are starting to amass a good deal of information on *how* our brain works, thanks to recent innovations in the neurosciences including sophisticated diagnostic imaging technology (such as CAT scans and PET scans). But they still have a long ways to go on *why* our brain does what it does. They do know the following.

Our brain has about 100 billion neurons—a cell membrane with a central nucleus and tiny, protruding dendrites and axons. Neurons connect to each other through a massive web of electronically charged synapses. Neurotransmitters, which include a range of chemicals in the brain, carry a signal or message between and among neurons, set off in turn by electrical signals that increase or decrease their rate of firing based on the stimuli received.

Within three-tenths of a second, our brain can detect a surprising or significant event ("The screen just went black"), set off a wave of neural activity that stimulates areas of our brain designed to respond to danger ("If this report's not done, I'm dead"), consider the significance of the event, and set off a surge of behavior-modifying chemicals in our brain and body ("Hello! Help Desk?!"). Such events are stored, albeit imperfectly, in our brain, adding to the storehouse of experiences that are constantly, and mostly unconsciously, accessed for comparison and definition purposes as new stimuli appear.

As inquiring humans, we know a lot about how our brain works—the technical, scientific stuff. We're far less clear about *why* it works. However, the answer to this question is the basis to understanding human behavior within the Organizational Family Tree and particularly to understanding why we do the things we do (or *don't* do) when dealing with corporate personality disorder.

The incredible complexity of our brain's electrochemical makeup allows consciousness to occur—we have a general awareness of ourselves within an organizational environment, we have memories of past experiences, and we entertain notions of the future. But it's sometimes harder for us to understand specifically *who* we are and *what* we are in relation to the world around us. We sometimes wonder if our colleagues and our boss fully appreciate the work we do. And we occasionally wonder how what we're doing brings any actual value and meaning to the organization.

We know that our personality is shaped through genetics, nurturing, culture, and the ongoing conscious and unconscious influence of our emotions. This knowledge has encouraged sociological, psychological, mystical, theological, neurological, biological, and psychiatric theories and models, with labels such as behaviorism; cognitivism; introspection; the organismic, mechanical, and dialectical paradigms; dualism; and reductionism—plus a big bag of other multisyllabic labels that we usually forget by the final syllable. Clearly, we have a propensity to label and characterize what we observe, because that's how we make sense of it all.

Most of us are driven toward having order and having everything "in its place"—even the words you are now reading are arranged in neat lines within precisely margined pages. For many, anything remotely disorderly creates discomfort—for some more so than for others. You'll know all about this if you've ever lived with a "neatnik" or a "slob" (or just happen to be one of those yourself).

PERCEPTION *IS* REALITY, AND IT'S DIFFERENT FROM COUSIN ELMER'S

Close your eyes for five seconds and think of the word "orange." Now open them. What did you think of—the very first image that came to your mind? I've asked this simple question in my group workshops, and so far I've counted twenty-seven different responses. People say, "a fruit," "the color of my car," "Agent Orange," "Apple" (as in "I remember buying oranges and apples"), "*A Clockwork Orange*" (the movie), "a sweater," and "getting a sun tan" ("I turned kind of an orange color because of the lotion"). It's a simple word with a variety of top-of-mind reactions, just like most of the word labels we use.

It's impossible for any two people to have exactly the same perception, recollection, or interpretation of a word or action, because no two people have *exactly* the same experiences or *exactly* the same historical and developmental history. Sometimes the results can be funny and sometimes they can be tragic. An airport snowplow driver was once asked to "clear" the runway and dutifully went out onto the landing strip in the way of a landing passenger jet, which swerved to avoid his tractor and crashed. (The word "clear," in this case, can also mean "get off.")

Dealing with an organizational personality means not only understanding *that* personality but also understanding *ourselves*. But when looking at ourselves, we're dealing with a constantly moving target. How we view ourselves often changes as we age and gain experiences and take the time to reflect. It's also possible that at some point we say, "Enough is enough!" Our self-image gets rooted in concrete. What we already know is just plenty—thanks anyway. Our view of the world can wrap us in an impervious cocoon of certainty. But here's the thing: We might lock the door and throw away the key on our conscious desire to learn or hear anything new, but the new stuff just seeps in under the door, around and over the top, and through the cracks. New experiences and learning are *always* entering our mental database, whether we know it or not. What happens afterward is where it gets interesting. It's what makes change easy or difficult for us, and why some people give in to badly behaving organizations while others fight back.

Sometimes our new experiences and learning serve to revise the nature and tone of our memories. But more often than not, our new experiences are judged and internalized according to the precepts, outlooks, opinions, and thoughts that have over many years gained seniority and influence in our brain. We all see the world differently, although we frequently share the same overall values and opinions. Perception *is* reality. But there are many realities. As neuroscientist Joseph LeDoux (1996) says,

> One of the main jobs of consciousness is to keep our life tied together in a coherent story, a self-concept. It does this by generating explanations of behavior on the basis of our self-image, memories of the past, expectations of the future, the present social situation, and the physical environment in which the behavior is produced.

The science author Mark Youngblood (1997) says, "The world we see is largely the world that we *expect* to see. In a very real sense then, we create our own reality." The lessons from psychology and neurology underscore why change within the Organizational Family Tree is so difficult to achieve. We may easily interpret organizational attempts to change system structures and actions as an attack on our deeply ingrained self-concept, our sense of coherence, and our expectations of the future. In large part, this perception of who we are and how we fit into the organization is driven by feelings buried deep within our brain.

Much of what we perceive with our five senses is subconscious. Every second, more than 11 million bits of information is absorbed by our sensory receptors, but fewer than 40 bits per second are consciously processed. We absorb what we think is critical to our survival and we interpret that information according to our past experiences, the composition of which changes over time. In turn, we communicate with others through both body and verbal language, but a significant portion of our communications, and therefore our external personality, we do not perceive. As social scientist Tor Norretranders (1989) says in his book *The User Illusion*,

> We experience not the raw sensory data but a simulation of them. The simulation of our sensory experiences is a hypothesis about reality. This simulation is what we call experience. We do not experience things themselves. We sense them. We do not experience the sensation. We experience the simulation of the sensation.... What we experience directly is an illusion, which presents interpreted data as if they were raw. It is this illusion that is the core of consciousness; the world experienced in a meaningful, interpreted way.

The quote above sounds a lot like what Socrates was describing in his metaphor of the cave dwellers. Today, thousands of years later, our fear of change is the one thing that hasn't changed. During dramatic or sudden change within an organizational climate, or when a corporate personality clashes with *our* personality, both our unconscious and conscious mind reacts, triggered by fear, the most protective and alert of all emotions. This neurological underpinning to human resistance and reaction is very little understood by most corporate managers.

Too often, managers attempt to soothe conflicts and neutralize negative energy within the Organizational Family Tree by using a cognitive, rational approach, hoping logic and facts will make things better. ("Our scientific studies show that you *will* like this.") But rational facts rarely dilute the powerful emotion of fear. My advice to many managers is "First find the fear." But to find fear, one must first be willing to understand it and admit its existence.

FEAR FUELS THE ORGANIZATIONAL FAMILY TREE

Fear is our natural friend, although we rarely treat it as such. Fear allows us to recognize threats and to take appropriate action in order to survive. Humanity's first programmed fear was the fear of death. Even basic life forms striving for survival billions of years ago had the deterministic chemistry that allowed them to recognize what was good and what was bad for survival. (That's big and ugly with huge teeth that will eat me.") Over time, as consciousness developed in the human brain, fear of *clinical death* was but one focus of our fear.

As we developed a sense of self and self-consciousness, fear of two other deaths became as prominent, if not more so: the death of self-image and the death of hope. This isn't surprising considering that humans are unique among species due to our well-developed sense of self and our ability to plan ahead and create hopes and expectations while at the same time being very aware of our fragile existence. Thomas Hobbes wrote, in his 1651 classic *The Leviathan*, that what distinguishes humans from other species on this planet is our awareness of death.

> Just as "man is famished by future hunger," so is he tormented by future sufferings. Accordingly, man not only fears death and seeks to avoid it in the here and now but also seeks to "secure himself against the evil he fears" for the future. He seeks not only to be secure but also to feel secure. He desires specifically to feel assured that he will continue to be secure in the future so that he may be free, not only from death but also from the gnawing fear of death.... The fundamental desire of the human animal is the unlimited desire for self-preservation.

Fear and a need for safety are key components of the human brain. Your brain, like my brain and Auntie Martha's brain, is naturally programmed to self-organize and to find order from anxiety. Ernest Beck (1997) uses the phrase "primal thinking" when describing how our brain automatically organizes itself in the face of a fear-inducing threat.

> When people become adversaries, their primal thinking may displace their adaptive skills, such as negotiation, problem solving, and compromise. The manifestations of primal thinking extend across a variety of situations: adaptive emergency reactions, dysfunctional interpersonal conflict, and intergroup conflict.

A developing area within psychology called *Terror Management Theory* says that our fear of death is linked to all manner of defensive and aggressive actions ranging from the creation of religions to controlling organizational systems (Pyszczynski, T., Solomon, S., and Greenberg, J. 2002). LeDoux (1996) maintains that emotional *feelings* and *thoughts* are very distinct and in fact emanate from different brain systems.

> When we are in the throes of emotion, it is because something important, perhaps life threatening, is occurring, and much of the brain's resources are brought to bear on the problem. Emotions create a flurry of activity all devoted to one goal. Thoughts, unless they trigger emotional systems, don't do this.

During organizational meltdown, or when we're picked on by a mean organizational personality, it's very natural for us to fear the death of our self-image and to be fearful about having a hopeful future. Our fear will automatically cause our brain to self-organize and try to find solutions that bring control and certainty to the situation. This is normal, despite those who squint their eyes at you and say, "You're getting too emotional." We are all genetically programmed to try to stay alive and further the survival of our species. But our genetically based electrochemical self-defense system is also very single-task focused.

For billions of years, the chemistry of survival has focused on identifying *physical* threats to self-perpetuation. In the past two million years in particular, mankind has used this survival chemistry to react to fearful stimuli, again mostly physical in nature (hungry lions, guys with sharp spears, etc.). But as mankind's consciousness evolved toward *self-consciousness*, there was a concomitant need to respond to not only the fear of clinical death but also the fear of the other deaths—of self-image and hope. But here's the thing: fear is fear, whether it's a coiled snake hiding in our computer bag or the metaphorical snake wearing a business suit.

Today, the physical threats to our existence are matched with equally powerful notional threats—*ideas* that could kill who we *think* we are or should be. So it should come as no big shock that a brain system that has for millions of years worked brilliantly in identifying physical death threats now applies the same efficiency to situations that we interpret as the death of self-image or the death of hope. To our ancient emotional brain system, dead is dead.

When a nuclear reactor begins to melt down, releasing deadly radioactive material, all manner of flashing lights, sirens, alarm bells, and safety warnings go off. When an organization melts down, it exhibits similar signs of meltdown: warning bells go off within our human survival system triggering multiple failsafe actions, both consciously and unconsciously.

In the next chapter, we'll look at why we're not alone in feeling (and I mean *feeling*, not just *thinking*) that it's time to do something about bad organizational behavior.

9

THE ROOTS, BRANCHES, AND GROWTH OF SOCIAL ACTIVISM

To quote Bob Dylan, "The times they are a-changin'." Today, as the tension between work life and personal life continues to rise, many wise and caring organizations are trying to provide at least some modicum of work/life balance. There's flextime, longer holidays, working from home, and many other emotionally intelligent good things going on.

Many corporations are seeing their personnel as more than cogs on a wheel. The trouble is, many still don't. Many organizations talk the talk, but that's as far as it gets. Mission, vision, and values statements make it as far as the brightest plaque on a wall or into that snappy multicolored annual report. And there the words stay, hermetically sealed, while the organizational personality stumbles about in its increasingly dysfunctional way.

In October 2006, a survey by employee assistance provider WarrenShepell found that 18 percent of employee assistance programs in Canada were being accessed by supervisors and managers. The survey showed 35 percent of managers reported high levels of stress on the job. In a Canadian Press story describing the survey, WarrenShepell president and CEO Rod Phillips is quoted, "The common attitude is that people at the top are not supposed to have problems that impact their performance or that of other employees. The truth is that they're not infallible. They're affected by the same daily hassles and struggles as everyone else."

Do we really need a survey to tell us this? And what's this about "the common attitude" that those at the top are somehow impervious to corporate personality disorder? The fact is there's nothing "common" about such an attitude anymore. Managers have started to figure out that they are not inert cogs on a wheel but are living, breathing humans with a lot of emotions. Many managers make decisions based on not what a SWOT analysis tells them but what their gut instinct says is right, and they are just as susceptible to having their self-esteem kicked out from under them by a dysfunctional organizational personality as their employees are.

Songs, fictional literature, and movies have for years portrayed the devastating impact of corporate personality disorder. In Sloan Wilson's classic 1956 book and movie *The Man in the Gray Flannel Suit,* Tom Rath (played by Gregory Peck in the film), just back from the war, is forced to make a moral and ethical choice between a fast-rising career in corporate America and more time with his family (at the cost of a major cut in pay).

In Arthur Miller's 1976 play *Death of a Salesman,* Willy Loman is an elderly salesman adrift in illusions and false hopes after his company decides he should work on commission rather than on salary. Trouble is, he can't pay the bills. In a classic example of human meltdown, Willy is abandoned by the company and spit out like "a piece of fruit" after thirty-four years of faithful service. His energy, self-image, and hope are torn away. In the end, Willy Loman sees suicide as the only way out. As he says to his friend Charley, "After all the highways, and the trains, and the appointments, and the years, you end up worth more dead than alive."

If we find that our human personality is in conflict with the organizational personality, if we find our insides starting to boil because of corporate meltdown, or, in the worst cases, if we lose our job or position within an organization, "don't worry about it," says the "common" thinking. There are plenty of career management consultants and human resource specialists who will be quick to tell us to stay low, keep our negative energy to ourselves, and definitely don't rock the boat or buck the system.

Such sage advice is straight from the instruction manual for building the perfect mechanical model of small-box organizational thinking. Such counsel, rather than recognizing corporate personality disorder for what it is, simply transfers blame to the individual. By telling us to stay mute, to never ask "Why?" or "Why not?" and to never say "no," the consultants and specialists are complicit in allowing badly behaving organizational personalities to get away with both psychological and physical abuse.

A great example of human meltdown caused by organizational meltdown and exploding in a backlash of negative energy is the 1976 movie *Network*. In this film, anchorman Howard Beale (played by the late Peter Finch) discovers his news department (of national TV network UBS) has been handed over to the advertising department for a ratings makeover and the aging Beale is given two weeks' notice that he's out of a job. Rather than meekly accept the fact that his job is over, he erupts. Preparing to read yet another scripted version of the evening news, Beale instead rises from his chair like a wild-eyed holy man and uses the airwaves as a conduit for his redirected energy. He screams out to millions of viewers:

> We sit in a house and slowly the world we're living in is getting smaller and we say, "Please, at least leave us alone in our living rooms, let me have my toaster and my TV and my steel belted radials and I won't say anything, just leave us alone!" Well I'm not going to leave you alone! … All I know is that first you've got to get mad! You've got to say, "I'm a human being, goddamn it! My life has value!"

In the next scene, we see tens of thousands of reenergized people throughout America sticking their heads out of windows and yelling, "I'm as mad as hell and I'm not going to take it anymore!" It is a huge energy surge of human power, complete with thunder and lightening. Today, hundreds of thousands of people are feeling the impact of corporate personality disorder—they are clearly mad as hell, and they don't want to take it anymore. Such people have been mad as hell for quite a while. This collective human energy is building to a volcanic pressure point, and it's ready to erupt—not through violence or dramatic law breaking—but through peaceful, determined, collective action demanding change.

What's happening today on a regional, national, and global scale is easily identified on the Organizational Family Tree. Corporate and institutional system structures that pay lip service to our emotional needs are seeing a natural and healthy backlash from those who will no longer put up with a debasement of their sense of self. Organizational structures that replicate historical mechanistic designs are finding they are lost in a world where connectivity, cooperation, and communications are based on holistic, networked models. And organizational personalities characterized by slick public relations and market "branding" rather than by deep values and virtues are increasingly clashing with human personalities that see through the phoniness of it all.

As we stroll through the corporate forest today, we see more than a few new healthy buds sprouting on the old Organizational Family Tree. Change is in the air, and a globally connected network of responsive and responsible human activism is spreading the organizational nutrients feeding this positive change. The activism is evident in hundreds of groups (such as Greenpeace), civil rights organizations, the antiwar movement, shareholder rights groups, environmental groups, gender and human rights groups, and corporate social responsibility advocates. But it hasn't always been this way.

PROTESTING BAD ORGANIZATIONAL BEHAVIOR IS GOOD FOR US

It wasn't that long ago that "experts" had a very critical view of anyone with the gall to challenge authority. "They're troublemakers. Communists. Never worked a day in their life. A bunch of granola-crunching tree huggers," was more or less the sophisticated thinking from those fearful of questioning the tight-thinking, small-box Organizational Family Tree.

Organizational experts and chiefly those in control of system structures argued that the psychopathology of primitive instincts (such as anger) produced riots, violence, and other nasty behavior. As William Gamson (1975) pointed out in his book *The Strategy of Social Protest*, "Movements were seen in general as providing a substitute for a spoiled identity." What the tight thinkers said to anyone who would listen (and there were plenty) was that you must have a screw loose to want to join a protest or to criticize the machinery of corporate structures. Fortunately, this shallow analysis of why we'd want to partake in a protest has mostly been washed away by a recent tsunami of common sense and scientific research. The fact is, our desire to react against threatening organizational actions is just as natural as our instinct to protect ourselves from a threatening predator.

The ability of any living thing to take responsive action, from a flatworm to a Chief Executive Officer, requires at least three basic ingredients: the ability to sense threatening stimuli; a memory by which to gauge the danger rating of the stimuli; and a protective response ("Whoa! That's a skunk! I'm outta here!" or "That decision to close the daycare stinks! Let's call a news conference!"). Basically, those who feel threatened by an organization are dancing to the same three-step tune as Andy the Alley Cat, who's just spotted Fido the Friendly Doberman.

All three biologically based survival mechanisms—sensing a threat, gauging the danger, and protecting ourselves—have direct parallels to the actions of protesters, who use communications, connectivity, and cooperation to counter badly behaving organizations. This human survival model also has a lot in common with the Organizational Family Tree, wherein human memory is represented by historical and developmental factors; the ability to sense stimuli is represented by emotion and knowledge factors; and the human protective response factor is found in the core Triangle of Trust components.

Here's specifically how the three-step protest waltz applies to a group of like-minded folks who've had it up to their eyebrows with the behavior of a nasty organization: The first step, "sensing stimuli," happens when our emotions are aroused (fear and anger) over organizational actions that we see as a threat to our sense of self. The second step, "gauging the danger based on memories," occurs when we quickly link the perceived existing threat with past negative organizational behavior (either exact or close enough and either your organization or others). The final step, a "responding to protect ourselves" draws on a repertoire of defensive actions available to us, including the creation of alliances with those who can help us (from lawyers to union officials); signing a petition; staging a public protest; alerting the news media; and going home on stress leave.

My point is that fear is fear. Survival is survival. These are basic, primordial responses to something that appears to be threatening our emotional wellness. Our survival response is rooted deep within our emotional brain, and a slick "good news" public relations brochure from headquarters certainly won't subdue it. Let's poke a little deeper into our three-pound brain to see where our natural defensiveness comes from.

Within our brain's first formed, primitive region are two small almond-shaped structures call amygdala. Like a dedicated police officer, the amygdala serves and protects us. But its policing actions operate in a split-second fashion, with no bureaucracy, second-guessing, or budgetary constraints. The amygdala helps orchestrate our safety and security through the use of neural receptors, chemical neurotransmitters, and direct connections to working memory in the prefrontal cortex, long-term memory in the hippocampus, and perceptions in the sensory cortex.

Like an effective protest organizer or police officer, the amygdala is all about dealing with *emotional* arousal. It's the ignition switch in our protective brain system. The amygdala draws upon our experiences—what are called *frames* and *schemas* of previously frightening or threatening events—to decide on our protective actions. In an organization, this is the storehouse of experience found in the historical and developmental factors rooted in the Organizational Family Tree. *Frames* and *schemas* are a pretty big deal with regard to how we behave and react to organizational behavior. As Bert Klandermans (1997) pointed out in his study of workers losing their job at a shipyard, feelings of injustice, threats to self-identity, and a sense of agency led to a group reaction that strongly supported protest demonstrations.

We take *action* because of a neurochemical fear response. We're *fearful* because the immediate stimulus reminds us of a past fear—either exact or "close enough." The actions we take are a combination of our fear alerting us to danger and our neocortex planning a response strategy. It's a balancing and codependency, much like the necessary balance between emotion factors and knowledge factors in the

Organizational Family Tree. When the amygdala processes multiple fears, it efficiently and subconsciously prioritizes our actions based on the greatest and most immediate threat before us. ("Okay, first I jump out of the way of the lunging alligator and now I avoid the quicksand.") It's the same process when the fear is created not by sharp teeth but by the threatening behavior of an organizational personality dressed up in a sharp suit.

Evidence from both social movement research and current work in neuropsychology shows that human emotion—particularly fear—plays a powerful role in kick starting actions like public protest. Our fear of certain organizational action is directly linked to our need to protect our self-image and to the ten emotion factors used to measure health within the Organizational Family Tree.

So, how does our fear of and anger toward organizational behavior eventually end up with 300 placard-waving protesters blocking the sidewalk outside the head office? We can find the answer by examining the growth structure of the Organizational Family Tree, where a healthy mix of *both* emotion and knowledge factors is the key to effective action.

It's important for our protest actions to be well organized, but without an emotional (chiefly fear-based) inducement, even the best organizational endeavors can fall flat. As Jo Freeman (1999) stated in *Waves of Protest: Social Movements since the Sixties*, "Nothing makes desire for change more acute than a crisis. Such a crisis need not be a major one; it need only embody collective discontent." In other words, get enough other fearful and angry people aware and organized, and you've got the beginnings of a hurricane-force wind of change. But wait! Before we start looking in a secondhand store for a cool-looking beret, remember that the key word here is *organized*.

Strong, emotional reactions to fear-induced stimuli that are *not* well organized through the application of knowledge, skills, and abilities can result in protests that lack direction, control, and sustainability. And so they quickly fizzle out, leaving us feeling worse than when we started. Powerful organizational actions occur when there's a blending of *both* emotion and knowledge. This means that the ten key knowledge factors found in the Organizational Family Tree are especially important when it's time to turn emotion into well-organized and *trusted* action.

OLGA AS A NOISY BRANCH ON THE ORGANIZATIONAL FAMILY TREE

When we combine high levels of emotional energy with strong knowledge, we get a powerful organizational ability to counter corporate personality disorder. I call this amalgam *knorganergy*, a creation of organizational energy through emotion and knowledge. The best way to explain how knorganergy can make a difference is to introduce you to my friend Olga. On a cloudy Friday in June, Olga is focused and determined to bring a well-worn industrial strength stapler back to life. It's big and heavy, made of shiny steel, and requires a firm, strong grip. She fires a half-inch staple into a wooden pole, impaling a freshly-minted leaflet promising action and a call-to-arms.

Olga is well acquainted with staplers and leaflets and especially the emotional punch of words. I was with Olga and dozens of others when she first learned and taught such things in the early fall of 1970, on the hot pavement spanning the Canada-U.S. border.

On that auspicious day, Olga's crisis developed within minutes of us blockading the popular border crossing. The action was part of a series of blockades across the country designed to raise public consciousness about American military plans to detonate a five-megaton nuclear bomb on Amchitka Island, near Alaska. Olga, complete with tangled hair, faded jeans, and a personality full of in-your-face, presented a semantic dilemma.

Specifically, the dilemma was the placard she'd made from cheap cardboard and borrowed red paint. "Fuck the Bomb!" her sign screamed out, in Olga's own literary version of a megaton explosion. A young officer with the Royal Canadian Mounted Police approached Olga and politely yet firmly explained that the word was an obscenity and the placard must be removed.

Olga agreed. "Damn right bomb is an obscene word!" she offered in a loud, clear voice.

The Mountie waited, and then retorted quietly, "No, it's the other word. That's the legally obscene word, ma'am."

Olga never missed a beat. "Oh, so *fucking* is a bad thing but bombing people to bits is okay. Is that what you're saying?" Mercifully for the Mountie (and ultimately for Olga), a few of us intervened, despite feeling as if we were sacrificing one principle for local peace by having Olga change "fuck" to "screw" on her placard. The Mountie was happy, and although Olga felt her prose now lacked punch, the show went on.

The year 1970 was a heady one for Olga. It was the year she and others, sitting on the wet sandy beach in Vancouver's inner bay, watching freighters drift slowly in from the Pacific Ocean, came to understand that human consciousness is inextricably intertwined with Gaia, the natural Earth force. Bob Hunter, a contemporary of Olga's, would go on about how the ecology movement was blessed by a higher power—it was in ecology that a new spiritual awakening was taking place, something transcendental, something spiritual and Zen-like.

He was absolutely right, of course, and many shared Hunter's thinking, including famed biologist Gregory Bateson, who told a conference in Austria in 1968 that human consciousness was badly flawed—that it contained "systematic distortions," which limited its ability to process information allowing for a balance between man, society, and ecosystems.

As Bateson told the conference in Austria, mankind is unique among all species in that it seeks to change its environment rather than its own behavior, while all other species make a determination "to adapt to the environment or adapt the environment to itself. In evolutionary history, the great majority of steps have been changes within the organism itself." Corporate personality disorder is evident when organizational structures refuse to regularly examine their inner working and to challenge assumptions, but instead seek to force or coerce others to change. Such was the case with the U.S. military and the mechanistic-thinking action to test an atomic bomb near Alaska, which in turn created an organic-thinking *re*action by a network of friends in Vancouver.

In the summer of 1970, the transcendental, metaphysical calling of natural forces to join with human ones became especially self-evident to Quakers Marie Bohlen and her husband, Jim, who, drinking their morning coffee and lamenting the pending blast at Amchitka, said, "What would happen if we sailed a boat of loving peaceniks straight into the detonation site? What if we got a ship and just confronted the war machine head on?" The concern was not just the symbolism of military aggression the bomb represented, or the ensuing radiation, but also a worry that the blast could destabilize the San Andres fault, leading to a massive earthquake.

Within days, Maria, Jim, Olga, and soon others banded together in a ragtag group called the Don't Make a Wave Committee and connected with someone who knew someone else with an old freighter. They christened the ship the *Rainbow Warrior*—borrowed from a myth by Cree Indians—networked themselves to others who connected to yet others, and soon had a shipload of volunteers and news media heading to Amchitka.

To Olga's consternation, the *Rainbow Warrior* was stopped short of its destination by the U.S. Coast Guard, protesters were arrested, and the bomb went off, but the San Andres fault did *not* rip open. Life went on. A new consciousness was indeed spawned, a lasting connectivity had been made with Mother Nature, and in the following year the Don't Make a Wave Committee changed its name to Greenpeace, going on to far greater challenges, including global trade, protection of endangered whales, and broad issues of sustainability and environmental protection.

Today, Olga and millions of other like-minded individuals have created an Organizational Family Tree that is international in scope and connected by a common consciousness and subconsciousness. Many are hearing the warning bells related to organizational meltdown. They are thinking about and planning actions, and their efforts are the best organized ever due to improved communications, connectivity, and cooperation thanks to the Internet.

THE ROOTS OF ACTIVIST ORGANIZATIONAL FAMILY TREES

Our brain is a wondrous organizational system that is attuned to threat, automatically takes remedial action to avoid death, and for the most part is adaptable to changing environments. Unlike mechanistic organizational systems, our brain has intricate networks of cooperation, connectivity, and communication. It's no wonder then that the design of the modern organization—with tightly prescriptive, mechanistic rules of how to behave on the job and within institutions—creates multiple points of conflict with how we adapt to the organizational world. Human personalities and the organizational personality just don't see eye to eye on many things, and there's a very long history of family feuding between the two.

While there have been clashes between organizational and human systems since modern civilization began in 3,500 B.C., the great disconnect began with the Industrial Revolution. It's at this time that public protests against sick organizational systems became both organized and violent. Rigid models of organizational design are unnatural acts that pose a threat to our emotional health as great as any physical threat we might encounter in a mean, dark alley. But we're also very alert to such threats. With over a hundred thousand years of collective experience with danger, humans have evolved a finely tuned early-alert system within an ancient area of our brain that now recognizes threats from both beasts and man alike.

We often think the purpose of public protests is to raise awareness, gain support for corrective action, and influence decision-making processes within the machinery of power. But when we dig deeper, we see that public protests against an organization's actions are really a reaction to how that organization is structured. Large-scale public protests have existed for hundreds of years, but when we dig into their history, we find that in all cases, the protests involved strong emotional reaction to a threat. That emotional reaction was then given focus and power through organizational knowledge.

In the distant past, protests against badly behaving organizations were highly localized, very specific, brief, and narrowly targeted; they involved violent actions dealing with, as Sidney Tarrow (2001) writes, "bread, belief, land, and death." One of the most significant wide-scale organized eruptions of dissidence occurred in 1517, when Martin Luther single-handedly began the Protestant Reformation, permanently shattering Western Christendom. But broad-based *social* (as opposed to religious) movements concerned with the negative impact of decaying organizational structures came much later.

In the sixteenth and seventeenth centuries and earlier, public uprisings were commonly associated with localized injustices, often linked to food supplies and religion, although there are also examples of slave revolts and occasional peasant revolts. In all cases, the organizational system structure failed to meet broad-based public expectations related to social, political, and economic needs. There were huge gaps in the Triangle of Trust's key points.

Ages ago, the actions of those suffering negative system impacts, although frequently violent, were narrowly directed and involved specific grievances, such as a Catholic Church being built in a Protestant district or millers selling grain outside a given boundary. Those participating in such uprisings usually had a connection not only among themselves but also to the target of their attack. Their actions were typically brief, focused, and lacking in communications or effective cooperation. They were, as Tarrow describes in *Dynamics of Contention* (2001), "like scattered sparks that were rapidly exhausted or snuffed out."

"Scattered sparks" indeed! Up until the nineteenth century, public revolts against badly behaving organizations were characterized by ideology, parochialism, direct action, and a lack of connectivity between the numerous events. In large part, the rebellions, riots, and sustained violent actions that occurred throughout Europe made a big splash only when driven by the organizational power of the church, which whipped worshipers into a frenzy of excitement, or by mad-as-hell peasants, who revolted against the establishment because they too wanted a block of land to call their own.

What did the church have going for it? Fear, mostly. The church had a well-ingrained system structure of unrivaled authority over its worshipers—despite its lack of responsibility or accountability. It was an Organizational Family Tree with very deep historical roots, a culture that was carved in stone, but it was also a system in decay.

The public reaction to how organizations treated them up to the late eighteenth century was influenced to a large degree by how Organizational Family Trees were structured at the time. Under these ancient systems, institutional authority, accountability, and responsibility were concentrated at the community level. Communication channels, including roads, were highly localized, connectivity was tight among groups because most people knew each other on a first-name basis, and cooperation, although sporadic, was relatively easy to organize. The chief target of protest activity was usually a figure within the township or the immediate area inhabited by those feeling aggrieved. ("Hey Jim, get hold of Sam and Trevor and let's meet tonight in front of the land baron's castle. Don't forget the torches.")

The growth of modern government systems in the eighteenth century brought plenty of new examples of organizational dysfunction and the spread of corporate personality disorder. National governments in both Europe and North America were gaining unprecedented power over how citizens conducted their lives as well as the social and economic quality of those lives. Associated with nationhood was the necessity to raise taxes to pay for wars, for various programs like sanitation and political junkets, and to support widespread systems of food production and distribution.

As institutions and corporations grew larger and more complex, their system structures and behavior grew more distant from the expectations of those they affected. The gap between authority, accountability, and responsibility widened, as did effective communications, cooperation, and connectivity. The seventeenth century, with it brutal factory floors, wretched working conditions, and capitalistic land barons, is ground zero for the historical factors found in many of today's Organizational Family Trees. That's why we call isolated corporate departments "silos" and "smokestacks" and why some misguided managers still want their employees to be part of a "well-oiled machine."

RENOURISHING THE ORGANIZATIONAL FAMILY TREE

In the eighteenth and nineteenth centuries, something dramatic occurred to the structure of the Organizational Family Tree. An entire new species was suddenly created. Imagine getting used to looking out your kitchen window at that old apple tree that's been there forever and then, one morning, looking out and seeing a giant cactus growing in its place.

The cause of this major reshaping was the Industrial Revolution, whose impact is still with us today. The vast industrialization in the eighteenth and nineteenth centuries throughout Europe and North America spawned a well-organized and bureaucratized system of government with far-reaching national roles operating in support of an industrial sector that benefited from economies of scale, standardization, and command and control. But as Einstein said, "For every action there is an equal and opposite reaction."

Dysfunctional organizational behavior, including the harsh treatment of employees and the amassing of wealth by a select few, gave rise to labor unions, political parties, and ideologies representing the working class. This is the thing about Organizational Family Trees. Just like a real tree, its growth and actions affect its environment, and the reactions in the environment come back to affect the Organizational Family Tree—sometimes positively and sometimes negatively.

From the late 1960s onward, the energy of public protests and large-scale public demonstrations in North America changed again, as badly behaving organizations triggered antiwar sentiments and protests against nuclear energy. As well, there were movements involving ecology, gay rights, animal rights, minority rights, alternative medicine, and anti-globalization. This panoply of grievances defied *traditional* institutional analysis of public protests that were chiefly locked in small-box thinking. Up to this point, studies of social movements had coalesced around theories of ideology, organization, and rationality—all in keeping with the machine metaphor of how things should work.

Inherent in this mechanistic, analytical approach was a tendency to study the economic and/or class characteristics of protesters and to measure their demands and their reasons for protesting against a standard ideology or philosophy that pigeonholed the group into a simple, one-size-fits-all box of understanding. In other words, if groups or individuals weren't behaving according to the status quo, if they were bucking the system with new and "radical" ideas, then they must obviously be troublemaking weirdoes who need to be put in their place.

The Organizational Family Tree of protest movements, especially those surfacing over the past ten to fifteen years, defies such simplistic characterizations. Human survival is a deeply buried natural instinct. The same brain chemistry that protects us from a leaping lion in the savannah protects us from lying Leo on the seventh floor. Basically, energy and protective action is produced within our protest group the same way our brain produces protective responses to scary things that can hurt or kill us.

The human reaction to badly behaving organizations has become progressively more sophisticated since the seventeenth century. It's clear that the Activist species of the Organizational Family Tree is very successfully adapting to the environment—*often at a much faster rate than within a traditional corporate Organizational Family Tree*. Protests, rather than getting more violent, are in fact becoming more peaceful. At the same time, they are becoming more common and having a greater impact due to the pervasive influence of the Internet and the domination of global television news.

In the past few years, throughout North America and Western Europe and to a lesser degree in authoritarian countries, nonviolent actions such as marches, protests, demonstrations, sit-ins, and numerous other tactics that still fall under the rubric of "civil disobedience" have become the staple of protest groups and social movements. Connectivity, cooperation, and communication channels between different groups have allowed them to spread their tactics globally, adapting them as the situation warrants. Perhaps most importantly, the general public and the political process (in nonauthoritarian systems) now recognize such tactics as a legitimate expression of dissent.

Today, social movement organizers are moving away from rough tactics and violence and are embracing more peaceful actions, as evidenced in the buildup to the large, February 15, 2003, antiwar rally in New York City. Social movement organizations, minding the principles of authority, accountability, and responsibility, have for the most part achieved a harmonious balance with the expectations of mainstream society. As social commentator Michael Morris wrote in an essay posted on the Indymedia Web site in May 2003,

> If you looked at the demographics of the march, there was a refreshing dynamic. Women in leadership roles and on the front line, large numbers of people of color, but the best part was that the people there were not all black clad Anarchists. We need to do different/new things and the other night was different.

The "difference," according to Morris' analysis, was that the "movement was growing up." In his view, events following the anti-globalization protests in Seattle had led to a soul searching by many social movement activists who clearly were rejecting violent actions in favor of political statements. What we're seeing is a healthy evolution of the social activist Organizational Family Tree—the maturing and protective adaptability of group action against badly behaving organizational personalities and sick systems.

ENGAGED, ACTIVE, AND VOLATILE GROUPS CREATE ORGANIZATIONAL CHANGE

The backlash against badly behaving organizations is not restricted to those of a certain age, gender, educational background, or income. Today, many of the formal and informal groups that engage in both small and large-scale public protests and demonstrations are a mosaic of personalities. For example, the ecology and environmental, children's rights, animal rights, antiwar, and anti-globalization movements, as well as gender and race-related groups, have supporters representing a wide range of age, gender, sexual orientation, and socioeconomic backgrounds, as well as professional, trade, and political affiliations.

As Gary Allgeyer wrote in the January 1996 edition of the *FBI Law Enforcement Bulletin*, "Protesters today are more likely to arrive at the scene conservatively dressed, some even wearing designer clothes. Protesters who once would have been considered reactionary now may be seen as courageous proponents of a cause." What's happening is that those previously labeled as nasty rabble-rousers impudently shaking the decaying Organizational Family Tree are now often seen as positive contributors to healthy—and essential—new growth. The natural eco-alarm bell that's going off in our subconscious and conscious mind, spurring us to take action against threatening organizational behavior, is waking up hundreds of thousands of people who've had it with sleepwalking through life.

What's consistently common to most social activism within North America and throughout Western Europe is an alignment with general public opinion that disapproves of violent lawbreaking. Numerous public opinion surveys (world values survey, 2005; Sopow, 2003) show support for such peaceful actions as petition-signing, lobbying of politicians, attending peaceful protests, and even getting arrested at a peaceful demonstration. And that's what 97 percent of public protests look like.

Once upon a time, I provided consulting services to the U.S. Department of Homeland Security as well as to other national organizations dealing with protest groups. What I shared with those august agencies was my research involving numerous public opinion surveys throughout North America regarding protests. Here's what I told them. There are basically three different groups of organizational change conductors—*engaged, active,* and *volatile.* Now, these definitions aren't carved in stone. They're more like shapes made from wet clay, alive to changes, blending, and also hardening. However, in general, I found the following in my research and in my direct experience:

Engaged conductors *strongly* support mild actions such as signing petitions, using the Internet, and writing to newspapers. They include up to 59 percent of the adult population, with women outnumbering men. The age groups include younger adults (18–24) and older adults (45–54). The profile of engaged conductors includes middle-incomes, both conservative and liberal political leanings, and university or college educations. The general tactics of this group include raising awareness and offering solutions to societal problems through letter writing and petitions, and a willingness to negotiate. The tone of the language used is moderate yet personal and linked to emotions.

Active conductors are strongly inclined to partake in all the actions of *engaged conductors,* but in addition they support attending peaceful protests. This group represents up to 27 percent of all adults. Typically, they include young adults (18–24) with equal support among genders. *Active conductors* are from middle-income households and have a range of educational backgrounds from high school to college/university. The tone of communications is similar to *engaged conductors,* with the use of descriptive language that is emotionally linked, personally directed, and simple to understand.

Volatile conductors are a very small minority (less than 5 percent) of the adult population and support illegal action such as getting arrested at a protest. The demographics of *volatile conductors* are young adults (18–24), with an equal mix of men and women, a large cross-section of educational backgrounds, and generally lower incomes. In my research and in my direct experience with protest policing, I found that what differentiates this group from the other two is both tactics and language.

Whereas *engaged* and *active* conductors are generally open to negotiation and discussion with "the other side," pursue nonviolent actions, and use dramatic but not doctrinaire language to get their point across, *volatile conductors* are more inclined to engage in violent action such as destruction of public property, attacks on police, and the use of ideology-laden, pejorative language.

Demanding Changes to a Decaying Organizational Family Tree

Here on the West Coast, those who try to save old-growth forests from logging are called "tree huggers." They're called that by those who prefer to cut down the trees (as if giving someone a hug is a bad thing). I think that the more we hear about the attributes of the *activist* Organizational Family Tree, the more we'll feel like jumping out of our bus stop shelter and giving this metaphorical, very green tree a huge hug. I want us to have a closer look at this particular species for a very important reason. The reason is that how the *activist* Organizational Family Tree adapts and grows is very different from how the *industrial* Organizational Family Tree grows. The first not only fits into the natural environment; it also protects it. The second often fears change and seeks to suck what it can from the natural environment. There's a lot we can learn from both species. But I suspect there's only one we want to hug.

In their assessment of what's called *new social movements*, Enrique Larana, Hank Johnston, and Joseph Gusfield (1994) point out that the global proliferation and presence of such movements escapes easy analysis through traditional academic theories associated with ideology, organization, and rationality. It's obvious that analysis of social movements and protest groups based on economic or class determinants is no longer helpful, and neither are simple labels such as "socialism," "capitalism," "conservatism," "communism," or "fascism." No, the activist Organizational Family Tree defies such simplistic labels. That's the stuff found in mechanistic small-box thinking. It's far more useful to use bigger-box thinking to understand what's behind social movements today.

We now know from our understanding of the Organizational Family Tree that today's actions are based on structures that draw from both historical and developmental organizational factors. It's the same for all system structures—whether it's an environmental group, a society of religious zealots, a police department, or the Ford Motor Company. Organizational actions today are an amalgam of history and lessons learned (culture) combined with system structures and the weight given to emotion and knowledge needs (climate). And so it stands to reason that *new* social movements, surfacing as antiwar, anti-globalization, ecological, and human rights champions, are also *old* movements.

There's no clean and simple ontology to the forms of collective action that surfaced at the World Trade Organization demonstrations in Seattle or at the Summit of the Americas in Quebec City. As political scientist Doug McAdam

(2001) pointed out, there's a cultural and ideational dimension to new social movements that goes beyond narrow rationalist, objectivist, or structural reasons for their being. The fact is, we can't use mechanistic models of organizational design to understand the workings of an organic system of bringing people together. A cactus isn't an apple tree.

Newer social movements contain cultural connections that can be traced back to social movements that existed decades ago, allowing cross-generational continuity to occur, one that is adaptive to modern needs. Basically, the growth and development of activist Organizational Family Trees is a healthy blend of culture and current operational climate.

The machine metaphor is a great way to describe how traditional Organizational Family Trees develop and operate. But an *activist* Organizational Family Tree needs a different perspective, that of a gardener. This perspective comes from a field of study called complexity science. In complexity science terms, social movements are a "complex adaptive system" with many points of interconnectivity among groups and individuals, constantly adapting networks of support, often decentralized operations, and no one single ideological focus.

In looking at the Organizational Family Tree of new social movements, it's important to acknowledge both what is known and not known. We know that the new groups exhibit a rich mosaic of supporters, including a range of gender, age, and socioeconomic backgrounds. We know that the new groups tend to champion causes that are less related to working-class economic issues and more related to issues of personal identity and empowerment, plus matters of values, ethics, and culture. This can include matters of an extremely personal nature such as gay rights and abortion, as well as issues involving food and ecology.

Here's another thing about social movements and activist groups today. There's often an easy mix of individual needs and goals and the collective needs and actions of the group. This means that while we might take part in large-scale demonstrations opposing the war in Iraq, we're just as likely to get involved in stuff of our own and *on our own*—individual actions to protect our beliefs and principles, such as boycotting a company's products, saying "why," "why not," and "no" to our organization, and writing a letter to a newspaper or calling a friendly local reporter with our concerns.

As we poke around the branches and roots of the activist Organizational Family Tree, you'll notice there's been new growth in the style and tactics of public demonstrations. Sure, we'll still find occasional disruptive and dramatic actions that garner a lot of attention. However, unlike protests in the early part of the twentieth century and before, most new groups generally subscribe to tenets of nonviolence and a Gandhi-like passive resistance to authority. The Organizational Family Tree of activist and protest groups has proven very adaptive to its environment, unlike the rigid Organizational Family Tree of many deeply rooted traditional organizations and institutions.

Unlike the inflexible Organizational Family Trees of many corporations and government institutions, where knowledge factors heavily outweigh emotion factors and command and control supersedes connectivity and cooperation, many activist groups are far more adaptive, decentralized, and delayered. The result is a far deeper, far more genuine, far more human connection to you than many sterile organizational personalities can offer.

What really stands out in the Organizational Family Tree of today's activism groups is how communications, connectivity, and cooperation with others are promoted through balanced structures of authority, accountability, and responsibility. The result is more positive energy, balanced power sources, the acceptance of resistors, and also the presence of organizational energy conductors—not just at the top of the structure, but latticed throughout the entire organization. Such a place can't help but feel good. It makes waking up in the morning worthwhile.

This feeling we get is very unlike that found in many corporations and institutions, where, as the story of Robert in the next chapter shows, any resistance to the status quo, any shaking of the branches on the Organizational Family Tree, is a signal that the organization must do all in its power to eradicate such aberrant behavior.

10

TRUST: THE ESSENTIAL ORGANIZATIONAL NUTRIENT

I'd like you to meet two Organizational Family Tree resistor-conductors. Their names are Ted and a guy I'm calling Robert. Both men clearly identified an organizational sick system that, if not dealt with, threatened the health and lives of many people. But the remedies they applied to their decaying and dangerous Organizational Family Tree were dramatically different.

Robert took actions that got many others involved in a supportive manner; he publicly exposed a sick system, and in doing so he got chewed up by a well-oiled corporate meat grinder. Ted was equally committed to his attack on a sick system. But his tactics, although fueled by human emotions similar to Robert's, were hugely different—and today Ted is in jail for murder.

When an Organizational Family Tree is in decay, when it's showing signs of corporate personality disorder, when we're feeling fearful or threatened by its behavior, we have a natural tendency to protect ourselves and to fight back (either that or become depressed and withdraw). This reaction creates what I call an organizational *resistor-conductor*. Our protective, emotional brain instinctively *resists* what the organization is doing to us, while at the same time both our emotional and higher-level thinking brain wants to *conduct* new actions to deal with a nasty organizational personality. We don't just want to fight back and defend ourselves. We want creative, logical, positive solutions to prevent bad things from carrying on.

In many cases, the actions of resistor-conductors results in positive new system structures and organizational behavior, such as greater corporate social responsibility, improved accountability and communications, an addressing of vital emotional needs, and a greater meeting of reasonable expectations. But it's not always so rosy. In some cases resistor-conductors are in the minority because their perceptions of the world and their reaction to organizational behavior is discolored and confused by their own personality disorders, caused by a host of historical and developmental factors. In such cases, their actions serve to hinder positive change. In very rare cases, resistor-conductors who are in a personal meltdown may physically harm—or even kill—others.

After a murder spree in which he targeted corporate leaders over a period of ten years, Ted Kaczynski, otherwise known as the Unabomber, was captured by police in 1995. He was captured in his barebones mountain cabin chiefly because his brother identified his writing style and the themes appearing in a lengthily article published by the *New York Times*. That treatise, titled "Industrial Society and Its Future," came to be known as the Unabomber Manifesto.

"Industrial Society and its Future" is a startling example of one man's dramatic personal meltdown in the face of what he perceived as a colossal *organizational* meltdown within industrial society. Kaczynski, a Harvard PhD in physics, had this to say:

> The Industrial Revolution and its consequences have been a disaster for the human race. They have greatly increased the life-expectancy of those of us who live in "advanced" countries, but they have destabilized society, have made life unfulfilling, have subjected human beings to indignities, have led to widespread psychological suffering and have inflicted severe damage on the natural world....

There are plenty of coffee shop, cop-on-the-street, sociological, and psychological explanations of Kaczynski's view of industrial society, and in particular why he took the extreme actions he did. In his own words, Kaczynski claimed, "In order to get our message before the public with some chance of making a lasting impression, we've had to kill people." He was, of course, acting alone in his killings. Kaczynski's use of the plural "our" and "we" was not designed to confuse authorities, but rather his belief was that the views expressed in his manifesto were strongly held by many others. And in some ways he was right.

Organizational decay and corporate personality disorder can directly and dramatically impact us. Our reactions can range from suffering personal stress to joining a peaceful protest along with others. Reactions to sick systems also include violent actions, such as those by the groups Earth First! and the Animal Liberation Front. Other responses to badly behaving organizational personalities range from corporate shareholder revolts and consumer boycotts to the rare spawning of personalities like Ted Kaczynski.

But here's the cold, hard, absolute truth: unless organizations begin to seriously examine how their Organizational Family Tree is affecting the environment they're rooted in (including the emotional impact on those they touch), there will be more Ted Kaczynskis, and at the very least there will be countless more people like Robert the tree planter.

Robert is also an organizational resistor-conductor, but his tactics are a world apart from Ted Kaczynski's. His self-designed role is to act as a resistor to what he sees as corporate behavior that poses a threat to the health of thousands, while at the same time being a conductor of positive energy and power. In the process, Robert is generating significant attention through his news media appearances and attendance at public forums.

Robert has three intertwined dimensions to his life. He's a dedicated environmental activist. He's also a tree planter who works for giant corporations that contract him to replant the valuable forest they have stripped from thousands of acres of virgin land. For over nineteen years, Robert has hiked and climbed through mountainous and rough terrain far removed from city life, packing a bag full of Douglas fir and spruce seedlings, inserting them delicately into the ground to replace the ancient trees logged off by lumber and pulp and paper manufacturers. He's also an occasional cab driver.

Lately, many corporate executives have become *very* interested in Robert, because he's been generating news media stories over his concern that industrial fertilizers used by forest companies are destroying the health of tree planters, natural water systems, and the environment.

Corporate executives and their public relations managers are nervous types. They want to know whether Robert is a kook or whether he has credibility, which would make him a threat to the reputation of their shareholder-sensitive company. As Robert outlines his thoughts I watch his body language, notice his suspicious glances, and mark how he speaks quickly while lacing his comments with occasional bravado and self-aggrandizement. I observe a man defining his sense of self through environmental activism, which is anchored in his hope that he's truly making a positive difference.

In most cases of human behavior, *emotional* truth has a deeper impact than *logical* truth, and this is especially true with Robert. Like all of us, Robert reveals his deep fears not in his carefully constructed sentences but in the emotions that lie under the words, the emotions that churn away within his inner self.

He's afraid that his value as a human is marginalized, he's afraid for the future of the earth, and he's afraid of not being taken seriously. That's why he's brought his "resume" to show me—a rumpled map with dozens of little red sticky dots commemorating all the mountainsides, flatlands, and deep forests that have felt his footsteps and been healed by the new growth he's planted.

Fear isn't an emotion we like to wear on our sleeves. It is an amalgam of powerlessness and the unknown, and how many of us are willing to admit that we're weak and stupid? Not many, at least not in public. It is, after all, the weak and the stupid who are easy prey for the strong and cunning. It's a lot safer to let our logical mind hide away our emotional fears.

But then we have Robert. Unlike many of us, Robert isn't afraid of articulating his fear and his anger. He uses words and phrases that telegraph, through phonetic code, what his outrage is all about.

> I want my work to be recognized as being part and parcel of a holistically managed working forest. I hate being used as a pawn in the industrial, biotechnological, agro-forestry, Franken-fiber scheme. We're second-class citizens in the woods. Our achievements are not recognized. We are never asked for advice.
>
> There is no understanding by university-educated foresters of our situation. They are too interested in mathematical plot formulas. I want to be more than a clone, a slave in silviculture. Tree planters need to be a respected part of silviculture. No one listens to me.

No one listens to me. A seemingly throwaway line tacked on to the end of a well-articulated and expansive argument against the nature of how big corporations operate. Yet those few words speak volumes. *No one listens to me.* The desire to be heard by others, particularly those who directly influence our life, is the crux to our self-identity, our sense of empowerment, and our access to knowledge and understanding. We all need this connectivity to feel whole, to feel we have purpose, and Robert is no exception.

If *no one* hears our pleas, our reaching out with our unique articulation of thoughts and ideas, of perceptions and feelings, then we in turn see ourselves as a *nobody.* The nature of human existence is to define ourselves according to how others see us. Not to be *heard* is to not be *seen*, to be invisible, the result being a great hollow of personal diminishment and a loss of self-worth, accompanied by a sense of powerlessness and unknown—the two ingredients of human fear.

Robert points out that the average age of a tree planter on the West Coast is thirty-seven years, with most having more than ten years of experience planting trees. But, he says, "What happens to a tree planter after age fifty-five?" For the past several months, Robert has garnered media attention in both newspaper stories and on television, warning the public that their health is at risk because of the massive doses of chemical fertilizer being dumped onto freshly planted forestlands.

And then there is the immediate danger to tree planters, who have to handle the potent chemicals often without gloves or other protection and who are now presenting symptoms of ill health. Robert is making waves because he's imbued with emotional energy and with the knowledge of how to put that fear, anger, and energy into action. But the waves will soon be fewer in number and weaker in strength, because time and system structures are on the side of the big companies.

It will in fact be the actions of one large forest corporation in particular that will kill Robert's energy, destroying him with the kind of premeditation reserved for literal first-degree murder. But Robert's death will not be literal—it will be the death of his self-image and death of his hope.

To deenergize Robert, the forest company will use a combination of tactics common to many large organizations (including corporations and governments) that see a threat to their authority from empowered voters, employees, and citizens. These people, like you, have had it with badly behaving organizational personalities, and they want changes. But change is scary to many staid old inflexible organizations, and so, instead of adapting, they go on the attack, using what I call the "3-D Defense"—*deny, delay, and destroy.*

THE SECRET "3-D DEFENSE STRATEGY" OF CORPORATE PERSONALITY DISORDER

Human resistor-conductors have what I term *C.O.R.E. strengths*—commitment and credibility, organizational skills, resources, and experience. At first they are outraged by an organization's behavior and they're spurred to take action, but for that action to bear fruit requires a strong emotional commitment to the cause, often fear based. However, *commitment* alone is never enough.

Organizational skills are required to plan strategy and tactics, to communicate and connect to others, and to find allies. This in turn requires both *commitment* and *credibility*. But this too is not enough to achieve a goal. Fighting back, taking a stand, and creating advocacy action requires *resources*—including funding (but not necessarily), knowledge, skills and abilities, plus a critical mass of support that's gained through communications, connectivity, and cooperation. Finally, all the above rolls out much more smoothly if people are *experienced* in this kind of thing, meaning they've stood up to badly behaving organizations before, they've helped organize others take a stand, and they know first hand what can go right and wrong.

The fact that people need C.O.R.E. strengths to stand up to and respectfully challenge an organization's dysfunctional actions is not lost on those in positions of power within a corporation, especially those who feel defensive about their authority, accountability, and responsibility being questioned. And so they defend themselves and the organizational personality with the 3-D Defense. First, they **deny** there's a problem. ("What problem? No one else says there's a problem. In fact, lots of people support us. It must be just you. So go away!")

But an organization can stick its head in the sand for only so long. Pretty soon it figures out that angry, fearful people still want to kick its butt. So now it's time for the second scene in this 3-D horror movie. After a period of sustained criticism, the organization may finally admit that yes, indeed, there's a problem. But the finger of blame will rarely point toward the dysfunctional system structure or the leadership and management spawned by the organizational culture. Organizational accountability is as rare as teeth on a duck. Instead, the problem will be grudgingly admitted, blame won't be explicitly accepted, and instead the organization will do what all organizations do well—drag its heels with **delayed** promises of reform. ("We'll definitely look into your concerns. How about being part of a five-year fact-finding committee?")

But this second scene will soon become a well-known, boring rerun for those who are still mad as hell about bad organizational behavior. So now the organization quickly jumps to the final scene of the 3-D morality play. Public relations spin doctors and steel-eyed corporate lawyers will try to **destroy** critics' commitment and credibility, limit their access to resources, and undermine their faith in their past experience. Such was the case with Robert.

Robert was highly organized and committed to his cause. But sustained public attacks on his credibility by the big forest company quickly depleted his meager financial resources and ate away at his personal resourcefulness. Without resources, Robert's personal energy ebbed and his commitment eroded. Soon his organizational strengths were critically weakened. The forest company managed to extract a small squeaky cog from the giant machine works of its Organizational Family Tree. But its troubles were far from over. Robert was but one small symptom of a sick system in meltdown. The continuing dysfunctional behavior of the company resulted in it becoming as vulnerable as Robert. The company's system structure, based on a rigid adherence to historical and developmental factors and a corporate culture that no longer aligned to a changing external environment and new public expectations, made it weak and vulnerable to a less-than-friendly corporate takeover.

Today, Robert is still Robert. He still holds tightly to his values. But the company is no more. Following the takeover, its name has changed, its senior executives are gone, and its mechanistic approach to dealing with resistors and positive conductors has been replaced by an Organizational Family Tree with a far more collaborative and consultative approach to dealing with a world full of change and challenges.

CREATING NEW TRUST WITHIN A DECAYING ORGANIZATIONAL FAMILY TREE

Revitalizing an Organizational Family Tree requires a series of interventions, similar to the ones counselors perform when dealing with human personality disorder. During my training as a peer counselor, my professors underscored the need not only to look at the immediate actions creating trouble for the client but also to explore the traits the person was born with and to delve deeply into her developmental background, including her early family life.

It's the same when treating an organization suffering from corporate personality disorder. It's important to look at each and every influence within the Organizational Family Tree, including historical and developmental factors (culture), emotion and knowledge factors, and especially the components within the Triangle of Trust (climate). While communications is the conduit of organizational energy, *trust* is the power source. Without trust, most organizational actions would be empty, they would fail to connect, and they would fail to sustain themselves.

There are only two professions in the Western world that consistently have public trust levels in the 70th to 80th percentile—the medical profession (including physicians and nurses) and law enforcement (including the military). Although there are pockets of demographics and certain communities that don't agree with these trust levels, generally it's very tough for us to lessen our trust in medical professionals or police officers regardless of what scandals or crises may befall the groups (unless you're a jailed serial killer with a botched appendectomy).

Police officers can create highly public sensations and still enjoy high levels of confidence. For example, in Vancouver, Canada, a few years ago, police picked up what they thought were young troublemakers, drove them out to a dark municipal park, and lay a beating on them. Even following the event they enjoyed a two-thirds trust rating. Medical doctors can make front-page headlines for molesting patients in their care and for wildly botching operations, as they have in many American cities, yet maintain an overall trust level in the high eighties.

This unwavering general public trust in police officers and medical professionals (and to a large degree the military in the United States) is due to an unconscious emotional imperative burrowed deep within our primitive brain structure. Police officers, medical doctors, and the military are the only professions legally mandated by society to protect us from serious harm and death. The simple fact is, we *must* trust these professions. Every atavistic, primordial impulse we have demands that we be supervigilant against harm and extinction. Without deep trust in those professions, we would feel unbearable anxiety and fear. This is what happens when we read scary crime stories in our local newspaper. These stories massively exaggerate the presence of fearful crimes and in doing so lower our faith that the police will be there when we need them.

We can live—literally *live*—without our local coffee shop, our favorite shopping mall, and even our smiling banker. If they closed or reduced service, we might be inconvenienced, but we wouldn't feel physically at peril. We'd simply find one of the many alternatives and take our customer loyalty elsewhere. But a reduction in police services or medical care, as is happening in many cities due to budget cuts and personnel shortages, is quite another matter.

Without those services, we would feel exposed, fearful, and anxious. We'd feel we couldn't live without them, and we'd do whatever was necessary to replace their diminished care with an alternative. That's why throughout North America today there are more private security guards than police officers, as police departments scale back their services to the public, and why the outdated physician-centric model of health care is being replaced with a galaxy of nurse practitioners, naturopathic medicine, and other alternatives to keeping us alive and well. We need to feel safe, without fear, and we'll support most actions that promise to protect us and bring us stability and security.

KNORGANERGY: BLENDING HUMAN EMOTION WITH ORGANIZATIONAL KNOWLEDGE

Today, instead of designing organizational system structures based on discredited and deterministic mechanistic models of how things are *supposed* to work, many organizational systems are being designed through a healthy blending of knowledge and emotion needs. This results in positive energy being produced (which I call *knorganergy*). There are plenty of examples of knorganergy around you.

Knorganergy is behind the strong resurgence of the antiwar movement, the hundreds of thousands who gather to protest against corporate globalization, the major restructuring of corporate accountability systems, and the increasing use of holistic, organic models in business planning, where lessons from complexity science and chaos theory are being used to replace the old and discredited machine models of how things are supposed to work.

Knorganergy is also evident in current efforts to stem organized crime and terrorism, as law enforcement researchers and analysts use the holistic lessons of social network analysis to study how crime groups and individuals are interlinked in complex webs rather than isolated boxes.

Knorganergy is behind what management consultant and educator Ralph Stacey calls "shadow systems," those highly creative and productive organizational interactions that occur among employees who work outside of formal structures and rules. Knorganergy is also behind the major shareholder rebellions, where corporate boards are being held to higher standards of accountability, transparency, and responsibility.

A greater emphasis on meeting and balancing knowledge and emotion needs within the modern organization is causing another shift, one that is quite huge. People today are reassessing what the concept of *trust* means—that powerful, must-have ingredient in a healthy Organizational Family Tree.

Without trust, the Organizational Family Tree is a place of decay and suspicion, of isolated silos of existence, of misaligned energy. An organization without trust is deep in meltdown, with vivid examples of corporate personality disorder. The fact is, much of our definition and understanding of trust is made of quicksilver. We need to appreciate this powerful concept not from an Industrial Age perspective but from an organic, adaptive one.

Scholars, social science researchers, and the passengers on cross-town bus no. 348 have a variety of definitions of *trust*. For example, Roderick Kramer (1996) states, "First and foremost trust entails a perceived vulnerability or risk that is derived from individuals' uncertainty regarding the motives, intentions, and prospective actions of others on whom they depend." J. David Lewis and Andrew Weigert (1985) say trust is the "undertaking of a risky course of action on the confident expectation that all persons involved in the action will act competently and dutifully."

Bernard Barber (1983) sees trust as a set of "socially learned and socially confirmed expectations that people have of each other, of the organizations and institutions in which they live, and of the natural and moral social orders that set the fundamental understandings for their lives." Christina Garsten (2001) states, "Trust is a specific form of power … trust is a social process through which control is affected in the sense of rendering people and events relatively predictable … trust is something which is constructed for and by people in organizations, thereby producing some degree of predictability."

Adam Seligram (1992) offers a clear distinction between trust and confidence. He states, "Confidence … is predicated on knowledge of what will be. And this knowledge may in turn be based on the ability to impose sanctions.… Trust is something very different. Trust is needed when there is no basis for confidence, for example, when behavior cannot be predicted or when strangers are part of the interaction."

When we apply the notions and technical definitions of trust to leadership and to our expectations of institutions and organizations, we refine the above definitions even further. Why do we trust leaders? John Gabarro (1987) found that perceived integrity, motives, consistency, openness, discreteness, functional competence, interpersonal competence, and decision-making judgment contributed to trustworthiness between vice-presidents and presidents. John Butler (1991), on the other hand, found that perceived availability, competence, consistency, fairness, integrity, loyalty, openness, promise fulfillment, and receptivity influenced subordinates' perception of an authority's trustworthiness. Sounds good so far. But how many people in a position of power can you think of who meet those definitions? How about even half the list? (And while we're at it, how well do *you* measure up according to either of the lists above?)

Tom Tyler and Peter Degoey (1995) as well as Tyler and E. Allan Lind (1992) have conducted some of the most systematic research on trust factors. Tyler and his associates discovered several important trustworthiness attributions. The factors include status recognition, benevolence, neutrality, and the existence of a common bond. In short, those who are trusted the most are seen as fully fledged members of a group, are well intentioned and honest, and are fair and impartial in their decision making. That's quite the list, and not many in positions of power make the grade judging from public trust levels in major North American institutions.

For example, according to a Harris national public opinion poll in February of 2007, 10 percent of Americans had a *great deal* of trust in Congress; 12 percent had a great deal of trust in the news media; 13 percent had a great deal of trust in law firms; 15 percent had a great deal of trust in organized labor; 16 percent had a great deal of trust in major companies; and only 21 percent had a great deal of trust in the courts and justice system.

Large-scale or highly emotional trigger events tend to test our level of trust. Two major recent events in particular stand out—the terrorist attacks of September 11, 2001, and the financial scandals involving WorldCom, Enron, and even Martha Stewart.

Following the collapse of Enron and WorldCom, an *NBC News/Wall Street Journal* national public opinion survey conducted in mid-2000 showed that 61 percent of Americans believed that wrongdoing among chief executives of major businesses was "a widespread problem in which many business executives were taking advantage of a system that was failing." The financial collapse of U.S. bastions of commerce resulted not only in a loss of public trust in American corporate executives but in the U.S. president himself.

A *Newsweek* national survey in July 2002 showed that 49 percent of Americans thought President Bush "took advantage of the system for personal financial gain" when he bought and sold stock as an executive at Harken Energy Corporation, and 42 percent thought President Bush "is knowingly covering up information about his stock transactions that could be damaging to his reputation."

In the summer of 2002, Americans thought that big business had too much influence on the Bush administration, that most corporate executives were dishonest, and that big business was four times more a threat to the country than big labor (CNN/*USA Today*/Gallup poll, July 2002; *CBS News* national poll, July 2002). At an individual level, three-quarters of Americans said in a national survey that they had only some or very little confidence in large business corporations (*ABC News/Washington Post* national poll, June 2002).

The news media as a key institution has not fared much better. The Pew Research Center reported in July 2002 that 58 percent of Americans thought the news media "gets in the way" of society solving its problems, while 56 percent of survey respondents thought that news reports and stories were often inaccurate. By 2006, the picture had not gotten much brighter.

Joel Brockner (1994) and others found that trust matters the most to people when they think the outcome of a situation is going to be bad. The researchers suggested a simple, straightforward reason for this. When a situation looks positive or at least poses little chance of having a negative outcome, we tend to assume that leaders know what they're doing and that their actions have contributed to the good news. However, when things are going badly, or when people have severe misgivings about a positive outcome, trust becomes a far more critical issue and leaders may receive far less support.

I saw examples of the above in two private research studies that I conducted for a client in 2005. The first involved residents of five adjoining Canadian cities who were asked to rate their trust in local police as well as indicate their perception of local crime rates. The second study was my analysis of national surveys of American's confidence in their military after a prolonged involvement in Iraq.

The study of police in a five-city region found a direct correlation between the levels of trust/confidence people had in their local police force and their perception of local crime rates. For example, in cities where people thought crime rates had increased dramatically, the level of public trust/confidence in police dropped significantly. However where crime rates were seen as having increased marginally, trust/confidence in police remained at previously high levels.

Desiring a more expansive example of the link between trust, fear, and confidence in institutions, I reviewed public opinion research related to (1) the terrorist attacks on September 11, 2001, and (2) American's confidence in their military during the peak involvement in Iraq. My review of forty-eight U.S. national public opinion polls, conducted by a variety of agencies in the year after the 9/11 attacks, uncovered a direct correlation between a relatively low level of personal fear related to terrorism and a high level of trust in government agencies designed to protect the public.

According to national surveys conducted on the day of the attack and in the following three days, the majority of Americans did not personally fear becoming a victim of a terrorist attack. On the actual day of the attack on the Word Trade Center, just under half of all adult Americans (43 percent) were personally fearful of being a victim of terrorism, a figure that had dropped to 37 percent by December 2001. By August 2002, the percentage of Americans personally afraid of being a victim of terrorism had dropped to 25 percent.

My research showed that the key reason Americans did not personally fear terrorism, although they had concerns about *other* Americans' safety, was that they trusted their military and other law-enforcement agencies—and not politicians—to protect them. For example, trust in the U.S. military to protect citizens from a terrorist attack reached 74 percent on September 11, 2001, remained relatively steady at 72 percent by March 2002, and only dropped to 60 percent in August 2002. This high level of trust wasn't because Americans didn't think there would be another terrorist attack on U.S. soil. In fact, from September 11, 2001, to September 11, 2002, the national sense that another attack was imminent never dropped below 62 percent.

On the other hand, my analysis of national public opinion related to confidence in the U.S. military and public attitudes toward the war in Iraq showed a different result. It showed that continuing American military presence in a war zone that most Americans had deep misgivings about was depleting the military of its bank account of goodwill.

In January 2002 a national Harris Poll showed 71 percent of Americans had a great deal of confidence in their military. This was shortly after the terrorist attacks of 9/11. Americans *needed* to trust the military to protect them from their fears of terrorism, and this was reflected in the high confidence levels. But by 2006, there was little fear of terrorism in the United States, plenty of concern about the affordability of health care, and a growing disenchantment with President George Bush's commitment to a military presence in Iraq.

In March 2006 a *CBS News* public opinion poll showed 20 percent of all Americans thought the war in Iraq was the most important problem facing their country—topping their list of concerns—while terrorism was cited as a concern by only 6 percent of those surveyed across the country. Meanwhile, a Harris Poll at about the same time showed that only 47 percent of Americans now had a great deal of confidence in the military.

The lessons from the above research studies are clear. Trust is a mercurial element. It's absolutely necessary for us to have trust in order to feel safe and secure, to believe that stable boundaries are there to defend us from the unpredictable, and that our fears brought on by a sense of powerlessness linked to the unknown will be mitigated by forces that promise power and knowledge. But when we're no longer afraid, when our fears have been abated, our need for blind trust is also extinguished. And when we see organizations and institutions behaving in ways contrary to our own values, when we see them no longer curbing our fears but instead building new anxiety and anger in us, our trust quickly evaporates.

THE MIRAGE OF ORGANIZATIONAL TRUST

My research on public trust and fear levels shows that we *need* to trust those institutions mandated by society to protect us. The more we trust such institutions, the less we fear those things that can hurt or kill us, such as war, terrorists, and vicious criminals. The less fearful we are and the more we trust institutions to protect us, the more compliant we are with system structures and the less chance there is for ignored fears to bubble into outrage and organized demands for action from institutions. But what if our concept of trust is but a house of cards? What if the notions we associate with trust, based in large part on a mechanistic, deterministic, cause-and-effect mindset from the Industrial Revolution are impossible to sustain? What if it's all a big lie?

In the various academic definitions of trust shared above, a common overarching theme emerges. Trust is collectively seen as a construct that brings predictability to uncertain situations, it exists when there's ample evidence of consistency, and it's based on promise fulfillment. Trust, at its core, is the guarantee of stability in our lives. It's another way of preserving the status quo and of taking away your fears. But the problem with this concept of trust is that it leads us to believe that the inevitable is also predictable. Unfortunately for trust, there is *nothing* completely predictable in our lives except death.

In organizational life, we often confuse inevitability with predictability and in so doing undermine trust. For example, crisis is inevitable—it is just a matter of time. Change is inevitable—it is just a matter of direction and speed. Inevitability means future actions *will* take place and changes *will* occur. However, as leaders, managers, and employees, we don't take kindly to change. We want the inevitable to be predictable so we can feel safe and secure and comforted by what we know. Even better, we want the inevitable to be not just predictable but also *controllable*, and it is from these demands for self-preservation that we design our neat, hermetically sealed definition of trust.

The reality is that there's a huge problem, a disturbing black fly in this ointment of trust, this supposedly soothing salve of organizational salvation whose ingredients were first mixed during the Industrial Revolution. The vexing problem with current definitions of trust is exposed by chaos theory, that close cousin of our friend complexity science. What the mathematically based science of chaos theory reveals through wondrous formulas is that the inevitable is not easily—if at all—predictable. Meteorologist Edward Lorenz first discovered this in 1960 during his attempts to use computer simulations of short- and long-term weather patterns. His simple tweaking of a mathematical formula, adjusting it by only the tiniest of degrees, produced dramatically different outcomes.

Lorenz's findings served as the bedrock to one of chaos theory's principal foundations, *sensitive dependence on initial conditions*, which means that small things can result in huge, unpredictable changes. This notion is popularly knows as *the butterfly effect*, based on the title of a paper by Lorenz (1972) in which he asks, "Does the flap of a butterfly's wings in Brazil set off a tornado in Texas?" The answer is, "Maybe yes, maybe no—it all depends on how a multitude of factors interact with each other." Now you might be thinking, "What's this got to do with my dealing with nasty organizational personalities hanging from decaying limbs on the Organizational Family Tree?"

One of the big downsides to living on a branch of a decaying, inflexible Organizational Family Tree firmly rooted to the past is that thinking ahead almost always means thinking backwards. It means unquestioningly accepting that what happened before will exactly happen again. But now, through the lens of complexity science and chaos theory, we can clearly see that this straight-line, nothing-ever-changes way of thinking is wonky. Things *do* change and events are impossible to perfectly predict. This means making plans about the future behavior of an organization is best done in a big, porous box of thought with plenty of elbow room for creativity and jumping around—not in a tight, tiny box of carved-in-stone certainty.

The phrase "sensitive dependence on initial conditions" (from chaos theory) means that big actions don't necessary result in big results. A good example of this foundational principle of chaos theory is multimillion-dollar marketing campaigns that have backfired. (Are you still drinking New Coke? Did you ever?)

Conversely, there are also many examples of seemingly small actions resulting in huge differences. For example, the civil rights movement got a major boost in December 1955 when Rosa Parks, a black woman, refused to sit in a designated seat on an Alabama bus and instead sat down in a "whites only" seat. The small fine she was levied was the kick-start to massive protest actions, the intervention of then little-known Martin Luther King, and the spread of civil rights marches throughout America. Later on I'll share other examples of when organizations have encouraged a few small positive steps to occur and then watched them multiply into a succession of interconnected actions. But before we go there, let's talk about conflict.

CONFLICT AS A VITAL ENERGY SOURCE IN ORGANIZATIONAL GROWTH AND CHANGE

Conflict surfaces every day and in every facet of our lives. Conflict is a disturbance to the status quo—to our sense of equilibrium. Conflict invariably results during change, and it's been proven over and over again that without conflict, without a rocking of the boat, positive change rarely occurs. But change can make us nervous. We like things to be predictable. We want to control the events in our lives. We want certainty. We've been taught that control and containment are essential to our lives. Indeed we base our notion of *trust* on our expectation that there will be control and containment—a no-surprises existence. But this solid definition of trust is the fly in the ointment.

The trouble with conflict and our definition of trust is that conflict is not completely—if at all—predictable. It can pop up here and there, and while it's often around in one form or another, we never know for sure what form it's going to take. And then, when conflict occurs, it's often difficult to manage, which makes our definition of trust a tough one to live up to. What happens next? Well, if we're living in a small-box machine metaphor of how life *should* unfold, we'll get very anxious and fearful when trust invariably starts to evaporate. So, what to do? We can start by sprouting some wings of thoughtful reflection, flying up to the ten-mile-high vantage point, and then take a cool, calm new look at the notions of change and conflict.

Looking down from up high, it's easy to see that we've defined trust too narrowly. The box is so tight that it's suffocating and keeping the Organizational Family Tree from sprouting out in a healthy evolutionary manner.

If the definition of trust today is based on our expectation that others will bring us control, certainty, and predictability, then how can trust *ever* be totally attained in a mercurial world where predictability over most organizational environments is an illusory ideal?

Once again we come to that pesky fly in the ointment. The problem is that much of our current expectation regarding trust is rooted in the Industrial Age concept of organizational life, in which events are *supposed* to unfold in a neat, linear, cause-and-effect manner. But the reality is that organizational life, like all living existence, is far from linear, far from predictable, and far more organic than mechanistic in behavior.

Our current expectations regarding trust can't possibly be met in the fluid, ebb-and-flow human and organizational environments we create and exist in. Such expectations merely create multiple points of anxiety and a feeling that we've been let down—or are letting others down. What's the answer? It's time to create a bigger box of thinking about trust. It's time for us to review and reconsider our expectations and to adapt our definition of trust to the realities of an ever-changing world. We're going to do this by shifting your mindset. We're going to reframe trust and see this important concept not from a mechanistic, nuts-and-bolts perspective but from a natural, organic, and evolutionary viewpoint. Basically, we're going to consider conflict, change, and the meaning of trust in the context of how natural systems have managed to fare throughout existence.

REPLACING MECHANICAL THINKING WITH EARTHY, NATURAL FEELINGS

Over time, natural systems survived and evolved based on their ability to recognize threats and to decide whether to fight, freeze, or flee. This process was made possible through rapid systems of internal and external communications, connectivity, and cooperation. When we take the ten-mile-high view of evolution, it becomes obvious that many species on this planet have very successfully adapted to their environment while others are still struggling.

For example, sharks have been around for over 250 million years, adapting to their environment with precision, while we humans, around for only 40,000 years, have basically been changing (or trying to change) our environment to meet our selfish human needs. When we look at the success-failure rate of our respective actions, the PowerPoint and Excel spreadsheets show a dismal record of human survival versus shark entrepreneurship. It's pretty obvious that we can learn more from natural, biologic systems than nuts and bolts, mechanistic management systems.

Mechanistic organizational thinking promises to bring us (and especially those heading up corporations, organizations, and institutions) comfort, control, and certainty, and to protect us from our subconscious fear of death—clinical death, death of self-image, and death of hope. In the blink of an eye, humans—with a lot of help from religious and industrial system structures—became fixated on the fact that we're surrounded by scary unpredictability. And so, detailed, box-like organizational systems were designed to act as a nice, safe, and warm security blanket.

Mechanistic, status quo-seeking approaches to keep the Organizational Family Tree straight, neat, and controlled show up in all manner of corporate systems and planning models. But regardless of what flavor-of-the-year system structure is being used, underneath it all is one basic management mantra: "control and certainty, control and certainty, control and certainty."

An organic system, by contrast, is based on adaptability and openness. To some people (especially managers), this notion sounds like something from some hippy-dippy place of peace and love, not the practical position of profits, bottom lines, and "stretch targets." Adapting and self-organizing and sharing authority and power can be pretty scary stuff to mechanistic, linear thinkers. But without this mindset, those folks might as well join the other dinosaurs sipping martinis at the Men-Only Club, wondering what went wrong.

LIVING, BREATHING, AND EVOLVING ORGANIZATIONAL FAMILY TREES

The organic model of system structure recognizes that crises or conflicting demands are inevitable and a natural part of evolution. Long-term predictability is impossible. General boundaries of authority, accountability, and responsibility are important, but tight prescriptions for behavior and actions are not. The organic model recognizes there must be opportunities for thinking on the spot *by those who are on the spot*, for a Plan "B" when necessary (or a Plan "C" or "D"), or for no precise plan at all but instead a set of general outcomes, employees with the freedom to experiment, and a flexibility to adapt and change course if necessary.

A key characteristic of organic, bigger-box thinking is that strength comes from networks—from communications, connectivity, and cooperation among many different interconnected agents in a system and in overlapping systems. Life is an energy-pulsating network where power ebbs and flows—not a neat, inert stack of perfectly aligned small boxes forever locked in the status quo.

Within the climate of a healthy Organizational Family Tree, the power and purpose of key components may constantly change. Who was strong yesterday could be weak today. Who was on the fringe of a network last month could be at the center today. The more things change, *the more they change*. In a networked environment, with continual ebbing and flowing of constituent parts, adaptation is a constant process. If it isn't, extinction occurs. In a healthy Organizational Family Tree there's no lasting and perfectly predictable equilibrium or status quo in the pattern of how things flow and the results they produce.

But there's no perfect system to deal with the perfect storm. A hospital emergency room admitting heart attack patients or a police S.W.A.T. unit deploying to deal with gunfire from drug dealers on a city street is no place for mind-maps and public opinion surveys. Decisions have to be made rapidly and through a single-point command structure. On the other hand, ongoing organizational life with continually changing environments and routine structures benefits from thoughtful planning, an awareness of social, political, economic, and technological trends, as well as teamwork and networks of collaboration. But it's not about separating these two approaches—it's about uniting them.

In both crisis-driven and longer term, strategically focused organizational systems, clear authority, responsibility, and accountability must be tied together through a framework of communications, connectivity, and cooperation among people. It's important to ensure that the urgency of the *here and now* is linked to the less immediate *then and there* of organizational actions. The two worlds must not only coexist but also collaborate and learn from each other. Circumstances may require different approaches to communications, connectivity, and cooperation, but they need to overlap through a coordinated system of authority, accountability, and responsibility. How do we link *here and now* actions to down-the-road *then and there* realities? Here's where we return to the importance and meaning of trust.

Trust in a healthy, networked organization is not about demanding precise predictability, never-changing consistency, total stability, and the status quo from others. Trust within the thriving, adaptable Organizational Family Tree needs room to stretch, to be flexible, and to jump up and down—but still within the clear, safe boundaries of a bigger box.

To this end, trust benefits from being adaptive rather than prescriptive. Instead of demanding predictability, consistency, and stability, trust should instead be comprised of openness, availability, fairness, shared values, and integrity among individuals. And like in the Triangle of Trust, these traits should be created and shared through ongoing communications, connectivity between individuals, and cooperation.

To expect ourselves and others never to change our behavior, to maintain high levels of competency, and to preserve us from the fears of changing circumstances is asking too much in a world of constant change and conflict. It's unreasonable to demand that our politicians, corporate executives and other leaders, and our colleagues in the next cubicle—as well as ourselves—provide us calm waters and sunny days at all times. It's too much to expect from them, and it's too much for others to expect from us. To create such expectations of trust is to guarantee its demise.

So how about this? Rather than seeking absolute certainty, let's design trust around our need to be adaptable, to be collaborative, and to apportion authority, accountability, and responsibility in a manner that enhances the flow of organizational energy rather than restricts it.

All action in life is a combination of emotion and knowledge. *Trusted* organizational action emerges when we skillfully combine our technical knowledge with our emotional energy, creating that powerful amalgam I call knorganergy. Action is a constant in our life, whether it's writing yet another report, taking our kids to their soccer game, joining an activist group upset with the chopping down of trees on our street, the beating of our heart, or the constant firing of our brain's neural connections.

Many of us, frozen by the vicissitudes of our daily challenges, too often gravitate to what we believe are tried and true remedies from the past. We believe yesterday's solutions can be easily transposed onto today challenges, forgetting Albert Einstein's dictum that we cannot solve today's problems with the same kind of thinking used to create them. In addition, it's so easy to automatically dismiss new ideas as old, saying, "We tried that ten years ago and it failed," forgetting that yesterday is not today. As the Greek philosopher Heraclitus said in the sixth century B.C., "You can never step into the same river twice."

11

CREATING A HEALTHY ORGANIZATIONAL PERSONALITY

Imagine living in a world so consumed with paranoia and anger that we're afraid of saying, "I'm sorry" to someone we've offended or hurt because our simple heartfelt apology could land us in jail or result in a giant court-imposed fine. This is not some Kafkaesque fantasy but the reality we're living in today—unless you happen to be living in California, Australia, or the Canadian province of British Columbia.

In March 2006, the provincial government of British Columbia was the first jurisdiction in Canada to pass a law—the Apology Act—saying it was okay for organizations to say "sorry" to people they had aggrieved without fear of legal liability. The law is similar to one in California and another in Australia.

The mind boggles that organizational system structures in North America have reached such a state that it takes official, protective legislation to be proclaimed before a company can say, "I'm sorry." However, it's also understandable. Organizational meltdown and corporate personality disorder have become so pervasive throughout Western society that an outraged public is prepared to use every weapon at its disposal to fight back against dysfunctional corporations and institutions.

Like the character Howard Beale in the movie *Network*, many people are ready to shout, "I'm mad as hell and I'm not going to take it any more!" Angry voters, customers, shareholders, and employees are taking direct action instead of curling up in a corner. The sought-after damages in class-action lawsuits brought on by disgruntled consumers and investors now totals billions of dollars a year. And while some governments have made it easier for corporations to say they're sorry, others are making it harder for them to get away with murder.

In Britain, the physical harm caused by corporations ignited both labor union and public demands for redress, resulting in the *Corporate Manslaughter Bill*

193

being drafted in 2004. As the preamble to the proposed law stated, the bill "will make it easier for companies who have shown little or no regard for safety of their workers or members of the public to be prosecuted for a specific and serious criminal offence." But in many cases of corporate personality disorder, saying "sorry" is just not good enough.

While giving corporations the legal protection to offer an apology may help convince them of the merit of such a simple act, and while hearing an apology from a giant company or institution may redress some wrongs, an apology is not likely to stop bad behavior emanating from corporate personality disorder. Just ask the Center for Corporate Policy in Washington, D.C. It reports that, "corporate crime causes far greater damage than violent street crimes each year."

To support its claim, the group cites Federal Bureau of Investigation statistics, stating that in 2001, "the nation's total loss from robbery, burglary, larceny-theft and motor vehicle theft was $17.2 billion—less than a third of what Enron alone cost investors, pensioners and employees that year."

The ability to say "sorry" with legal impunity is not very likely to change organizational behavior whose actions are deeply rooted in the past. Bad behavior by corporations and institutions, just like bad behavior by individuals, won't stop until the root causes of such behavior are recognized and addressed. Regenerating the Organizational Family Tree—building meaningful levels of trust—requires not a simple tinkering with overt actions, not a weekend workshop on leadership, but an examination of the whole system of affective factors—an examination that requires a mindset quite different from the thinking that created problems within the network in the first place.

By taking the first step—by acknowledging we're not destined to be trapped in what the sociologist Max Weber called the "iron cage of certainty," by having the power to say the enormous but simple word "no" to dysfunctional organizational circumstances, we're one huge step closer to saying "yes" to building healthy organizational systems of living and working together. This first frightening, tentative step in looking at our life through a new lens of existence, if even for a moment, is huge.

HEALING SICK SYSTEMS WITH NATURAL SCIENCE

We now know that the problem with most badly behaving organizations is an inability to break free from past negative influences—chiefly mechanistic management models that treat personnel like cogs on a wheel. What's needed is a healthy alternative to the machine metaphor of organizational life—something based on natural, adaptive systems. Luckily for us there is such an alternative, and it works.

The study of *complex adaptive systems* (a.k.a., complexity science), like those found in trees, plants, and other biological systems in nature, teaches us there's no absolute control over many events in society, organizations, and corporate life. In fact, some big thinkers in complexity science say that a dash of human anxiety, as long as it's served within safe boundaries, is essential for creativity to spawn and for a system to emerge into something new and positive.

For example, Brenda Zimmerman at McGill University maintains that the emergence of positive energy and creativity happens when information flows freely and openly and when people can respectfully question organizational behavior. She and other complexity science adherents, such as Ralph Stacey, call this fertile area the *edge of chaos*—the area between a system being at rest and in total chaos. As Zimmerman says in her 1998 book, *Edgeware* (together with Curt Lindberg and Paul Plsek),

> In human organizations, the creative destruction phase may require dismantling systems and structures that have become too rigid, have too little variety and are not responsive to the current needs of the community.... This can be a very disturbing, unsettling time for organizations as assumptions need to be exposed and re-examined in light of changing needs and environments.

Unfortunately, many organizations are still stuck in an Industrial Age mindset, convinced that *management* is about preserving the status quo, rigidly controlling outcomes, and designing business plans with carved-in-stone predictability. But a *healthy* Organizational Family Tree is a place of constant change, of unpredictable tides of turbulence, and a bubbling brew of human emotion and knowledge. This is the stuff of creativity, of adaptability, and of growth. But it's also the stuff that can freak us out if we're still stuck in small-box thinking.

In reality, we have limited control over our organization's environment and how it responds to its environment. We'll never know everything, we'll never always be right, and we can't stop an avalanche by standing in its path. General Colin Powell (1996) once said that he made major decisions if there was enough information in hand to give him a 40 to 70 percent probability of success. Ralph Stacey (1995) uses the 30 percent rule, saying managers have only 30 percent control over the activities they're responsible for.

Those few who, because of fear of change, try to prevent their organization from being in tune with natural forces affecting its growth and development are the same folks who plop a big rock into a fast-moving stream thinking they're going to stop the flow. The water simply goes around, under, or over the rock and finds its own path. It's the same with the turbulent natural forces affecting the organizational environment. By using the big rocks of command-and-control structures, linear thinking, and precise prediction and management of events, those making such small-box decisions not only block the natural flow of energy and growth within the Organizational Family Tree, but they're forcing the growth of a parallel structure hidden in the shadows.

Stacey calls the type of under-the-radar parallel process described above a "shadow system." In Stacey's terms, organizations can have both a legitimate system with official rules of conduct, behavior, and reporting relationships and an *unofficial* system of behavior that encourages creativity to achieve aims. While I suggest that *all* organizations have a shadow system, I also think there's a wide range of depth to those shadows. They can be light or dark or somewhere in between.

It's easy to see how nature-based complexity science is a direct challenge to the linear-thinking machine metaphor used by leaders and managers in many organizations, including government departments and corporations. In a mechanistic, rigid Organizational Family Tree, managers and leaders (and many others) feel safe and secure. They feel this way because no matter how unsound their thinking is, subordinates never dare to challenge their authority, knowledge, and decision making. The title on their door is what counts, and their accountability is measured not by meaningful outcomes but by numerically neat and tidy outputs that fit into predesigned, predictive performance measurements. But such rigid Organizational Family Trees that can't bend with the winds of change are not destined to be around for long.

In working with and for dozens of private-and public-sector organizations over the past thirty-five years, I've learned that there are no 100 percent replicable "best practices," no one-size-fits-all systems, and no magic management solutions. The healthy Organizational Family Tree is alive with human energy. It's constantly swaying and moving. It's inhaling and exhaling. It has both chaos and calm. In such places of growth and adaptability, thoughtful leaders and managers are often situational—they take what measures are necessary to deal with the pressures of the moment but at the same time remain true to a few overarching, guiding principles. But this too can be tricky, particularly if the overarching, guiding principles are out of synch with what the majority of others believe is right and true. Let me share a few stories to illustrate my point.

STORIES FROM THE SHADOWS OF ORGANIZATIONAL LIFE

On December 4, 1999, Dr. Jorge Denegri, citing "unsafe, unsanitary and unsuitable for patient care" conditions at Vancouver Hospital and Health Sciences Centre, announced he was resigning as president of the hospital's medical staff. He said his resignation came after years of quietly battling the various administrative and political powers that ran the Canadian province of British Columbia's major trauma center.

A week later, on December 11, 1999, Dr. David Harrison, faced with an overflowing emergency ward at Vancouver Hospital, "started working outside of the box," as he described to reporters. With the assistance of nurses and other staff, he started an unorthodox system of emergency treatment that served to alleviate pain and suffering among numerous patients backed up in the hallways.

A couple of days later, on December 13, 1999, in the city of Victoria, Canada, Dr. Bill Cavers and Dr. Dave Doty called the news media to report a significant event. Cavers was head of the medical organization representing all general practitioners in the province, while Doty was president of the parallel organization representing all surgeons and specialists.

The two doctors said local physicians had unanimously voted not to release patients before they were absolutely ready to be released from hospital, contrary to the pressures being put on them by administrators. They also encouraged the public to contact their government representatives if they were unhappy with the health care system. Doty told reporters,

> I've been in Victoria for 15 years now and this is the most militant I have ever seen the physicians here. I think they have just had enough…. They have reached the final point where they are just going to put their hands up and say, "Look, I am not going to make any more excuses for you. If you want to make excuses, you have to do it directly to the patients."

The comments by physicians Denegri, Harrison, Doty, and Cavers created a news media frenzy, because what they said and did was out of the ordinary and unexpected (full of action, conflict, and emotion—the definition of news). Their comments created a stir especially among those who assumed that the management of a health care system should just hum along in a nice, neat, controllable fashion.

But thing were definitely *not* in control. Normally stoical and reserved medical doctors were breaking rules. They were zigging and zagging rather than obeying bureaucratic conventions and walking a straight line. They were exposing how things *really* worked, regrouping their thoughts, and then moving in an entirely unpredictable direction. What on Earth was going on? To outsiders, there was definitely a major storm threatening this particular forest of Organizational Family Trees.

To some, the news reports of a *crisis* in health care in the province of British Columbia painted a chaotic picture. Just who were these trembling souls? Well, they were easy to spot, because they all lived in a very small box of organizational thought. Inside this tight-thinking little box was a carved-in-stone view that events should have well-defined predictability; that there is a consistent cause and effect; and that past actions are clear and exact indicators of future actions. This deviation from the cozy perception of how things were *supposed* to be had a scary and unsettling effect. People felt their boat of reality being crushed by a giant wave.

People were scared out of their wits over what appeared to be a crisis in health care because their perception of how organizational systems *should* operate was trapped in a very small box of mechanistic logic. If things weren't predictable, stable, and rooted in the way things always were, then—well—the alternative was chaos, powerlessness, uncertainly, and big-time fear.

But here's the thing: What if their perception of how a health care system (or any organizational system) should operate hadn't been trapped in such small-box thinking? What if their—what if *our*—perception of an organizational system came from a *big* box, where there was plenty of elbowroom to move around and do organizational-thinking back-flips? What if in this bigger box it was *normal* to see a great deal of change, shifting directions, and unpredictability? How would our behavior, expectations, and relationship with our organization be affected? Would our actions in this realigned bigger-box reality be significantly different than in the smaller-box rigid view? The evidence says yes, and it's found in a theory of psychology called cognitive restructuring therapy (CRT), which is often used in the counseling of individuals.

Founded in part by Rian McMullen, cognitive restructuring therapy essentially says it's possible for us to change our beliefs, to reframe our perceptions and see the world more clearly, and to exchange negative outlooks with positive ones that enhance our life and give us more control. Usually CRT is used with clients in a counseling setting, where they're provided skills to look at their lives through a different lens—to *reframe* their world in a far more optimistic perspective. (We'll talk about "frames" a lot more later.)

The principles of CRT can help us deal with corporate personality disorder. Remember, many of us are fearful of organizational change because we've been *conditioned* to fear such change. We've been taught and told in mechanistic-model management studies, by employers, and by an army of organizational development consultants that tight control is essential, that "if it can't be measured it can't be managed," and that precise predictability is possible. This form of thinking pretty well sums up what creates corporate personality disorder. Can we change this reality by reframing how we see the modern organization? I think that it's possible, but it takes a lot of work, and first we need to understand our own reality.

We must understand that there's nothing wrong with wanting control—it's just *how much* and *what kind* of control that matters. Harvard psychologist Daniel Gilbert in his highly entertaining and informative book *Stumbling on Happiness* (2006) points out that humans are the only species with the ability to imagine future scenarios, but in so doing we also desperately need to *do something* about all the things we imagine. As he says, knowledge is power and "our brains want to control the experiences we are about to have." The problem is, as many others point out and as we know from our own experience, expectations of just how much control we have is very much blown out of proportion. Despite the mechanistic models of management taught to sponge-like MBA students, control is made of quicksilver—just as soon as we think we have some, it shape-shifts into something else.

One more important thing to consider: as we prepare to deal with badly behaving organizations and actually take steps to reenergize the Organizational Family Tree, many of the conflicts we will encounter within our organizational life will involve not so much our *doing* but our *seeing*. We run into problems because we allow Industrial Age thinking to superimpose its management reality upon our own natural instincts and in the process displace our sense of self and our inner core of worth.

This not-so-little matter of our personal perception, how we see ourselves, is critical for our emotional and physical well-being within the Organizational Family Tree. In a *complex adaptive system*, the way nature puts *its* systems together, there are frequent periods of turbulence or conflict that trigger communications among all the various parts in the system, leading to new connections and cooperation among the parts, which in turn leads to a period of self-organization and the emergence of new activity or growth. This natural, recurring pattern fosters evolution and has a track record stretching over three billion years—not bad when we consider the average corporation is lucky to live to the ripe old age of fifty.

In a mechanistic system of organizational life, one of the biggest problems is overcoming our programmed notion of how things work. There are times when our natural instinct, our gut feel, tells us that an organizational decision or course of action is just plain wrong. But too often this natural alarm bell is silenced by what we have been taught to believe is right.

When you come to that moment, ask this question: "Just who says organizational life is supposed to be this way (your boss, that $500-an-hour MBA consultant, your teacher from the fifth grade)?" As events and actions swirl about us and impact our state of being, just *what and whose* perception of reality is really being addressed? Often we're asked to believe that there's one constant and stable reality in organizational life, a happy and achievable one-size-fits-all status quo. But what if there are *multiple* realities based on *multiple* perceptions and consequently a lot of natural instability, inconsistency, pegs not fitting into holes, and a constant challenging of assumptions?

The fact is, that's *exactly* how organizational life is. The way we think about the organizational personality and its actions will never be exactly the way George or Alma down the hall, Judy at the counter, or the boss thinks about it. This may seem like a "no-brainer," but neuroscientists and psychologists tell us there's no single reality and that each of us perceives an event, action, or issue in a unique manner.

We absorb what we think is critical to our survival and interpret that information according to our past experiences, the composition of which changes as time passes. That's why witnesses to crime are notoriously inaccurate when recounting the event later. Hindsight is not 20/20 at all—our hindsight is full of blind spots. We communicate with others through both body and verbal language, with the vast majority being body language that we can't see or control.

Even how we physically see ourselves is a big lie. Our physical image of ourselves is for the most part based on a mirror's reflection (unless you have out-of-body experiences), but what we see in the mirror image is the exact opposite of how others see us. That's why we're often shocked or perhaps mildly puzzled by our image on video or in photos. The camera reports back how others see us, not how we see ourselves. We go through the day and through our life convinced that our nose turns slightly to the left when in fact it turns slightly to the right, that our right eye is bigger than the left when it's actually the other way around, and so on.

Just as our mirror image presents us with an opposing view of reality, our brain takes from our immediate environment only the reality it believes is necessary for our survival and disregards the rest. As the psychologist Robert Ornstein (1991) writes, "The neural underpinnings of the mind evolved in part to select only that which is of use to survival. Consequently, the mind tends not to care too much about frills that modern, well-educated human beings are trained to think important, such as self-understanding and accurate perception."

When I was slaving away on my doctorate at the Fielding Graduate University in Southern California, I was fortunate to have many tremendous professors, some of whom I still count among my friends. I'll never forget an elderly professor in systems theory whose thinking was far from the traditional mechanistic manner that many scholars rely on when explaining how organizations function. Will McWhinney had developed what he called the four dimensions of reality: unitary reality, sensory reality, mythic reality, and social reality. It's useful to think of these when considering what to do about that organizational personality in our midst.

According to McWhinney, sensory reality is based on what our senses tell us and is "the reality of the practical person, of science and commerce." Social reality is a humanistic view of mankind and centers on the feelings and values people have. Unitary reality is monistic and deterministic. This is the world of true believers, of ritual, sacred art and architecture, and of "the machinations of bureaucratic regulations." Finally, mythic reality "combines belief in free will with a monistic concept of the universe."

Although McWhinney makes it clear that no one person ever operates entirely out of one reality, he points out that "conflict and thus issues are founded in differences. The differences in belief ... are fundamental. There are no grounds on which we can resolve these differences."

Like sociologist Terrell Northrup, who makes a strong case that we'll do anything to protect our sense of self—our self-image, McWhinney states that "our beliefs are very important to our security." He adds, "Conflict, the processes of change, and beliefs about reality are deeply intertwined." This means that you, being unique in your perceptions, have a unique, personal view of what the organizational personality is doing to you through its behavior.

Our perception is chiefly based on what we have led ourselves to *believe* will happen. There's no cookie-cutter formula for organizational change or management, because you are not a cookie. And your very human, very emotion based, very unique beliefs are key to how you see the world and how change affects you. As Carl Sorensen from Stanford University says in a quote cited in Mark Youngblood and John Renesch's *Life at the Edge of Chaos* (1997), "There's an old expression, 'Seeing is believing.' But it's more accurate to say that 'Believing is seeing.' That is, you tend to see what you believe you're going to see. You bring to a situation what you expect you are going to experience."

So what's this got to do with how we deal with a badly behaving organizational personality? Everything. For starters, there's no such thing as a *real* reality. The organizational behavior that's impacting us is what we *believe* should be happening. "Believe based on what?" you might ask.

How many of us see an organization today, what we expect from it, is what we've been taught to see and expect. In large part, our perceptions and expectations have come from ordinary (albeit quirky) humans, who gave us command-and-control organizational structures, the mechanistic management models of Fredrick Taylor, and the continuing lessons of MBA schools, which preach the doctrine of linear thinking, tightly prescriptive rules, and micro-measured outputs rather than common-sense and useful outcomes.

We can now see how easy it is to be squeezed into a small box of organizational tight thinking and why it hurts to stay stuck in that box. Our emotional brain is constantly sending us unconscious survival messages ("Get me out of here!"), while our logical, mechanistic knowledge brain believes what it's been programmed to believe ("Follow the rules, don't rock the boat, just do your job.").

"Okay," you say, "how the Mary Poppins do I levitate out of this cramped space?" The answer is going out on a very scary but safe limb of the Organizational Family Tree.

CREATING A COMMON REALITY THAT RESPECTS DIFFERENCES

The Oxford English Dictionary defines a system as "A set of things working together as a mechanism or network ... an organized scheme or method ... orderliness." Organizational systems (at least the ones that aren't mechanical, sticking you into a round hole like an interchangeable peg) are all that, but much bigger. Systems, at least successful ones, are what I call *reality spanners*.

Here's how it works. A successful organizational system structure takes our reality, the reality of the person next to us, our boss's reality, and hundreds of other individual realities and finds common ground. A successful system's job is to have you look out the window and see the same tree that I see, which is the same tree a hundred other people see. This is an incredibly tough task considering that each of us will see that maple tree differently based on our immediate emotions, our short- and long-term memories, our culture, our gender, and our experience with trees. But well-functioning organizational systems try to do this rather than jam one reality—usually that of those at the top of an organization chart—down our throats and in the process trigger our gag reflex.

How is this done? In a healthy Organizational Family Tree, we take our individuals views, called *schemas*, and organize them into "frames." In looking at this idea of frames, psychologist Daniel Goleman (1994) says,

> A frame is the shared definition of a situation that organizes and governs social events and our involvement in them. A frame, for example, is the understanding that we are at play, or that "this is a sales call," or that "we are dating."

The notion of frames and schemas first made a big impression on me when I was researching my doctoral dissertation about what triggers and sustains public protests. The answer evolved not only from my academic review of what others have learned but also from my direct experience with many protest groups and demonstrations since the late 1960s, as well as my brief consulting stint to the U.S. Department of Homeland Security, where I taught police officers about the dynamics of crowd psychology.

Public protests in reaction to ill-informed or insensitive decisions by a government or corporation aren't that much different from the dynamics that bubble up during organizational change affecting a handful or many employees. A line of thinking called *new social movement theory* says that protest actions are a marriage of emotion and knowledge—a complex mix of resource mobilization, a reaffirmation or a definition of self-identity, and a commitment to cultural and ideational factors. In simple terms, it's like this: "Politicians are shutting down the women's shelter because of budget cuts. Well, to hell with them! Let's stage a protest at the capitol. Alert the media, and let's spend the night painting placards!" What really shapes and guides such human actions are "frames" and "schemas" that create meaning for us. Think of frames and schemas as big boxes of meaning, places where there's lots of elbowroom to safely jump around and be creative.

The writings of Scott Hunt, Robert Benford, and David Snow back in 1994 explained that frames are mental processes that place individuals within a common time and space, linking them ideologically and attributing to them specific and identifiable characteristics—what I term a *common reality*. As well, the research by William Gamson (1988) says that frames often involve a sense of injustice, an element of identity, and something called *agency*—meaning that people think they can actually effect change through collective action. This idea of *agency* is vital, because, as I have sadly found in trying to organize protest groups, unless we think that we're actually going to achieve a quick win, we're not all that keen to tear ourselves away from other things.

Social movement *action*, according to Gamson, Snow, and Benford, is the result of raising both *emotional* and *cognitive* awareness that there's need for action and then supplying the *organizational* wherewithal to channel all that emotional energy and knowledge into action. The experts say that the driving force behind such action is the preservation or actualization of our self-identity—how we see ourselves.

This link between self-identity and social movements has long captured the attention of social-movement scholars. In both Gamson's and Snow and Benford's models of framing, *emotion* plays a key role. For example, *framing* involves raising awareness of perceived injustices and spurring supporters to take remedial action. Gamson's focus on the importance of identity and sense of injustice also has an emotional underpinning. As Klandermans (1974) points out in his assessment of framing, anger is the emotion expressed by people who hold others responsible for an unwanted situation, whether it involves discrimination, abortion, or drunk driving.

What constitutes a *frame* in society or in organizational life can sometimes be hard to define, but a frame is certainly easy to spot if it's broken, such as when protesters are violent or when employees don't behave according to management's wishes. The real challenge is figuring out why things have reached the point of meltdown. Because of our varied realities, groups and individuals within a group may disagree widely as to what constitutes a frame—what we all agree on or how we collectively look at an issue. Why does this happen? It's because most disagreements within organizations are about the *being* and not the *doing*. Allow me to explain.

Organizations do a lot of dumb things that our emotional brain often perceives as bureaucratic lunacy. Many of the conflicts between our personality and the organizational personality occur not so much because we are *doing* dumb stuff but because the organizational personality is deathly afraid of *being* in a state of uncertainty. Predictably, after all, is the core function of mechanistic, small-box thinking. The conflict that arises is between our deeply rooted emotional brain, where *believing is seeing* and our Industrial Age rational-knowledge brain, which is trained to *believe what it sees.*

Let me add just a little more to this difference between what *we* think is key to survival and what that organizational personality that we hang out with thinks is important. Neuroscientist Joseph Le Doux, author of the 1996 book *The Emotional Brain*, says,

> One of the main jobs of consciousness is to keep our life tied together in a coherent story, a self-concept. It does this by generating explanations of behavior on the basis of our self-image, memories of the past, expectations of the future, the present social situation, and the physical environment in which the behavior is produced.

The challenge to having a healthy, evolving Organizational Family Tree is to somehow align our needs and our reality with the needs and reality of the organizational personality.

IT'S OKAY TO FREAK OUT A BIT

So, how do we create this positive bond, this common purpose? First, we have to understand that building such positive linkages won't happen in an organization that is standing still, that is afraid of change. Conflict, rather than being an organization bogeyman, is in fact the ignition switch to renewed energy and innovation, and yet organizational life is about stopping conflict—hence the terms "damage *control*," "change *management*," and "crisis *management*."

The lessons from complexity science tell us there's no absolute control over many events in society, organizations, and corporate life. In fact, many complexity scholars say that anxiety, within certain boundaries, is a necessary trigger to allow a system to emerge as something better and new. They say that such emergence is the product of communications, new relationships, and creative thinking at what's called "the edge of chaos"—that area between a system being at rest and in total chaos. As complexity scholars Zimmerman, Lindberg, and Plsek write in their 1998 book *Edgeware: Insights from Complexity Science for Health Care Leaders,*

> In human organizations, the creative destruction phase may require dismantling systems and structures that have become too rigid, have too little variety and are not responsive to the current needs of the community.... This can be

a very disturbing, unsettling time for organizations as assumptions need to be exposed and re-examined in light of changing needs and environments.

Unlike rigid, bureaucratic, mechanistic organizations that resist change, complex adaptive systems (such as a healthy Organizational Family Tree) are never stuck in status-quo quicksand. They can be very sensitive to seemingly small things that people say or do, and the *perceived* conflict and resultant anxiety can quickly move the organization into a state of instability or to the *edge of chaos*. But then communication feedback loops, group self-organization and cooperation, and new connections can lead to the emergence of something quite different. This process means, as is often stated in chaos theory (using the metaphor of a butterfly flapping its wings and causing a thunderstorm), that one person doing something small can indeed make a big difference.

Human anxiety, whether about a lost job, a vexing issue, or the fear of death (in whatever form), is rooted in how the key points of the Triangle of Trust are configured. Our sense of self—our identity—is built on the interrelationship between our connectivity, the efficacy of our communications, and our ability to cooperate. It also hinges on how an organization empowers us with authority and how expectations are linked to our responsibility and accountability.

WHAT HAPPENS WHEN PLANETS ARE OUT OF ALIGNMENT?

In August 2006, a group of astronomers got together and officially decreed that Pluto wasn't a planet after all. Now, this is quite immaterial to Pluto, which never asked to be in some human-centric club in the first place and still continues to spin around as it always has. But the decree has created a lot of anxiety in my astrologically driven Scorpio brain, which is now in a dither about how to interpret my daily horoscope.

It's easy to get anxious when disorder emerges from order, be it our neatly arranged solar system or our neatly stacked organization chart, resplendent with its own galaxy of special stars, meteoric careers, and space cadets. When things start rattling and rolling in our perfectly aligned organizational lives, the first thing that's stretched is trust.

We may feel anxiety when we *perceive* the absence of one or more of the key factors within the Triangle of Trust, or when we sense conflict between the categories. Conversely, our anxiety is reduced and our sense of self is enhanced when the factors within the Triangle of Trust harmoniously align. For example, enhancing our connectivity with others in the face of sudden anxiety or fear can lead to positive communications, which can lead to increased cooperation, which in turn can boost our sense of self and identity.

What's key to reenergizing the Organizational Family Tree is remembering that all organizational systems are made up of *people*. It's not about separating "people stuff" from "process stuff" but understanding that the two are inextricably intertwined. You can't have organizational systems and structures, "strategy maps," "decision trees," and processes without human emotion.

Our human body is itself a fabulous example of a complex adaptive system, embedding multiple feedback loops, changing conditions, and self-organization. As the fields of neuroscience and psychology tell us, we often make decisions based on emotions, not cognitive thought, with fear in particular being a very powerful emotion and our *perception* of events serving as reality. This means others may not share our perception of cooperation, connectivity, or communication. At another level, we may not even be aware of the reality that we have created for ourselves, since a great deal of human behavior occurs at a subconscious level.

Therefore, now it's time to ask a few questions of ourselves, such as whether the organizational world we live in, our reality, is the reality shared by many—or *any*—others in our organization. It may be that the conflicts we face have been created not by *our* subconscious beliefs but instead by what *others* have convinced us is the right way to be and to think. There's a chance we're not doing or thinking things because of our unique perception of what should be. We're doing and thinking things based on the influence of *others'* reality—how they think we should be, how we should behave, what organizational systems are "supposed" to look like, and what shape of box we should work in.

For example, small-box thinking argues that organizational accountability is achieved by slavishly adhering to a set of micro-measurements that minutely calibrate outputs of behavior, with little or no thought to *outcomes*—what actually ends up getting done at the day's end. As an example of this bizarre behavior, a certain federal agency measures effective external communications by the number of news releases it distributes every year. They do not care what impact such activity has—neither whether public attitudes have changed nor if awareness of programs has increased. What's important to senior managers is merely achieving that numerical target.

What would bigger-box thinking do in the above case? What would the lessons from complexity science teach us? Well, for starters, we would recognize that effective communications is not a tick on a scorecard of activity but a measurement of human attitudes, including awareness, behavior, and attitudes. To reframe or redefine a sense of self, whether it's the corporate personality or our own, we must review the quality of our communications and connectivity to others and seek cooperative efforts that allow us to recognize ourselves for who *we* need to be—not the image in the mirror created by outdated, mechanistic models of what organizational and human behavior is *supposed* to be.

I'm talking about a process requiring safe and open self-exploration, and a system of reality spanning and inquiry needed for healthy growth within the Organizational Family Tree. This new reality often turns out not to be new at all, but a releasing of our natural instincts. Really, we're doing what made sense in the first place.

THE DISCOVERY OF A HEALTHY NEW REALITY

In small-box thinking, things are supposed to work consistently and predictably and to fit into very tight boxes of certainty. In fact, the language of organizations often reflects this thinking, with phrases like "containment," "control," and "management." But of course events don't follow this orderly path, not in biology and not in business. Small-box thinking generally follows six basic rules. Those rules are:

SIX RULES OF SMALL-BOX THINKING

1.   Detailed planning guarantees predictability.

2.   History *always* repeats itself.

3.   The status quo *must* be protected.

4.   Emotions are bad—so don't show any.

5.   Don't ask questions—just do it.

6.   Keep information tightly controlled.

The six basic rules of small-box thinking are of course based on myths. And like a lot of mythology, they bring us comfort, assurance, and usually disappointment. So, if small boxes are cramping us, giving us corporate claustrophobia, how do we get out of this tight fix? (You don't want to jump "out of the box," because that's just a whole lot of empty space with no safe boundaries or nets.) Well, to get away from tight thinking, we have to stretch out the organizational box. To create positive energy within the Organizational Family Tree, to build a bigger box, means reframing how we think about organizational systems—and not just reframing, but ripping the staid black-and-white picture out completely and replacing it with a free-form painting that's full of vibrant color, imagination, and especially human emotion.

Reframed thinking is not about the precision of machines but about the power of nature (and networks and in particular), the power within us to wage peace, not war, with our constantly changing circumstances. One way to do this is to abandon the language that creates negative and fearful realities within organizational life. Words are symbols for the powerful emotions we feel, but they also create emotions, because we associate their meaning with past actions and feelings.

GETTING RID OF WARFARE WORDS

Some people can't keep a job—I can't keep a career. Over my years, I've worked in a sawmill pulling boards off a conveyor belt, as a construction worker, as a newspaper and television journalist, as an associate deputy minister and senior advisor to a government cabinet, as a vice-president with an international consulting firm, as a department head with a national agency, and as a university instructor.

I've heard many people refer to their reality as a *battlefield* as they dealt with seemingly intransigent bureaucracies, inadequate funding, and challenges to their professional status. In fact, warfare analogies are common in organizational systems throughout North America. In my conversations with clinical care providers, I've heard professionals cynically refer to their work as the *bunker* and physicians refer to the *war* with government and the need to have a *war chest* to do *battle* with the *enemy*.

In my experience attending government cabinet meetings, I've heard various politicians, cabinet ministers, and a head of government discuss their *battle* with groups and the need to *fire the first shot*. Terms like *doing battle* (with a company or government) and *firing a missile* (in reference to political and advocacy campaigns) commonly fit into the lexicon of adversarial relationships between groups. It's a model based on positional rather than interest-based relationships.

It's tough language from the Industrial Age and from a corporate mindset that sees only winners and losers. There's nothing positive in this language that speaks to establishing communications, connectivity, and cooperation or sharing authority, responsibility, and accountability.

Language, especially emotion-laden words, plays a powerful role in how we frame our environment. LeDoux (1996) says, "Not surprisingly, the development of language has often been said to be the key to human consciousness." His point is that we categorize, label, and store our experiences in linguistic terms, using words as labels, and thereafter retrieve that information linguistically.

When we use loaded words like "held hostage" or "do battle" in reference to the administrative and bureaucratic goings on within our organization, the odds are pretty good (as neuroscience and psychology tell us) that the words in fact conjure up a literal visual image of that action, often at the subconscious level. LeDoux explains:

> The difference between fear, terror, apprehension, and the like would not be possible without language. At the same time, none of these words would have any point if it were not for the existence of an underlying emotion system that generates the brain states and bodily expressions to which these words apply.

Here's the problem with sprinkling battle language into our communications like sesame seeds onto chow mien. Our emotional brain, the really deep-seated part that was created before any cognitive, smart thinking was developed, doesn't have an imagination. Just *hearing* the language of warfare, even used metaphorically, creates a split-second physiological response to what our subconscious mind sees as a *literal* threat (that of actual war). This in turn elicits a conscious defensive response that, depending on the nature of the response, can lead to an even more confrontational situation. Yell at me and I get angry and yell back, which causes you to yell back because I'm yelling at you. And so it goes as the temperature rapidly escalates and human meltdown occurs.

If we're going to change bad organizational personalities, if we're going to create bigger-box thinking, then we need to start with our own perceptions of the world and our own behavior. One way to do this is to understand the pathways of choice facing us when a dysfunctional organizational structure is creating conflict, when corporate personality disorders are starting to create upsets in our work and private life. There are two paths we can follow—the rousing waging war path to battle and confrontation, where we're looking for "wins" and domination over others, or the inspiring waging peace path, where the idea is to find positive solutions and to work with others.

Let me draw you a picture of what I mean. I call it the *Dynamic Tension Loop*, and it illustrates the options facing us when we think that our sense of self is threatened by the actions of an organizational personality. The waging war approach calls for a rousing and reactive response, usually fueled by anger, to the perceived threat. This behavior is typical during organizational meltdown because both the culture and the climate of the place is build around an "us vs. them" mentality.

Dynamic Tension Loop

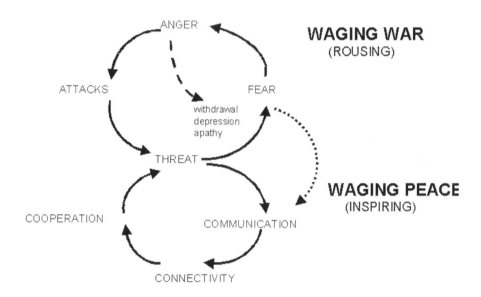

The perceived threat to us in such an organizational environment creates a lot of anxiety, which results in fear and then anger, leading to either withdrawal and depression or an attack on the perceived source of the threat. All this does is escalate conflict to the point where you and the other side reach an intractable state, increasingly seeing each other as the hated enemy. Unfortunately, this is what often happens.

This Waging War loop is behind most of the workplace depression throughout the Western world, it's behind labor strikes, and it fuels consumer boycotts.

For example, it was the cause of the troubles at a small city newspaper where I was a young reporter about a zillion years ago. The editor of the humdrum publication single-handedly created a sick system and an organizational meltdown that sent a shudder throughout the entire Organizational Family Tree. But that's the way it often is. One person in a position of authority—just one person—whose bizarre or cruel behavior is either ignored or supported by the organizational personality (including senior management) can eventually pump enough hot air into the tight-thinking, small organizational box that soon the walls simply explode.

At the newspaper in meltdown, the organizational box was overflowing with toxic behavior. It included rampant sexism, racism, drunkenness, bullying, the imposition of grueling work hours with no extra pay, and blatant political cronyism. For example, a political opponent to the editor's favorite candidate was cropped out of a group shot appearing on the front page. And every time the editor looked out his office window and spotted an attractive woman walking down the street below, he would shriek out, "Hoo yeah! Look at that!" This was his order that those around him get to the window and join his gawking.

The dysfunctional office environment finally came to a head. First, we naïve and junior reporters went to the publisher with our complaints (in keeping with the Waging Peace approach). In return, we were offered a few freeze-dried platitudes and a soggy promise that he'd "look into it." We left his office totally freaked out. Quiet consultation didn't seem to be working, and we were now fearful of getting fired for our presumptuous behavior. But our fear quickly turned to anger and protective action. We walked off the job in protest, contacted a labor union, and got the entire newsroom certified as an official local outlet of an international union. In short order, the editor was fired and we ended up with a raise in pay—all in accordance with union wage scales.

If the above sounds like a happy outcome and a cure for corporate personality disorder, there's also a warning. Throwing sand into the machinery of long-established organizational systems can have many outcomes. You may introduce more emotional awareness and caring into an organization, but in doing so you may also suffer the consequences of challenging the status quo. In my case, I was branded a troublemaking union organizer and for the next two years had trouble finding another job as a news reporter. But it was well worth it.

If, as in my experience at the city newspaper, you face an anxiety-creating threat within your organizational environment, I strongly urge you to "wage peace" and act in an inspiring fashion—using communication to understand the nature of the anxiety, connectivity to create alignment with other individuals and groups, and cooperation to refine the organizational climate and even eventually rebuild and heal the organizational culture.

Now, you may be noticing that even in waging peace, we eventually move on to another threat. "So, what's the point?" you're thinking. "Just give me a solution that fixes the place for good." Sorry, that's impossible. There are no finite fixes in real life, versus the mechanistic mentality of corporate life. Just like our personal lives, the organizational personality has highs and lows, ebbs and flows, and is never in a static state. And there's absolutely nothing wrong with this. In fact, it's perfectly normal, despite what management gurus tell you about the need to have control and containment.

Having another threat down the road (which is really not a threat but an inevitable bit of natural turbulence in the rolling river of life) is in keeping with the continually evolving nature of all systems on the planet, including biological ones and those dreamed up in corporate planning retreats. When we embrace the Waging Peace model, we won't see organizational threats as *threatening*. Instead, we'll accept "threats" as natural, recurring events leading to emergence and something new, through communication, connectivity, and cooperation. We'll experience less anger fueled by fear. We'll find less reason to go into withdrawal, depression, or apathy. And we won't think the solution to what's bugging us, or the organization, is to attack others.

THE SLINKY NATURE OF CHANGE: WHAT WAS ONCE CAN'T BE (EXACTLY) AGAIN

Life within the Organizational Family Tree is a continual ride on the whitewaters of life. It's not a straight line with neatly prescribed demarcations of events guaranteed to occur on a certain date because a strategic planning exercise dictated so. Life within the Organizational Family Tree is more like a Slinky toy.

I learned this sophisticated theory of organizational life from two experts on chaos—my sons Nikolas and Michael, when they were toddlers. As we sat together in the middle of assorted action heroes and building blocks, I watched them move a multicolored Slinky up and down, never exactly repeating a pattern but nevertheless staying within the overall boundary of the Slinky's design.

I was struck by the action of the Slinky compared to my own desktop toy. It was a Newton's cradle, comprised of five suspended metal balls that, when set into motion by the action of an end ball hitting others, would engage in a cause-effect action lasting until they eventually came to rest. What I learned from my children's toys was that most corporate small-box thinking emulates Newton's cradle. Yet human life and organic life and life inside bigger-box thinking follow the pattern of the Slinky.

We often hear, "The more things change, the more they stay the same." That phrase suggests that patterns and actions really do not change, regardless of surface changes. I think the phrase is characteristic of linear thinking and Newtonian logic. The phrase comes from a small, protected box of corporate logic. This protected box keeps us fearful of lifting the lid—even a wee bit—and taking a quick peek out. I suggest a different phrase, one that is born from the world of complexity: *The more things change, the more they change.*

Let me share with you another model of life. In looking at the properties of complexity science, in thinking about Slinky toys, and especially in considering bigger-box thinking, I have taken inspiration from Eastern religion and designed what I call the *anicca wave* to describe the ebb and flow within the Organizational Family Tree. *Anicca* is the Buddhist word for the notion that nothing stays the same. It means the impermanence of all things and the discomfort that naturally accompanies sudden change.

THE ANICCA WAVE

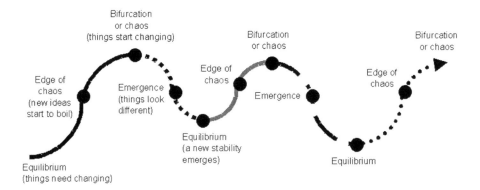

In the *anicca* wave, an unexpected event or crisis or moment of change moves an organization from equilibrium, where things are generally in a stable state, to the edge of chaos, where a great deal of anxiety-fueled creativity can take place based on communication, connectivity, and cooperation between groups and individuals.

The area of equilibrium on the *anicca* wave is definitely not a place where you sit around staring at the fish on your screen saver. This is where the dark and soft shadows that we talked about earlier exist, a place where people informally get together and creatively find solutions not obvious to, or accepted by, the formal system of strict rules and regulations.

The next area on the *anicca* wave is called a *bifurcation point*, where either total chaos results within the organization, resulting in its structural collapse, or emergence into something new happens. This organizational emergence, this something new and different, comes from the self-organization between those who have experienced the communication, connectivity, and cooperation found at the edge of chaos. But here's the really important point. If emergence does happen, it's not a clean slate—not a giving up of what was good and positive and nourishing from the organization's historical and developmental factors, which represent its culture. What's new also incorporates what's old, building upon the best of past experiences.

In the *anicca* wave, the emergence of new ideas and actions is followed by a period of equilibrium, where things settle down again and you start incorporating the new thinking into everyday life. Then, inevitably, the process starts all over again. It's impossible to predict just how long it will be between waves, no matter how many PowerPoints are presented with snappy timelines and critical paths. But this much is known: waves of change in society and organizations are coming far quicker than ever before.

In my various research collaborations with the Virginia-based Issues Management Council, I've noticed a dramatic shrinkage of time between an emerging issue—something that may pose a threat to organizational reputation or viability—and a full-blown crisis requiring immediate action.

A common saying is that, "It's too late to be thinking about draining the swamp when you're up to your ass in alligators." Today there are more alligators around than ever. I've observed that twenty years ago a sensitive issue, if left unmanaged, could take up to eighteen months to develop into a crisis. Ten years ago, the gap between an emerging issue and a full-blown crisis took up to six months. Today, an emerging issue can turn into a major crisis of confidence within a matter of weeks, if not days.

Because of modern technology and rapid global communications, there is no place left to hide, no time to think strategically, and no room for error. Our reputation and our trusted relationships are precariously balanced in a publicly exposed, daily high-wire act performed without a net.

Our anxiety at the edge of chaos can bring us together in new ways that stimulate creativity and foster communication. All this activity at the edge can create a new and unpredictable direction (bifurcation and then emergence) or things can fall apart (chaos). But not for long. The *anicca* wave shows that even if total chaos was the result, this state would eventually self-organize into something new, would emerge and find stability again—at least for a while. Life goes on, one way or another. *The more things change, the more they change.*

One place where the *annica* wave has a major impact is in what organizations call environmental scanning—researching the impact of social, economic, political, and technological factors on the ability of the organization to do what it's supposed to do. Often organizations, like one high-profile national one I know of, conduct environmental scanning as if they were in a forest picking different types of berries. Raspberries are dropped in one basket, strawberries in another, blueberries in yet a different basket, and so it goes. At the end of the day, in the kitchen of environmental analysis, the dedicated researchers must busy themselves counting how many individual berries are in each basket.

Such organizations never ask themselves how strawberries and raspberries might be combined to make a tasty pie, nor do they consider that the aggressive blackberry bushes are overwhelming the strawberry plants (as blackberry bushes tend to do). To switch metaphors on you, the researchers get so absorbed counting how many pine needles are on a branch that they don't see what's happening to the overall tree, never mind the whole forest.

Organizations that get wrapped up in tightly prescriptive and predictive environmental scanning activities—trying to predict what social, political, technology, and economic factors will do in the future—are just tying themselves up in knots. It's much more useful to seek general patterns and look for linkages between such various factors rather than to carve the future in stone (or embed it into a memory stick). That's what the *annica* wave describes—general patterns and trends in natural, evolutionly growth within the Organizational Family Tree.

It's easy to see how the ideas from complexity science are a direct challenge to the linear machine metaphor commonly used by managers in many organizations, including government departments and corporations. But don't worry—there's something here for everybody. It's not so much an either/or situation but a choice of what approach best fits the situation.

12

BIGGER-BOX THINKING

In this concluding chapter, I want to stress that there's room—and indeed a need in the Organizational Family Tree—for both situational leadership styles that focus on the here and now as well as transformational leadership, which is far more inclusive and visionary. It's never one cookie-cutter, one-size-fits-all formula.

In my own management experience, I've found that short-term situations with a very direct correlation between cause and effect, requiring specific outcomes, can lead to very controlled actions. Examples would be crises or emergencies, although even here I would suggest two questions: "Why are we doing this? Is there a better way?" However, situations requiring longer term planning, where there is a degree of uncertainty and unpredictability and a strong chance of variable outcomes, are well served by the ideas found in complexity science.

I don't want you to think that we're straying into pointy-headed academic stuff and ideas best suited for some crunchy-granola organization, so let me offer an example from the trenches. Even the quintessential command-and-control organization, the United States Marine Corps, understands the concept of blending complexity principles with hierarchical management. For example, USMC Training Manual No. MCDP6, *Command and Control*, recommends that the Marine Corps use the biology metaphor associated with complexity science:

> Like a living organism, a military organization is never in a state of stable equilibrium but is instead in a continuous state of flux continually adjusting to its surroundings. Command and control is not so much a matter of one part of the organization getting control over another as it is something that connects all the elements together in a cooperative effort.

As U.S. Marine Corps Captain Mary Leonardi said in a 1999 documentary about complexity science,

It's simply not possible to control in the traditional sense of command and control. In fact, in some of the Marine Corps professional journals we are actually moving to a different term called command and coordinate.

When thinking about an Organizational Family Tree and how we can make it grow stronger and healthier, consider complexity science a big bag of super-nutrients picked up at the local horticulture shop. Within this bag of healthy organic compounds are all manner of ingredients that can help us weed out the bad stuff and bring new life to a living and breathing organizational system structure. A great source of tips to reenergize an Organizational Family Tree by using the principles of complexity science is the Plexus Institute in Allentown, New Jersey (www.plexusinstitute.com)—an organization I've been a member of for many years.

Curt Lindberg is one of the major forces behind the Plexus Institute. I first encountered him in the late 1990s at a complexity systems conference in Philadelphia. As I mentioned earlier, Curt, together with Brenda Zimmerman and Paul Plsek, wrote a fabulous book in 1998 called *Edgeware: Insights from Complexity Science for Health Care Leaders*. This, in my opinion, is the best layperson's primer on complexity science and on caring for the Organizational Family Tree. Here are just a few examples of bigger-box thinking found in the book:

The concept of 15 percent: Gareth Morgan, an expert in organizational development, says the amount of real influence any organization's manager has in influencing change is about 15 percent. But this is not a bad thing. Morgan says that 15 percent can accomplish a great deal when you stop thinking like a machine and instead realize that even a small change or action can ripple out to eventually create huge changes.

Minimum specifications: This is one of the most mind-twisting concepts for small-box thinking managers. The idea is that successful outcomes within an organization aren't based on carving in stone a bunch of detailed instructions and rules and then micromanaging and second-guessing what employees are doing. Successful outcomes, truly creative ones, emerge from leaders and managers who provide just the essential basics of what needs to get done and then give work groups and individuals the freedom and space, the responsibility and accountability, to get on with it.

Wicked questions: This is Brenda Zimmerman's term for the kind of hard-hitting challenges to which managers need to subject their plans and schemes. As she says, "Wicked questions serve to dislodge self-fulfilling prophecies, open the ground for new experimental possibilities and increase communication in a system." The result is often a new and creative way of looking at things. Too often, employees who ask the "wicked questions" are seen as disloyal, poor team players, or rude.

Good-enough vision: There's nothing like a detailed strategic planning exercise to get you off the tracks and locked in small-box thinking. The fact is, many strategic plans fail to achieve their goals, as we saw in an earlier chapter and the examples from Harvard's Robert Kaplan and McGill University's Henry Mintzberg. They fail because they create minutely measurable goals and outputs based on a set of rigidly predictable factors found in straight-jacketed environmental scans. But the reality is that organizational environments ebb and flow based on the interaction of multiple variables, most of which are not entirely predictable.

Healthy growth and positive energy occurs in an Organizational Family Tree when leaders and managers think about the outcomes they hope to achieve rather than be mesmerized by narrow outputs. The Organizational Family Tree flourishes when managers trust those around them with minimum specifications and a general sense of direction and then, based on the Triangle of Trust model, provide plenty of empowered authority, clear responsibility, and wide accountability measures, and finally wrap up the package with ongoing two-way communications, connectivity, and cooperation.

This bigger-box thinking approach encourages individual autonomy, creativity and self-organization, and the ability to adapt to change. The principle suggests, for example, that intricate strategic plans be replaced by simple documents that describe the general direction the organization is pursuing, as well as a few basic principles for how the organization should get there.

I heard examples of how the above tools of complexity could be put to use when I attended the Third Annual VHA Complexity and Health Care Conference in Philadelphia in December 1999.

Jim Taylor, a tall, dapper man with a bow tie, explained how as the new president and chief executive officer of the University of Louisville Hospital (ULH) he gingerly introduced complexity science to a medical setting. Taylor said, "Organizations are *processes* of being, not states of being. The future cannot be implemented through a controlled and directed manner. It is communication flow and connectivity that leads to creative change."

At ULH, Taylor faced a hospital that was very much in transition, with its status recently going from for-profit to not-for-profit. In addition, the administrative structure had just changed when two not-for-profit hospitals and former competitors of ULH formed an alliance and succeeded in getting the management contract for the hospital, creating a new entity called University Medical

Center. The transition and planning challenges were great, not the least being the need to rationalize delivery of services.

Taylor introduced the tools of complexity in a disguised form because he thought the language and principles might be a bit overwhelming. "It's better to translate these ideas into behaviors within the environment. Once people experience it, the ideas make more sense."

Over time, the center's need for a formal strategic plan gave way to "min-specs" and "good enough planning." The bureaucracy was trimmed and decision-making power was spread throughout all levels. Soon after, Taylor introduced staff to the formal concepts of complexity. The financial bottom line improved at the center, and so did efficiency and effectiveness.

The staff at Taylor's hospital told him they needed a sense of personal control over their jobs as well as open communications. Trust, they told him, was essential, and they wanted to be respected for who they were and what they did. In addition, the staff wanted to have a common purpose, personal responsibility, and accountability. Again, all of the above is what produces positive energy within the Organizational Family Tree.

In turn, Taylor shared a number of his leadership principles. For example, he told us,

> Lead by example, be a relationship manager, have confidence that you will get to the right place, even if you don't know—and in fact cannot know—where it will be. Be willing to forgo your own advantage for the benefit of the organization as a whole.
>
> Be willing to forgo the advantage of your own organization for the benefit of the larger community of which the organization is a part. It is liberating to accept the reality that no one has *the* answer, and that you can say, "I can make a difference doing what I do best."

In his address, Taylor also described liberation:

> There is liberation about saying that nobody has the answer, that nobody *can* have the answer. I can make a difference in doing the best I can. That's an important recognition for me to make, for anybody to make for themselves. That doesn't mean I don't sometimes feel anxious. I do. So I'd say it's not a matter of whether you are anxious or not; it's a matter of dealing with your anxiety.

BIOLEADERSHIP AND THE ORGANIZATIONAL FAMILY TREE

Taylor's suggestion that we should take steps to deal with our anxiety is similar to the thinking that brings together cooperation, connectivity, and communication in the Triangle of Trust. Such outreaching also means that the Organizational Family Tree, based on the principles of complexity science, requires a different model of leadership—one that combines transformational leadership with situational leadership, one that recognizes not only the value of Robert Greenleaf's servant leadership but also the vital role of followership. I call this leadership style *bioleadership.*

How does bioleadership help positive growth within the Organizational Family Tree? Let's start with a definition and expand that to actions you can take. Bioleadership is *creating conditions of trust and adaptability.* My notion of bioleadership is not cut from whole cloth but is a patchwork of ideas from a variety of thoughtful folks.

For example, Uri Merry (1995) says, "Design and guidance to some degree appear to be possible, but not control. It is impossible to predict when a transformation will take place and what exact form it will take." In addition, Ralph Stacey (1996) says in a slightly more academic way, "It seems to me that we have no realistic alternative but to accept that we cannot be in control of the kind of complex co-evolutionary process that drives all nonlinear feedback networks but can only participate in producing emergent patterns." That's the key to bioleadership—our participation in helping produce new patterns of organizational and human behavior using the basic principles of my Triangle of Trust.

Here's another way to adopt bioleadership in your daily life. With mechanistic, small-box thinking, there are six basic rules, based on myths, designed to offer artificial comfort and get you to think in a certain narrow manner. In bioleadership, there are no rules, but I have developed ten touchstones to help you incorporate the six guiding principles I mentioned earlier.

BIOLEADERSHIP TOUCHSTONES

1. Accept crises as part of positive change.

2. Challenge assumptions on a regular basis.

3. Accept that small actions can lead to huge changes.

4. Set general, flexible goals, then go with the flow.

5. Know that what happened before won't *exactly* happen again.

6. Focus on creating outcomes, not outputs.

7. Believe that perception *is* reality.

8. Accept that the more things change the more they change.

9. Believe that emotions trigger all human action.

10. Reduce fear through shared power and communications.

Now, here are some more nutrients to help us deal with organizational root rot. I've packaged the following as the *Principles of Bioleadership Behavior.* In the bag, you'll find a sprinkling of healthy ingredients from the field of emotional intelligence plus a large dollop of my own original research on what creates and sustains trust within an organization.

PRINCIPLES OF BIOLEADERSHIP BEHAVIOR

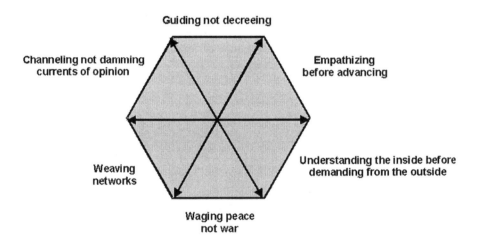

Guiding not decreeing

Channeling not damming
currents of opinion

Empathizing
before advancing

Weaving
networks

Understanding the inside before
demanding from the outside

Waging peace
not war

Guiding rather than decreeing means moving away from the old command-and-control mindset. Stop seeing the organization as a clockworks that can be wound up and tuned to specific precision. Instead, play an active role in helping shape outcomes through communications, cooperation, and connectivity.

Guiding also speaks to the Triangle of Trust and the benefit of sharing, not hoarding, authority, accountability, and responsibility. And finally, guiding calls for being adaptable and looking at the big picture with respect to systems and organizations rather than getting tied up with detail and control. It calls for using the "min-specs"—the minimum-specifications approach advocated in complexity science. It's also understanding that it's best to focus on the small percentage of organizational life that we can do something about rather than try to control all elements.

Empathizing before advancing means seeking to understand others—including the reasons and rationale for others' behavior and attitudes—before advancing our own position. It means actively listening and searching for the emotional reasons that others adopt the positions they have (particularly those based on fear) and appreciating that no two realities are the same. This principle is particularly attuned to the Triangle of Trust.

Understanding the inside before demanding from the outside calls for continual self-reflection and personal growth before imposing demands on others. It means challenging personal assumptions about the world and about our own sense of self. Most importantly, it means having the strength to say, "I don't know," "Why/Why not?" and "No" in a principled and polite way.

Waging peace, not war calls for collaboration and nonconfrontational tactics. It means using a new lexicon of relationships. This means using language that explores possibilities, gives credit when credit is due, and recognizes the power of occasionally doing nothing in the face of confrontation. It particularly recognizes that words can be as powerful as a bullet, that what others say figuratively is first absorbed in our brain as a literal representation with linkages to past events and memories that are unique to us.

Weaving networks speaks to the importance of communication flows and connectivity at the edge of chaos, especially with groups that in the past we may not have been seen as allies. It means understanding that openness in communications does not equate with vulnerability—and that vulnerability is not weakness.

Channeling, not damming, currents of opinion means recognizing it's impossible and fruitless to try to stop the flow of events. Building a dam to block a river results simply in the water backing up and eventually going over or around the dam. It's better to redirect the flow by constructively building new channels and new directions that take the water—or events—to the most positive spot.

Guiding, empathizing, understanding, waging peace, weaving networks, and channeling summarize the core principles of bioleadership, but the attributes also speak to a certain style of leadership—one that is *transformational* rather than *transactional*. Transformational leaders shape, alter, and elevate the motives and values of followers, while transactional leaders focus on rewards and punishments and rely on their official positions of authority to make things happen.

Transformational leaders inspire and motivate others not only to perform beyond organizational expectations and to achieve goals beyond the norm but also to inspire people to be the best individuals they can be. On the other hand, transactional leaders operate on a system of exchanging rewards for effort, usually in accordance to some form of contract. Transformational leaders are open to change and challenge, while transactional leaders are stick-in-the-muds who are comforted by tight command and control.

As I indicated, my bioleadership model also embraces the notion of *servant leadership*, forwarded by Robert Greenleaf, Max DePree, and others. Here's an example of what Greenleaf means by servant leadership, as quoted in a book by Larry Spears (1995):

> It begins with the natural feeling that one wants to serve, to serve first. Then conscious choice brings one to aspire to lead. The difference manifests itself in the care taken by the servant—first to make sure that other people's highest priority needs are being served. The best test is this: Do those served grow as persons; do they, while being served, become healthier, wiser, freer, more autonomous, more likely themselves to become servants? (Reflections on Leadership: How Robert K. Greenleaf's Theory of Servant Leadership Influenced Today's Top Management Thinkers)

In my experience (including more deaths of self-image and death of hope than a mangy alley cat has lives), I have found that a science-based tendency to offer unquestioned prescriptive actions is one of the major underlying problems facing many organizations. So instead of offering a magical shopping list of specific dictates to follow, I'm suggesting a number of questions that may stretch the walls of the small organizational box that you're trapped in. I'm not guaranteeing success or enlightenment, but instead offering a way to take that first step, that tiny, frightening step that can ultimately create a wave of change.

The questions are designed to have us look inside ourselves for answers, to discover what we really believe rather than follow the beliefs that have been programmed into our mindset from a very early age. I do promise this: I believe that if you find even one answer that surprises you, that makes you wonder, that gets you to ask even more questions, then you are setting off a chain reaction of change whose boundaries are limitless.

When we speak out on behalf of our beliefs and values, when we seek to build new connections in our community, and when we contribute to communication flows between individuals and groups, we will have a tremendous impact on the world around us. We can indeed be like a pebble creating ripples on the water or the metaphorical butterfly creating a thunderstorm far away.

Six Guideposts and Many Questions for the Self

1. Who do you see in the mirror?

In the Organizational Family Tree, a sense of self and personal identity is one of the keys to sustaining meaningful relationships.

- What are my assumptions about my role in society, in my work and career, with my family, and with friends? Who says it has to be that way?

- Is my assumption about myself shared by others? How do I know?

- Have I ever met a personal assumption that I didn't like? Which one? Why not?

- What would happen if I said, "I don't know" to someone who has an expectation that I *should* know?

2. Who do you hear when you communicate?

Communication is more than the dissemination of information. Communication builds relationships and reduces fear by addressing the constituent parts of fear—powerlessness and a sense of unknown. In the Triangle of Trust, communications has a partnership with connectivity and cooperation as well as with authority, responsibility, and accountability.

- What's the average length of silence between others' speaking and my replying? Is that good? Why? What communications do I receive in that period of silence? What do I communicate in that silence?

- How many ways of listening do I employ when hearing others speak? How many are there?

3. Does a true network need a powerful center?

Organizations and systems emerge in part because of communications, connectivity, and cooperation between groups. Anxiety and a diminished sense of self are created when there's a poor fit between relationships or connectivity, communication, and cooperation and when there's a poor alignment between authority, responsibility, and accountability.

- What is most threatening to me—the loss of positional power, personal pride, or financial profit? Why are any of those important?

- Where can new relationships help me reduce personal anxiety? How can communications build relationships?

- What group, individual, or organization is most threatening to my sense of self and professional identity? Why? What positive things do I have in common with those threatening to me? How can I build on those common interests?

- What is leadership and what is my role in followership? Am I more comfortable as a leader or follower? Why?

4. How do you behave in the shadows?

Earlier, I described Stacey's work with shadow systems and also suggested a system may have multiple hues of shadow. Such a system could range from dark shadows of negative behavior to soft shadows of positive response to negative actions within a system.

- Where am I in the organizational "shadows" of a company or organization or even my personal life? What ideas do I have that are outside the "legitimate" system of how things should unfold? How am I sharing those ideas with others?

- How can I move negative, reactive behaviors, actions, and attitudes found in the dark shadows of an organization into the soft shadows of the system, where there is opportunity for positive change?

5. Are you still trapped in a small box?

Small-box thinking is being brainwashed by Newtonian logic, which states there's a very orderly universe in which cause and effect is predictable and future actions are based upon similar past experiences. But as the *anicca* wave shows, events are often unpredictable, changing in nature, moving at an increasingly rapid pace, and not replicating past behaviors in response to seemingly similar situations.

- What are three examples of my own "small-box thinking"? Who put me into this box? What prevents me from getting out?

- Do I think others sometimes just don't get it when it comes to understanding my ideas and my role? Why do I think they are wrong and I am right? What would happen if I were wrong? Who defines right and wrong?

6. What are you afraid of?

Fear is a lack of power and knowledge. Fear can also lead to anger and withdrawal or attacks on others. Or it can be looped into connecting with others and finding mutual gains.

- Where do I feel a sense of powerlessness—the perception that I can't influence events? What would it take for me to feel as if I had direct influence and the ability to guide events? How would communications play a role, and what relationship structure could make this happen?

- Where do I feel "in the dark" about what's going on and why? Is this information gap a result of a disparity between my reality of events and the reality of others? What communications actions could I take to enhance my level of information and understanding?

- What is my deepest fear? What or who has defined this fear for me? Can my reality be redefined to eliminate the fear? How?

SOME CLOSING THOUGHTS

I'm hoping you agree that it *is* possible to revitalize and renourish the Organizational Family Tree and, in so doing, to reenergize ourselves—to break free from the Iron Cage of Certainty imposed by traditional mechanistic thinking.

There's little doubt that organizational meltdown is at epidemic proportions throughout the Western world, and not a day goes by that we don't experience a dysfunctional sick system or hear about such a system in the news. But I don't want to totally bum us out. The fact is, there's also a lot of good news. The good news is that the way organizations are designed and run is changing, and that change—like all change today—is happening at an exponential rate. Organizational Family Trees, like many real trees, have a way of adapting and surviving, even if it involves a dramatic rerooting. It's only natural.

Even vast forest fires don't spell the end of a forest, regardless of how charred the ground may look afterward. Eventually new growth appears, and it thrives on the soil and nutrients left behind. In time, a new forest appears. It may not be the same species (and it usually isn't), but it definitely is a natural forest. *The more things change, the more they change.* It's only natural—just like our natural, subconscious propensity for survival.

Deep in our brain's primitive limbic system, formed many millennia prior to development of our "rational" cognitive brain systems, lies an instinctual desire for human self-preservation. The Industrial Age and the mechanical nature of most organizational systems have done a great job scaring many of us away from being influenced by this "hopefulness gene," as neuroscientist Antonio Damassio calls it. But things *are* changing.

Fewer of us are willing to be unheard, to put up with dysfunctional workplaces and the bad behavior of sick systems and nasty organizational personalities. More of us are willing to live our values, to ask the "wicked questions," and to demand that organizations operate with a reasoned balance of authority, accountability, and responsibility, which includes all of us in systems of communications, connectivity, and cooperation.

Changes will come—they are coming—to the outdated mechanistic model of organizational structure and behavior. *They must come.* To have otherwise is a recipe for both human and ecological disaster. The human meltdown now evident in many organizations suffering from corporate personality disorder has triggered a countervailing, atavistic survival response from those affected, be they employees, customers, shareholders, or members.

It is not just about FEMA, or Arthur Andersen, or Duke Energy, or Enron. It is not just about the hundreds of millions of dollars in class-action lawsuits ongoing throughout the Western world, about the mounting levels of workplace burnout and stress, or about the meltdown in public trust in our major institutions. It is about all of those and much, much more.

Thank you for sharing this journey with me into the psyche of the organizational personality. There's an old saying: It's impossible to ever leave a situation in exactly the same state that we were in when we entered it.

I'm hoping that somewhere in the preceding pages, something touched you, made you question an assumption, or maybe gave you hope. I'm also hoping that you realize you are not alone—that many thousands think just like you, feel what you feel. And that the very next thing you think and do after closing this book can change you forever. And finally, I invite you to share your thoughts with me at our Web site, www.orgenome.org.

REFERENCES

ABC News/*Washington Post* national poll. 2002. *Confidence in institutions.* Retrieved September 12, 2006 from www.pollingreport.com.

Allgeyer, G. 1996. Social protests in the 1990s: Planning a response. *The FBI Law Enforcement Bulletin*, January issue: 12–14.

American Institute of Stress. 2006. *Job stress.* Retrieved January 9, 2007 from www.stress.org/job.htm.

American Psychiatric Association. 2000. *Diagnostic and Statistical Manual of Mental Disorders-IV-TR.* Washington, DC: American Psychiatric Association.

Amis, J., T. Slack, and C. Hinings. 2002. Values and organizational change. *The Journal of Applied Behavioral Science* 38, no. 4: 436–65.

Angus Reid/*Bloomberg Business News* national survey. 1996. Retrieved August 9, 2006 from www.pollingreport.com.

Ashkanasy, N., C. Wilderom, and M. Peterson, eds. 2000. *Handbook of organizational culture & climate.* Thousand Oaks, CA: Sage Publications.

Ashkenas, R., D. Ulrich, T. Jick, and S. Kerr. 2002. *The Boundaryless organization.* San Francisco, CA: Jossey-Bass.

Associated Press national poll. 2003. *Confidence in institutions.* Retrieved June 19, 2003 from www.pollingreport.com (retrieved June 19, 2003).

———. 2003 Associated Press national poll. 2003. *Confidence in institutions.* Retrieved October 23, 2006 from www.pollingreport.com.

Axelrod, R. 1997. *The complexity of cooperation.* Princeton, NJ: Princeton University Press.

Babiak, P., and Hare, R. 2006. *Snakes in suits.* New York, NY: HarperCollins.

Backhaus, G. 2000. Emotions: The Fetters of Instincts and the Promise of Dynamic Systems. In *The Cauldron of consciousness, motivation, affect, and self-organization: An anthology*. D. Ellis, N. Natika, eds. xxii, 223–42. John Benjamins Publishing Co. Philadelphia, PA.

Bak, P. 1996. *How nature works*. New York, NY: Springer-Verlag.

Bakan, J. 2004. *The corporation: The pathological pursuit of profit and power*. Toronto, ON: Viking Press.

Tuchman, B. 1985. *The march of folly*. New York, NY: Ballantine Books.

Barber, B. 1983. *The logic and limits of trust*. New Brunswick, NJ: Rutgers University Press.

Baskin, K. 1998. *Corporate DNA*. Woburn, MA: Butterworth-Heinemann.

Bateson, G. 1999. *Steps to an ecology of mind*. Chicago, IL: University of Chicago Press.

Beck, A. 1976. *Cognitive therapy*. New York, NY: Penguin Books.

Becker, E. 1973. *The denial of death*. New York, NY: Free Press Paperbacks.

Beiter, M. 2003. *Strategic organizational change*. Greensboro, NC: Practitioner Press International.

Benedict, A. 1991. *Imagined communities,* 2nd ed. London, UK: Verso Publishing.

Benjus, J. 1997. *Biomimicry*. New York, NY: William Morrow and Company.

Blackmore, S. 1999. *The meme machine*. Oxford, UK: Oxford University Press.

Block, P. 1981. *Flawless consulting: A guide to getting your expertise used*. Indianapolis, IN: CWL Publishing Enterprises.

Bloom, H. 1995. *The Lucifer principle*. New York, NY: Atlantic Monthly Press.

———. 2000. *Global brain*. New York, NY: John Wiley & Sons.

Blumer, H. 1969. In B. McLaughlin, ed. *Studies in social movements: A social psychological perspective*. New York, NY: The Free Press.

Bridges, W. 2000. *The character of organizations*. Palo Alto, CA: Davies-Black Publishing.

Brodies, R. 1996. *Virus of the mind*. Seattle, WA: Integral Press.

Burden, O. 1992. Peacekeeping and the thin blue line: Law enforcement and the preservation of civil rights. *The Police Chief* 59, no. 6: 16–26.

Butler, J. 1991. Toward understanding and measuring conditions of trust: Evolution of a conditions of trust inventory. *Journal of Management* 17(3), 643-663.

Cameron, K., and R. Quinn. 1999. *Diagnosing and changing organizational culture*. Menlo Park, CA: Addison-Wesley.

Capra, F. 1982. *The turning point*. New York: Simon & Schuster.

———. 1996. *The web of life*. New York, NY: Bantam Doubleday Publishing Group.

Carroll, W., and R. Ratner. 1996. Master framing and cross-movement networking in contemporary social movements. *Sociological Quarterly* 37, 601–25.

CBS News national poll. July, 2002. *Confidence in institutions*. Retrieved August 9, 2002 from www.pollingreport.com

———*New York Times* national poll. 2004. *Confidence in institutions*. Retrieved November 2, 2004 from www.pollingreport.com

Chandler, A. 1977. *The visible hand*. Cambridge, MA: Harvard University Press.

Childre, D., and B. Cryer. 1999. *From chaos to coherence*. Woburn, MA: Butterworth-Heinemann.

Clegg, S., C. Hardy, and W. Nord, eds. 1999. *Managing organizations*. Thousand Oaks CA: Sage Publications.

CNN/*USA Today*/Gallup poll. July, 2002. *Confidence in institutions*. Retrieved September 14, 2002 from www.pollingreport.com

Cohen, P. 1979. *Policing the working class city*. In B. Fine, R. Kinsey, J. Lea, S. Picciotto, and J. Young, eds. *Capitalism and the rule of law*. London, UK: Hutchinson Publishing.

Coleman, A., ed. *Oxford dictionary of psychology*. Oxford, UK: Oxford University Press.

Cook, T. 1989. *Making laws and making news: Media strategies in the House of Representatives*. Washington, DC: Brookings Institute.

Coveney, P. 1995. *Frontiers of complexity*. New York, NY: Fawcett Columbine.

Crozat, M. 1998. Are the times a-changin'? Assessing the acceptance of protest in Western democracies. In D. Meyer, ed. *The social movement society*. Lanham, MD: Rowman and Littlefield.

Csikszentmihalyi, M. 1990. *Flow*. New York, NY: HarperCollins.

Damasio, A. 1994. *Descartes' error*. New York, NY: Avon Books.

———. 1999. *The feeling of what happens*. Orlando, FL: Harcourt Brace.

———. 2003. *Looking for Spinoza*. Orlando, FL: Harcourt Books.

Das, T. 2001. Trust, control, and risk in strategic alliances: An integrated framework. *Organization Studies* (Spring): 27–45.

Dawkins, R. 1989. *The selfish gene*. Oxford, GB: Oxford University Press.

De Becker, G. 1999. *The gift of fear*. New York, NY: Random House.

De Vries, M., and K. Balazs. 1999. Transforming the mind-set of the organization: A clinical perspective. *Administration & Society* 30, no. 6: 640–75.

della Porta, D. 1995. *Social movements, political violence, and the state: A comparative analysis of Italy and Germany*. Cambridge, UK: Cambridge University Press.

———. 1996. Social movements and the state: Thoughts on the policing of protest. In D. McAdam, J. McCarthy, and M. Zald, eds. *Comparative perspectives on social movements*. Cambridge, UK: Cambridge University Press.

———. 1997. The political discourse on protest policing. In M. Giugni, D. McAdam, and C. Tilly, eds. *How movements matter*. Minneapolis, MN: University of Minnesota Press.

———and M. Diani, eds. 1999. *Social movements: An introduction*. Malden, MA: Blackwell Publishers Ltd.

Denison, D. 1996. What is the difference between organizational culture and climate? *The Academy of Management Review* 21, no. 3: 619–54.

Dozier, R. 1998. *Fear itself*. New York: Thomas Dunne Books.

Eckersley, R. 2005. *Well & good: How we feel and why it matters*. Melbourne, Australia: The Text Publishing Company.

Eisenstadt, S. 1995. *Power, trust, and meaning*. Chicago, IL: University of Chicago Press.

Eisinger, P. 1975. The conditions of protest behavior in American cities. *American Political Science Review* 67: 11–28.

Elwell, F. 1996. *Verstehen: Max Weber's home page*. Retrieved January 14, 2007 from www.faculty.rsu.edu/felwell/Theorists/Weber/Whome.htm.

Eoyang, G. 1997. *Coping with chaos*. Cheyenne, WY: Lagumo Corp.

Ettner, S., and J. Grzywacz. 2001. Workers perceptions of how jobs affect health: A social ecological perspective. *Journal of Occupational Health Psychology* 6, no. 2: 1-24.

Eve, R., S. Horsfall, and M. Lee, eds. 1997. *Chaos, complexity, and sociology*. Thousand Oaks, CA. Sage Publications.

Fekete, S., and L. Keith. 2003. *Companies are people too*. Hoboken, NJ: John Wiley & Sons.

Ferree, M. 1992. The political context of rationality. In A. Morris and C. Mueller, eds. *Frontiers in social movement theory*. New Haven, CT: Yale University Press.

Fineman, S. 2000. *Emotion in organizations.* Thousand Oaks, CA: Sage Publications.

Flacks, R. 1994. The party's over—so what is to be done? In E. Larana, H. Johnston, and J. Gusfield, eds. *New social movements.* Philadelphia, PA: Temple University Press.

Forbes Magazine. 2002. *The corporate scandal sheet.* Retrieved January 11, 2007 from www.forbes.com.

Foucault, M. 1977. *Discipline and punishment: The birth of the prison.* London, UK: Penguin Books.

Frederick, W. 1995. *Values, nature, and culture in the American corporation.* Oxford, UK: Oxford University Press.

Freeman, J., and V. Johnson, eds. 1999. *Waves of protest: Social movements since the sixties.* Oxford, UK: Rowman and Littlefield.

Friedman, D. and D. McAdam. 1992. Collective identity and activism: Networks, choices, and the life of a social movement. In A. Morris and C. Mueller, eds. *Frontiers in social movement theory.* New Haven, CN: Yale University Press.

Fromm, E. 1941. *Escape from freedom.* New York: Farrar and Rinehart.

Frost, P. 2003. *Toxic emotions at work.* Boston, MA: Harvard Business School Press.

Fukuyama, F. 1999. *The great disruption.* New York: Simon & Shuster.

Gallup poll. 2000. *Attitudes in the American workplace.* New York, NY: Gallup.

———. 1999, 2002, 2003, 2004, 2005. *Confidence in institutions.* Retrieved October 10th, 2006 from www.pollingreport.com.

Gamson, W. 1975. *The strategy of social protest.* Homewood, IL: Dorsey Publishing.

———. 1992a. *Talking politics.* Cambridge, UK: University of Cambridge Press.

———. 1992b. The social psychology of collective action. In A. Morris and C. Mueller, eds. *Frontiers in social movement theory.* New Haven, CT: Yale University Press.

———. 1995. *Constructing social protest.* In H. Johnston and B. Klandermans, eds. *Social movements and culture.* Minneapolis, MN: University of Minnesota Press.

———. B. Fireman, and S. Rytina, eds. 1982. *Encounters with unjust authority.* Homewood, IL: Dorsey Publishing.

Garsten, C. 2001. Trust, control, and post-bureaucracy. *Organization Studies* 26 (March): 24–37.

Gerde, V. 2001. The design dimensions of the just organization: An empirical test of the relations between organization design and corporate social performance. *Business & Society* 40, no. 4: 472–77.

Gerlach, L. 1999. The structure of social movements: Environmental activism and its opponents. In J. Freeman and V. Johnson, eds. *Waves of protest.* Lanham, MD: Rowman & Littlefield Publishers, Inc.

Gilbert, D. 2006. *Stumbling on happiness.* New York, NY: Random House.

Gilbert, R. 1992. *Extraordinary relationships.* New York, NY: John Wiley & Sons.

Glassner, B. 1999. *The culture of fear.* Reading, MA: Perseus Books.

Gleick, J. 1987. *Chaos.* New York, NY: Penguin Books.

Goffman, E. 1974. *Frame analysis.* New York: Harper Press.

Goldstein, J. 1994. *The unshackled organization.* Portland, OR: Productivity Press.

Goleman, D. 1985. *Vital lies, simple truths.* New York, NY: Simon & Schuster.

———. 1994. *Emotional intelligence.* New York, NY: Bantam Books.

———. 1998. *Working with emotional intelligence.* New York, NY: Bantam Books.

Greenleaf, R. 1998. *The power of servant leadership*. San Francisco, CA: Berrett-Koehler Publishers.

Greenspan, S. 1997. *The growth of the mind*. Reading, MA: Perseus Books.

Guastello, S. 1995. *Chaos, catastrophe, and human affairs*. Mahwah, NJ: Lawrence Erlbaum Associates.

Gundelach, P. 1995. Grass-roots activity. In J. van Deth and E. Scarbrough, eds. *Impact of values*. New York: Oxford University Press.

Gurr, T. 1970. *Why men rebel*. Princeton, NJ: Princeton University Press.

———. 1997. Cited in B. Klandermans, *the social psychology of protest*. Oxford, UK: Blackwell Publishers.

Gusfield, J. 1994. The reflexivity of social movements: Collective behavior and mass society theory revisited. In E. Larana, H. Johnston, and J. Gusfield, eds. *New social movements: From ideology to identity*. Philadelphia, PA: Temple University Press.

Harris Poll. 2006. *Confidence in institutions*. Retrieved March 8, 2007 from www.pollingreport.com.

———. 2001. *Confidence in institutions*. Retrieved September 25, 2001 from www.pollingreport.com.

———. 2004. *Confidence in institutions*. Retrieved October 19, 2005 from www.pollingreport.com.

Harris, P. 2003. Big Brother takes grip on America. *London Observer* (September 7), 8.

Helliwell, J., and H. Huang. 2005. *How's the job? Well-being and social capital in the workplace*. Cambridge, MA: National Bureau of Economic Research, working paper 11759.

Hersey, P., and K. Blanchard. 1993. *Management of organizational behavior*. Englewood Cliffs, NJ: Prentice-Hall.

Hetherington, M. 1998, December. The political relevance of political trust. *American Political Science Review* 43: 56–74.

Hickman, G., ed. 1998. *Leading organizations.* Thousand Oaks, CA: Sage Publications.

Hobbes, T. 1651. *The Leviathan.* Retrieved March 14, 2005 from www.thomas-hobbes.com/works/leviathan.

Hoffer, E. 1951. *The true believer.* New York: Harper and Row.

Holland, J. 1995. *Hidden order.* Reading, MA: Perseus Books.

———. 1998. *Emergence.* Reading, MA: Perseus Books.

Hunt, S., R. Benford, and D. Snow. 1994. Identity fields: Framing processes and the social construction of movement identities. In E. Larana, H. Johnston, and J. Gusfield, eds. *New social movements.* Philadelphia, PA: Temple University Press.

Ipsos Reid. 2006. *Half of Canadians say they have no control over stress levels.* Toronto, ON: Ipsos R.

Irwin, W., ed. 2002. *The Matrix and philosophy.* Peru, IL: Carus Publishing Company.

Jasper, J. 1999. Recruiting intimates, recruiting strangers: Building the contemporary animal rights movement. In J. Freeman and V. Johnson, eds. *Waves of protest.* Lanham, MD: Rowman & Littlefield Publishers, Inc.

Jennings, M. 2006. *The seven signs of ethical collapse.* New York, NY: St. Martin's Press.

Johnston, H. 1995. A methodology for frame analysis: From discourse to cognitive schemata. In H. Johnston and B. Klandermans, eds. *Social movements and culture.* Minneapolis, MD: University of Minnesota Press.

———, and B. Klandermans, eds. 1995. *Social movements and culture.* Minneapolis, MN: University of Minnesota Press.

Kaczynski, T. 1995. *Industrial society and it's future*. Retrieved January 4, 2006 from www.thecourier.com/manifest.htm.

Kaplan, R., and D. Norton. 2001. *The strategy focused organization*. Boston, MA: Harvard University Press.

Kelley, R. 1992. *The power of followership*. New York, NY: Doubleday.

Kennamer, J., ed. 1992. *Public opinion, the press, and public policy*. Wesport, CT: Praeger Publishers.

Kern, R., and Peluso, P. 1999. Using individual psychology concepts to compare family systems processes and organizational behavior. *The Family Journal: Counseling and Therapy for Couples and Families* 7, no. 3: 236–44.

Klandermans, B. 1997. *The social psychology of protest*. Oxford, UK: Blackwell Publishers.

Klein, N. 2000. *No logo*. Toronto, ON: Vintage Canada.

Knights, D. 2001. Chasing shadows: Control, virtuality, and the production of trust. *Organization Studies* (March): 45–57.

Kornhauser, W. 1959. *The politics of mass society*. Glencoe, IL: The Free Press.

Kramer, R. 1999. Trust and distrust in organizations: Emerging perspectives, enduring questions. *Annual Review of Psychology* 3: 23–31.

————, and M. Neale, eds. 1998. *Power and influence in organizations*. Thousand Oaks, CA: Sage Publications.

Kramer, R., and T. Tyler. 1996. *Trust in organizations*. Thousand Oaks, CA: Sage Publications.

Kriesi, H. 1996. The organizational structure of new social movements in a political context. In D. McAdam, J. McCarthy, and M. Zald, eds. *Comparative perspectives on social movements*. Cambridge, UK: Cambridge University Press.

Kubler-Ross, E. 1997. *On Death and Dying*. New York, NY: Touchstone.

Larana, E., H. Johnston, and J. Gusfield. 1994. *New social movements: From ideology to identity*. Philadelphia, PA: Temple University Press.

Lasora, D. 1991. Political outspokenness: Factors working against the spiral of silence. *Journalism Quarterly* 68: 131–40.

Lazlo, E. 1996. *The systems view of the world*. Cresskill, NJ: Hampton Press.

Le Bon, G. 1960. *The crowd: A study of popular mind*. New York: Viking Press.

LeDoux, J. 1996. *The emotional brain*. New York, NY: Touchstone.

———. 2002. *Synaptic self*. New York, NY: Viking Press.

Lewis, J., and A. Weigert. 1985. Trust as a social reality. *Social Forces* no. 63(4): 967–85.

Linsky, M. 1986. *Impact: How the press affects federal policymaking*. New York: Norton Publishing.

Lorenz, E. 1993. *The essence of chaos*. Seattle: University of Washington Press.

Lovelock, J. 2006. *The revenge of Gaia*. New York, NY: Penguin Group.

Marion, R. 1999. *The edge of organization*. Thousand Oaks, CA: Sage Publications.

Marktrend. 2001, 2002. *Activism survey of British Columbia adults vol. 1 & 2*. Vancouver, BC: Marktrend Research.

Marwell, G., and Oliver, P. 1988. Social networks and collective action: A theory of the critical mass iii. *American Journal of Sociology* 94, 502-534.

McAdam, D. 1996. Conceptual origins, current problems, future directions. In D. McAdam, J. McCarthy, and M. Zald, eds. *Comparative perspectives on social movements: Political opportunities, mobilizing structures, and cultural framings*. Cambridge, UK: Cambridge University Press.

McAdam, D., J. McCarthy, and M. Zald, eds. 1996. *Comparative perspectives on social movements*. Cambridge, UK: Cambridge University Press.

McAdam, D., S. Tarrow, and C. Tilly. 2001. *Dynamics of contention.* Cambridge, UK: Cambridge University Press.

McCarthy, J., and C. McPhail. 1998. The institutionalization of protest in the United States. In D. Meyer and S. Tarrow, eds. *The social movement society.* New York, NY: Rowman and Littlefield.

McCarthy, J., and M. Zald. 1973. *The trends of social movements in America: Professionalism and resource mobilization.* Morristown, NJ: General Learning Press.

McCarthy, J., C. McPhail, and J. Smith. 1994. *The institutional channeling of protest: The emergence and development of U.S. protest management systems.* Paper presented at the World Congress of the International Sociological Association, Bielefeld, Germany.

McCarthy, J., J. Smith, and M. Zald. 1996. Public, media, electoral, governmental agendas. In D. McAdam, J. McCarthy, and M. Zald, eds. *Comparative perspectives on social movements.* Cambridge, UK: Cambridge University Press.

McMullen, R. 2005. *Taking out your mental trash.* New York, NY: Norton & Co.

McWhinney, W. 1997. *Creating paths of change.* Thousand Oaks, CA: Sage Publications.

Melucci, A. 1994. A strange kind of newness: What's "new" in new social movements? In E. Larana, H. Johnston, and J. Gusfield, eds. *New social movements.* Philadelphia, PA: Temple University Press.

Merry, U. 1995. *Coping with uncertainty.* Westport, CT: Praeger Publishers.

Meyer, D. 1999. Civil disobedience and protest cycles. In J. Freeman and V. Johnson, eds. *Waves of protest: Social movements since the sixties.* Oxford, England: Rowman & Littlefield.

———, and S. Tarrow. 1998. *The social movement society.* Oxford, England: Rowman & Littlefield.

Mintzberg, H., B. Ahlstrand, and J. Lampel. 1998. *Strategy safari*. New York, NY: The Free Press.

Misztal, B. 1996. *Trust in modern societies*. Cambridge, UK: Blackwell Publishers.

Mohrman, S., R. Tenkasi, and A. Mohrman. 2003. The role of networks in fundamental organizational change. *The Journal of Applied Behavioral Science* 39, no. 3: 301–23.

Morgan, G. 1997. *Images of organization*. Thousand Oaks, CA: Sage Publications.

———. 1997. *Imaginization*. Thousand Oaks, CA: Sage Publications.

Morris, A. D., and C. M. Mueller. 1992. *Frontiers in social movement theory*. Binghampton, NY: Vail-Ballou Press.

Nagura, H., and H. Honda. 2001. *Success to corporate genome*. Tokyo, Japan: Nomura, Research Institute, NRI papers no. 35.

NBC News/*Wall Street Journal* national public opinion survey. *Confidence in institutions*. 2000. Retrieved March 2, 2005 from www.pollingreport.com.

Neilson, G., B. Pasternack, and D. Mendes. 2003. The four bases of organizational DNA. *Strategy and Business Magazine* (Winter 2003). Retrieved February 14, 2004 from www.strategy-business.com/press/16635507/03406.

Newsweek national survey. *Confidence in institutions*. July of 2002. Retrieved August 20, 2005 from www.pollingreport.com.

Ng, D. 2003. The social structure of organizational change and performance. *Emergence* 5, no. 1: 99–119.

Noelle-Neumann, E. 1977. Turbulences in the climate of opinion: Methodological applications of the spiral of silence theory. *Public Opinion Quarterly* 41: 143–58.

Norretranders, T. 1989. *The user illusion*. New York, NY: Penguin Books.

Northrup, T. 1989. The dynamic of identity in personal and social conflict. In Louis Kriesberg, Terrell Northrup, and Stuart Thorson, eds. *Intractable conflicts and their transformation.* New York, NY: Syracuse University Press.

Offe, C. 1985. New social movements: Challenging the boundaries of institutional politics. *Social Research* 52, no. 4: 817–68.

Olson, E., and G. Eoyang. 2001. *Facilitating organization change.* San Francisco, CA: Jossey-Bass/Pfeiffer.

Olson, M. 1968. *The logic of collective action: Public goods and the theory of groups.* Cambridge, MA: Harvard University Press.

Opp, K. D. 1989. *The rationality of political protest.* Boulder, CO: Westview Press.

Ornstein, R. 1991. *The evolution of consciousness.* New York, NY: Touchstone Press.

Oshry, B. 1995. *Seeing systems.* San Francisco, CA: Berrett-Koehler Publishers.

Pearse, W., and S. Littlejohn. 1997. *Moral conflict.* Thousand Oaks, CA: Sage Publications.

Pierce, J., and D. Gardner. 2004. Self-esteem within the work and organizational context: A review of the organization-based self-esteem literature. *Journal of Management* 305: 591–622.

Pinker, S. 1997. *How the mind works.* New York, NY: W. W. Norton & Company.

———. 2002. *The blank slate.* New York, NY: Penguin Books.

Piven, F., and R. Cloward. 1971. *Regulating the poor.* New York: Vintage Books.

Powell, C. and J. Persico. *My American journey.* New York, NY: Random House.

Powell, W., and P. DiMaggio. 1991. *The new institutionalism in organizational analysis.* Chicago IL: University of Chicago Press.

Prigogine, I. 1996. *The end of certainty.* New York, NY: The Free Press.

Probst, T., and T. Brubaker. 2001. The effects of job insecurity on employee safety outcomes: Cross-sectional and longitudinal explorations. *Journal of Occupational Health Psychology* 6, no. 2: 139-159.

Public Health Agency of Canada. 2004. *Exploring the link between work-life conflict and demands on Canada's health care system.* Ottawa, ON: Queens Printer.

Pyszczynski, T., S. Solomon, and J. Greenberg. 2002. *In the wake of 9/11: The psychology of terror.* Washington DC: American Psychological Association.

Rafaeli, A., and M. Worline. 2001. Individual emotion in work organizations. *Social Science Information* 401: 95–123.

Reiner, R. 1998. Policing, protest, and disorder in Britain. In D. della Porta and H. Reiter, eds. *Protest policing: The control of mass demonstrations in Western democracies.* Minneapolis, MN: University of Minnesota Press.

Richardson, K., ed. 2005. *Managing organizational complexity.* Greenwich, CT: IAP Information Age Publishing.

Ridley, M. 1999. *Genome.* New York, NY: HarperCollins.

———. 2003. *The agile gene.* Toronto, ON: HarperCollins.

Roberts, J. 1992. *The history of the world.* London, UK: Penguin Books.

Robinson, O., and A. Griffiths. 2005. Coping with the stress of transformational change in a government department. *The Journal of Applied Behavioral Science* 41, no. 2, 204–21.

Rodney, P. 1988. Moral distress in critical care nursing. *Canadian Critical Care Nursing Journal* 5, no. 2, 9-11.

Scarf, M. 2004. *Secrets, lies, betrayals: The body/mind connection.* New York, NY: Random House.

Schein, E. 1992. *Organizational culture and leadership.* San Francisco, CA: Jossey-Bass.

————. 1999. *The corporate culture survival guide.* San Francisco, CA: John Wiley & Sons.

Scheufele, D., J. Shanahan, and E. Lee. 2001. Real talk: Manipulating the dependent variable in spiral of silence research. *Communication Research* 28, no. 3: 304–24.

Seligram, A. 1992. *The idea of civil society.* New York, NY: Free Press.

Semler, R. 1993. *Maverick.* New York, NY: Warner Bros.

Senge, P. 1990. *The fifth discipline.* New York, NY: Doubleday.

————, A. Kleiner, C. Roberts, R. Ross, G. Roth, and B. Smith. 1999. *The dance of change.* New York, NY: Doubleday.

Sewell, W. 1980. *Work and revolution in France.* Cambridge, England: Cambridge University Press.

Shamir, J. 1995. Information cues and indicators of the climate of opinion. *Communication Research* 22 (February): 24–53. Thousand Oaks, CA: Sage Publications.

Smelsner, N. J. 1962. *Theory of collective behavior.* New York, NY: The Free Press.

Smyth, M. 2006. *Liberals great at shirking responsibility.* Vancouver Province (March 5, 2006), A-6.

Snow, D. 1983. *A dramaturgical approach to collective behavior.* Paper presented to the American Sociological Association, Detroit, Michigan, August 31–September 4.

————, and R. Benford. 1992. Master frames and cycles of protest. In A. Morris and C. Mueller, eds. *Frontiers in social movement theory.* New Haven, CT: Yale University Press.

————, B. Rochford, S. Worden, and R. Benford. 1986. Frame alignment processes, micromobilization, and movement participation. *American Sociological Review* 51: 464–81.

Solomon, R., and F. Flores. 2001. *Building trust in business, politics, relationships, and life.* Oxford, UK: Oxford University Press.

Sopow, E. 2002. *Ticking, clicking, and ready to explode: A quantitative study of British Columbia baby boomers and their attitudes toward protest action.* Vancouver, BC: Mediascope International Inc.

———. 1991. *Taking charge! A survival guide to media relations.* Victoria, BC: Mediascope International.

———. 1994. *The critical issues audit.* Leesburg, VA: Issue Action Publications.

———. 1997. *The age of outrage.* Victoria, BC: Mediascope International.

———. 2000. *Leadership at the edge of chaos: Physicians, anxiety, and a complex, adaptive health care system.* Victoria, BC: Master's dissertation, Royal Roads University.

———. 2000. *The age of outrage: The role of emotional and organizational factors on protest policing and political opportunity frames.* Santa Barbara, CA: Fielding Graduate University, PhD dissertation.

Soule, S., and S. Tarrow. 1991. *Acting collectively, 1847-1849: How the repertoire of collective action changed and where it happened.* Presented to the annual conference of the Social Science History Association, New Orleans, October.

Sparks, G., M. Pellechia, and C. Irvine. 1999. *The repressive coping style and fright reactions to mass media.* Communications Research (April): 176–92. Thousand Oaks, CA: Sage Publications.

Stacey, R. 1996. *Complexity and creativity in organizations.* San Francisco, CA: Berrett-Koehler Publishers, Inc.

———. 1992. *Managing the unknowable.* San Francisco, CA: Jossey-Bass.

———. 1997. *The implications of complexity theory for psychoanalytic thinking about organizations.* Paper presented to the Symposium of the International Society for the Psychoanalytic Study of Organizations, Philadelphia, PA.

Stryker, S., T. J. Owens, and R. W. White. 2000. *Self, identity, and social movements*. Minneapolis, MN: University of Minnesota Press.

Synovate Research. 2003. *Public support levels for protest action*. Unpublished report. Vancouver, BC: Synovate Research Inc.

Tarnas, R. 1991. *The passion of the western mind*. New York, NY: Ballantine Books.

Tarrow, S. 1998. *Power in movement: Social movements and contentious politics*. Cambridge, UK: Press Syndicate of the University of Cambridge.

Tilly, C. 1978. *From mobilization to revolution*. Reading, MA: Addison-Wesley.

Tipton, R. 1992. In T. Kennamer, ed. *Public opinion, the press, and public policy*. Wesport, CT: Praeger Publishers.

Touraine, A. 1981. *The voice and the eye: An analysis of social movements*. A. Duff, trans. Cambridge, UK: Cambridge University Press.

U.S. Department of Labor. 2004, 2005. *Mass layoff statistics*. Retrieved October 10, 2006 from www.bls.gov.

U.S. Government Accountability Office. 2006. *Agency management of contractors responding to hurricanes Katrina and Rita*. Washington, DC: U.S. Government Accountability Office.

Vince, R. 2001. Power and emotion in organizational learning. *Human Relations* 5410: 1325–51.

Waddington, D. 1998. Controlling protest in contemporary historical and comparative perspective. In D. della Porta and H. Reiter, eds. *Policing Protest: The control of mass demonstrations in Western democracies*. Minneapolis, MN: University of Minnesota Press.

———, K. Jones, and C. Critcher. 1989. *Flashpoints: Studies in public disorder*. London, UK: Routledge.

Waldo, D. 1980. *Sincerity and authenticity*. New York, NY: Harcourt, Brace.

Waldrop, M. 1992. *Complexity*. New York, NY: Touchstone.

Warren-Shepell. 2005. *Workplace mental health indicators.* Toronto, ON: War-ren-Shepell Group.

Weick, K. 2001. *Making sense of the organization.* Malden, MA: Blackwell Pub-lishing.

⸺, and K. Roberts. 1993. Collective mind in organizations. *Administrative Science Quarterly* 38: 357-381.

Westley, F., B. Zimmerman, and M. Patton. 2006. *Getting to maybe.* Toronto, ON: Random House.

Wheatley, M. 1992. *Leadership and the new science.* San Francisco, CA: Berrett-Koehler.

Whyte, D. 1994. *The heart aroused.* New York, NY: Currency Paperback.

Wilson, E. 1998. *Consilience.* New York, NY: Alfred A. Knopf.

World Values Survey. 1981–2000. Retrieved April 18, 2005 from www.worldvaluessurvey.org.

Wright, R. 2004. *A short history of progress.* Toronto, ON: House of Anansi Press.

Yen, H. 2006. *Audit: Millions wasted on Katrina response.* Associated Press. Retrieved March 16, 2006 from www.afscmeinfocenter.org/privatization update/auditsreporting/

Young, J. 2003. The role of fear in agenda setting by television news. *American Behavioral Scientist* 46, no. 12: 1673–95.

Zimmerman, B., B. Lindberg, and P. Plsek. 1998. *Edgeware: Insights from com-plexity science for health care leaders.* Irving TX: VHA Inc.

BIOGRAPHY: ELI SOPOW PHD

Eli Sopow is an international-award-winning "scholar-practitioner" whose involvement with change processes and leadership has taken him from South America to the Arctic Circle. Over the years, Eli has worked as a newspaper and television journalist, a senior advisor to a government Cabinet, a vice president of an international consulting firm, a director with a medical association, and as a consultant to environmental groups and law enforcement agencies interested in collaborative processes.

Eli holds a PhD in Human and Organizational Systems from Fielding Graduate University in Santa Barbara, CA, where his studies resulted in creation of the "Organizational Family Tree" leadership/management system. His work on change processes, particularly the role of human emotion in organizational conflict, resulted in his receiving the international Howard Chase Award for outstanding issues management, presented in Washington DC in 2000. He has also received three national awards for outstanding corporate issues management and eight regional awards for investigative journalism.

Besides his PhD in human and organizational systems, Eli holds a master's degree in Human Development, a second Masters degree in Leadership and Training, and an undergraduate diploma in Public Sector Management. In addition, he holds a Certificate in Peer Counseling granted by the University of British Columbia.

He is a team leader of organizational research and human development at the west coast headquarters of the Royal Canadian Mounted Police in Vancouver, Canada, where he also serves as an expert on crisis communications and issues management. Eli is also a partner with Sopow & Wilde Organizational Consulting in Vancouver where he provides individuals and groups with advice and training related to leadership and managing change. He is also an Associate Faculty member at the Royal Roads School of Leadership in Victoria, Canada.

Over the past 25 years Eli has provided leadership and change management advice to a broad array of clients including Starbucks Coffee Company, Greenpeace Canada, the U.S. Department of Homeland Security, numerous national and international resource and financial corporations, a wide range of professional and not-for-profit associations, as well as government agencies and politicians. He has presented over 250 workshops to groups throughout the United States and Canada, as well as having his work published in numerous professional journals. Eli lives in Vancouver with his wife Lindsay who is also his consulting partner. He has two sons, Nikolas and Michael, as well as his extended family including Wesley and Loralee.

INDEX

978-0-595-42560-0
0-595-42560-7

Made in the USA
San Bernardino, CA
02 December 2015